The Glasgow (

The Glasgow Curse

My Life in the Criminal Underworld

William Lobban

BIRLINN

To my beautiful daughter, Tamara, my grandparents,
William and Easter Manson, and all those who have
lost their lives due to the Glasgow Curse

First published in 2013 by
Birlinn Limited
West Newington House
10 Newington Road
Edinburgh
EH9 1QS

www.birlinn.co.uk

ISBN: 978 1 78027 126 2

British Library Cataloguing-in-Publication Data
A catalogue record for this book is available from the British Library

Typeset by Iolaire Typesetting, Newtonmore
Printed and bound by Gutenberg Press, Malta

Contents

Acknowledgements

I'd like to say a special thank you to all the staff working at Birlinn Limited, especially Hugh Andrew, Andrew Simmons, Neville Moir, Tom Johnstone, Jan Rutherford and Edward Crossan. I'd also like to thank Peter Urpeth for all his hard graft in the early stages of bringing this book to life. Thank you to Patsy and Christine, Donald Findlay, Jillian Powery, Kirsten McCormick, Mark and Anmarie, Kate Higgins from Children 1st, and last, but certainly not least, to Kelly, for her love, support and understanding while the pages of this book came together.

Introduction

Glasgow people are amongst the warmest and most humorous on the planet, but underneath the surface of a friendly, vibrant community lurks a brutal criminal underworld that has blighted the city and its inhabitants for generations. Glasgow is, in fact, one of the most violent places in the UK – in fact a recent article on the BBC News website shows that Scotland's largest city ranks as the most violent part of Britain, with 2.7 homicides per 100,000 of population as opposed to 1.0 for the rest of the country.

Over the years thousands of people have been drawn into this vile and insidious underworld. Once entered, it is almost impossible to escape; many who have been sucked into it have paid for their involvement with their liberty and, in many cases, their lives. This is what I mean by the Glasgow Curse, and I should know what I'm talking about, as I was born into one of the most notorious crime families in the city: the Mansons. Back in the day my uncle, Billy Manson, was a criminal boss who controlled a tight ship and, along with his loyal friend and partner in crime, Scotland's most notorious gangster Arthur Thompson, had an iron grip on an underworld dominated by fear, armed robbery and protection rackets. Vincent and Robert Manson, my other uncles, were equally hardcore villains with a proclivity for law-breaking and violence. It was their way of life and nothing could change that.

Crime was my way of life from as far back as I can remember; over the years, I have been responsible for all manner of offences – fraud, armed robbery, grievous bodily harm, drug dealing, prison riots. You name it, I've done it.

1

Except for one thing – I have never killed anyone.

This highlights another facet of the Glasgow Curse: that you can trust no one; the person you regard as a brother can turn round and stab you in the back.

One of the main reasons for writing my life story is to clear up all the lies and inaccuracies that people have written about me over the years in a number of tabloid newspapers and books, most notably Paul Ferris, a criminal I first met decades ago when we were both teenagers together in a Young Offenders Unit. Ferris and I crossed paths many times, and I worked closely with him when he was at the height of his career in crime during the early 1990s. There was no code of honour with Ferris, as he had me and others believe. In his books *The Ferris Conspiracy* and *Vendetta*, Ferris accuses me of murdering Arthur Thompson's son, while I have also been linked by some to the death of two other Glasgow criminals, Joe Hanlon and Robert Glover. Neither accusation has any basis in fact.

This is my chance to repudiate their claims, and to put forward my side of the story. But this is not the only reason. If by writing a book that tells the truth about the consequences of a life of crime, that doesn't sensationalise what is truly an awful, degrading and hopeless way of life, it might in some small way help finally break the curse that has destroyed too many Glaswegian lives for far too long.

Chapter One

Born in a Prison

The first six months of my life were spent in Exeter Prison, at that point a female only borstal, where my mother was incarcerated for her part in a family plot to steal valuable antiques and the contents of a safe inside an English country mansion.

Although I don't know all the ins and outs relating to the wild scheme, I do know it was well planned but went tragically wrong. My mother was keeping lookout while her brothers tried to get into the property, and it was at this stage the police turned up and she quickly got apprehended. During a fierce struggle with the arresting coppers, my mother thought it was wise to sink her teeth into a police sergeant's hand, almost severing his thumb in the process. She received a two-year borstal sentence for her stupidity.

While most newborn babies come into the world in a hospital setting with possibly their fathers or other family members there to witness the event, I arrived surrounded by prison guards. What a dreadful thought, and how unpleasant it would've been for any woman to give birth in that way. My mother, Sylvia Manson, was only 19 years old when she had me in February 1968, but she never did talk much about this episode in her life. I never really took the chance to ask her about it when I was growing up because, frankly, I wasn't that interested. Over the years I did pick up certain details relating to my mother's incarceration, and I do know she served the full two years of her sentence – the maximum length of time that any borstal inmate could serve.

For many years I knew next to nothing about my father, David Lobban. A respectable and quiet man who never had any

3

criminal leanings, he must have found my mother extremely difficult to live with. At any rate he left us when I was 18 months old.

In contrast to my father's law-abiding ways, Sylvia's family were always disrespectful towards the law and they wholeheartedly stood by the criminal code of silence. In my mother's case, while she was no angel, during the court proceedings against her she never once incriminated any of her brothers. She took it on the chin and was sent down on her own.

Was the court aware of my mother's pregnancy before passing sentence? Surely not, as her borstal sentence was punitively steep. Prison rules of the time stated that a female prisoner could keep her baby with her for up to six months, after which time a family member had to take over the care of the infant.

In my case, my grandparents, who lived in the East End of Glasgow, travelled all the way to Exeter to collect me and, like some little parcel, shipped me all the way back home with them. Oblivious to what was going on around me at the time, I now look back and find it hard to imagine what it must've felt like for everyone concerned.

It would've been heartbreakingly difficult for my mother when the time came for her to hand me over to my grandparents, but this was typical of a hardened family, just doing whatever it was they had to do and simply getting on with it. I've no idea if Sylvia saw me again during the remainder of her sentence; perhaps not, since the distance from Glasgow to Exeter and back is approximately 900 miles – quite a trek.

Adding to my mother's dismay at having to hand me out to be looked after elsewhere would most certainly have been a cutting reminder that I wasn't the only baby that she'd had to part with so young. My baby sister, Patricia, died of pneumonia aged just six months – or so the story goes.

There are rumours within the Manson family that suggest little Patricia died when Alex Manson, one of my uncles, fell asleep on an armchair while holding her in his arms, accidently smothering her. I genuinely don't know what to believe when it comes to my baby sister's death, but the uncle in question was an insufferable alcoholic who was held responsible for another atrocity within the family, so I wouldn't put it past him to have inadvertently smothered the baby when he fell asleep full of booze. Whatever the case, growing up with siblings wasn't to be for me. I've always wondered what it would've felt like to have a sister.

My granda, William Manson, also known as Hector, died in a manner that I still find very hard to accept. In a drunken fit of rage it was alleged Alex Manson attacked him in his flat in 1985. I was in prison at the time and my aunt Patsy had to take care of all the funeral arrangements. Hector was frail, a wheelchair user since he'd had a leg amputated. (Gangrene had set in to his foot after he got an infection in his toes. In the habit of using razor blades to cut his toenails, he accidentally cut his toe then neglected the wound.) He relied on help, but Alex was volatile and violent when he had a drink in him, which was most of the time.

The attack was savage, deranged. Before Hector slipped into a coma during the beating, the urinary catheters fitted to his bladder had been ripped from his body and he was stamped on so hard in the assault that the imprint of a training shoe was left on his forehead and neck. A lack of evidence meant that no one was ever prosecuted for this despicable act of extreme violence, but Alex spent time on remand in Barlinnie jail having been accused of this crime.

Alex was different from the rest of the Manson family, especially his brothers, but only because he wasted his life with booze. When my grandmother died soon after old Hector, a pal and I intended to drive Alex to Hawick to collect his half-brother, Archie Gourlay, so that he could go to the funeral, but the dark country roads spooked Alex. Paranoia got the better of him – maybe he had a guilty conscience – and on the way there he jumped out of the car at a busy roundabout and started shouting at motorists for help. After several hours at a local police station he made his way home. There's no doubt in my mind he thought that my friend and I were going to do him in.

My mother was born in Glasgow and, as a young woman bursting with acumen, she left school with top qualifications and passed her driving test when she was just seventeen. People would often tell me that she and I looked alike. She had natural long dirty-blonde hair which complimented her fine-looking facial features. Her high cheekbones and piercing green eyes set off her lovely smile. She was very attractive in her day, and she knew it. She was also very assertive. But she possessed a violent streak so terrifying that whenever she started boozing you were better off staying well out of her way.

I witnessed this violent side of my mother's personality on numerous occasions, especially when she was steaming drunk, and when she flipped she would change into a completely different woman. Born with only one kidney, she should've known better and stayed well clear of alcohol, but she took no notice of this pitfall. In the end she endured a slow and agonising death alone in her bed in a filthy house in 1999. She was just 52 years old.

Sylvia was the youngest member of the Manson family, and just like the rest of them she possessed a somewhat twisted streak. She could change rapidly from being a tender and loving person, an avid reader, especially of horror stories, Mills and Boon romances and the *Bunty*, to one who was instinctively horrible, uncaring and evil. She always had a book in her hand along with a can of Carslberg Special Brew and a fag.

I had to share a bed with my mother when I was small, and when she was drunk she would often wet the mattress and I would have to sleep on towels to try to keep dry. There was no heating in the room and on cold winter nights I was often freezing with the wetness of the bed. I remember my mother trapping me in the kitchen once when she was drunk and severely beating me with a pot. She hit me so hard that the pot was completely dented and useless for cooking. On occasion she would also whack me over the buttocks with a thick leather belt.

When I was eight or nine years old, she would put me on the train on my own at Glasgow Central Station and send me to visit my aunt Patsy in Dundee. One time she dressed me up in girls' sandals for the journey. When I arrived, Aunt Patsy had to go straight away and buy me boy's shoes. Your mother is your mother at the end of the day, but I could never understand growing up why mine was so cruel towards me. I know now that it was all down to the booze.

After completing her borstal sentence Sylvia never went back to prison, not even for a single day on remand, which I find incredible considering the damage she meted out to so many different people. Somehow she always managed to dodge the law for her various violent offences, which included stabbings, slashings and even biting one of her old boyfriend's ears clean off. Sylvia wasn't someone you wanted to mess with. When I look back, I'm amazed she never killed someone. My mother was nuts.

Having liberated me from Exeter Prison, my grandparents flitted from Budden Street in Parkhead to Penicuik Street in Carntyne, still in the East End of Glasgow.

Penicuik Street was a typical row of three-storey tenement blocks, and my grandparents and I lived in one on the bottom right-hand side as you walked in the close. It was quite a small street, with only four blocks of houses on either side. The house was tiny, with only one bedroom, a kitchen and a bathroom. The three of us slept in the same room in the same double bed. At one stage I remember having my own little fold-away bed that converted back to a cabinet when not in use for sleeping.

At the back of the house there was a huge back court, a sort of wasteland which all the households from three different streets had the displeasure of having to share. People used this waste ground as a shortcut from street to street, but you did get kids playing there even though broken bottles and other dangerous objects littered the place.

The first eight years of my life were spent growing up in Carntyne, and despite the hardships of life there I have many fond memories from that period. This was a very exciting and significant time for me. Looking back, I was taught how to be independent and fend for myself from a very young age. The truth is, I wasn't cared for properly as a child. My grandparents would often go on drinking benders. During the worst of these binges I took on the role of a kid twice my age because my granny and granda were never in a fit state to care for me when they were plastered. You could say they lived a sort of double life, having a kind of Jekyll-and-Hyde syndrome, where one day they'd be sober and the next they'd be drunk. With no supervision, it meant I could do whatever I wanted, when I wanted, and there was no one there to discipline me. It was not all bad, however, and there were times when my grandparents would stay sober for short periods. To be honest though, I preferred them drunk – what child wouldn't, when it meant you could do anything that came into your head?

My grandparents, Nessie and Hector, married in the 1930s and they were a devoted couple when they weren't drinking. My grandmother already had a son, Archibald, before they married, and together they produced six more children: Alex, William, Vincent, Patricia, Robert and my mother, Sylvia.

My grandmother was a heavy-set woman with long dark hair that she always kept tucked under a headscarf. She was originally from the Outer Hebrides and was a fluent Gaelic speaker. Nessie always had her own seat right next to the coal fire, and because of the incessant heat her bulky legs would turn a blotchy red colour. She had a heart of gold when sober, a typical Glaswegian granny who doted on her grandchild. As a little boy I called her 'Nana' and she called me her 'Silver Son'.

During sober periods she was really on the ball. She would hang out her washing and keep to her daily chores. Every morning, in rain, sleet or snow, she had a routine of making the short journey to the local grocery store, Jamison's on Carntyne Road, to pick up a copy of the *Daily Record* and a quarter of cheese for the breakfast. It was always cheese; we ate loads of the stuff. Some mornings there would be spam too and on occasions my grandfather would make a pot of porridge, which he would put into bowls and leave on the windowsill to cool down.

When the drinks were flowing, Nessie loved nothing more than to belt out a few old-fashioned songs. She was a lovely singer and one of her favourites was 'Stormy Weather', an Ethel Waters number, which she would sing with real vigour. Another was 'My Yiddishe Mamma', made famous by Anne Shelton.

Every week she would fill out the spot-the-ball coupon from

the newspaper, and she always betted on the Grand National when it came round. I remember having to close my eyes and pierce the newspaper with a sewing needle, and whichever horse the pin landed on was the horse you backed.

Our television was a black-and-white set with wooden shutter doors, a fancy TV at the time, a gift from their son, my uncle Billy, after whom I am named. *Coronation Street* was a big hit with Nessie and you wouldn't dare utter a word when it was on the telly. Every night when the programmes finished and the national anthem came on my granny would turn the volume up and my grandfather would shout: 'Nessie, fur fuck sake, hen, will ye turn that fucking thing doon,' before rushing over to switch it off himself. Hector was a staunch Celtic supporter, which explained his anti-royal sentiments.

Hector was born in 1915. He was a very proud and well-turned-out man for his years. Even when drunk he made an effort to look after his appearance. His head was nearly bald, with bits of grey hair sticking out from each side, which he tended to regularly with the comb he always kept in his back trouser pocket. He smoked Woodbine cigarettes and he liked nothing more than to sit sucking on a bar of Highland Toffee, the only time, I remember seeing him without his false teeth.

At night he washed his white dress shirt before going to bed. As a young boy I would stand in the scullery and watch him shake the shirt several times to get rid of the excess water. He would then hang it on the pulley so that it would be dry for him first thing in the morning. He would also polish his shoes to a clear shine, and then iron his trousers, which he wore with braces, using the old iron heated on the gas stove. Immaculate, he was a credit to a man of his age. At the weekend I loved nothing more than to walk with him to the Barras market where he was well known for years. With his street trader's badge pinned to the lapel of his overcoat, he sold Wilkinson Sword razor blades. I would have to run to keep up with his brisk walking pace as we headed to the market. The Barras was always very busy at the weekend, with crowds of shoppers searching for a bargain, and I couldn't get enough of the frenetic atmosphere.

At one time Hector worked as a ships' rigger for the Glasgow shipyard Harland and Wolff. He also had a wooden barrow with large wheels that he would push around the streets of the Gorbals selling fruit and veg. During World War II Hector served his country in the Merchant Navy. He had a dramatic escape when his ship, HMS *Forfar*, was sunk while he was not aboard. HMS *Forfar* was torpedoed on 2 December 1940, 500 miles west of Ireland, by a German submarine, *U-99*: 130 members of her crew lost their lives in the attack. Hector and one of his mates had failed to return to the ship from a short spell on leave, and he would often reminisce with Nessie about how lucky he was to be alive.

When his singing head was on, he would try his best at a verse or two of the Tony Bennett favourite 'I Left My Heart in San Francisco'. My granda was also a fantastic impersonator and he would have people in stitches when he mimicked acting legend James Cagney.

When Nessie and Hector were drinking, they would always start with a single bottle of Eldorado fortified wine. It was always Eldorado, or LD, as people called it. The local off-licence must have made a small fortune just from selling bottles of LD to Nessie and Hector. After the first bottle had been knocked back they would take it in turns to walk the short distance back to the off-licence for another. Well into their drinking sessions, the atmosphere would turn foul and the tension would thicken between them. I knew what signs to look out for, and I knew what would happen next. Nessie would be sitting in her favourite chair, arms folded, and the insults would come pouring out of her. She would start by saying to Hector: 'You're nothing but a dirty cow' or 'You're a baldy bastard . . . nothing but a brass-nail.'

After the last swig of LD she would stand up, walk over to an unsuspecting Hector and smash the empty bottle right over his skull. My poor old granda! I can see him now, sitting there with his head and face drenched with blood. He had that many wine bottles cracked over his nut I don't know how his body coped with the abuse. His bald head was covered with scars. It was always comical for me as a wee boy to sit and watch the pair of them turn from being a loving couple to cursing each other.

One day Hector was so drunk he took off all his clothes, every stitch, and wandered around outside naked. They had been arguing all day and he decided to demonstrate his love for Nessie. He stood on the grass verge that ran along the street in front of the houses and, with his arms held aloft, he began shouting in a high-pitched Glaswegian voice: 'Nessie, I luv ye, hen . . . I luv ye . . . Nessie, I dae luv ye.' This sort of incident didn't seem to upset or offend the neighbours. They simply laughed; it was nothing out of the ordinary.

If Hector and Nessie had a bad fall out, he would sometimes pack a bag and head off to the Great Eastern Hotel on Duke Street. The Great Eastern Hotel is one of Glasgow's best-known landmarks and is of historic significance to the city. It was built originally as a cotton spinning mill and was previously known as Alexander's Mill. In 1907 it was converted into a hostel for homeless people and Old Hector spent many a night there. It was finally closed amid some controversy in 2001.

Hector was also no stranger to crime. He served a five-year sentence for stabbing a man who had apparently been bothering Nessie; a family member suggested that, in fact, my granny had concocted a story after they had been seen together up a close. Whatever the case, I believe it was the only long-term prison sentence my granda served. Like my mother, Hector was lucky in evading capture for violent crime. A family recollection has it that on one occasion Hector, in his bare feet, crept up behind a copper who had been harassing him and hit him on the head with the hob of a cooker. Suspecting Hector of the serious assault, the polis (Glaswegian for 'the police' or 'police officer') went to the house looking for him, but he was already in his bed. They decided that it couldn't possibly have been him. If only they had checked his feet, they would've seen they were dirty and would probably have charged him!

As a child I always looked at life through rose-tinted spectacles. With no real discipline in my early years, I felt I had a sort of licence to do whatever I wanted. My grandfather acted as a fatherly figure; I cannot remember him lifting his hands to me ever. At no time did my grandmother hit me either.

Growing up in Carntyne was a happy and exciting time for

me, not because I was cared for properly as a child, but because I could do as I pleased, which I suppose is every kid's dream.

I remember the ragman with his horse and cart, walking his horse along the street blowing his bugle, enticing all the kids from their houses. It was always a treat exchanging a few old rags for a big balloon on a stick or simply following the horse and cart along the road in the hope you'd get one for nothing. Then you had the hawkers who sold their homemade candy-apples around the back courts. Whelks and mussels were another customary trade for most of the residents from the neighbour-hood. Men carrying cardboard boxes stuffed with little white paper bags full of seafood they'd just picked from somewhere along the Ayrshire Coast would walk about shouting erratically in a fancy tune, 'Get your whelks and mussels!'

Kids would be playing in the streets, dodging the lorries as they delivered their bags of coal. Women would hang out their windows talking to each other. Others would be shouting at their kids, telling them their supper was ready. Packs of dogs would roam the streets and back courts rummaging for food. Some-times you would catch a glimpse of an old woman throwing a pail of water over a couple of strays who'd become over-amorous and got stuck together in her garden. On every street corner there was something exciting happening; it was a very spirited and fulfilling time in my life.

From as far back as I can possibly remember, it was drummed into me time and time again never to talk to the police. My grandparents were forever telling me that if I were naughty then the man wearing the uniform would take me away and put me in a home for bad boys. We even had a budgie called Billy that could say 'fuck the polis' as clear as day! The Mansons also had a characteristic whistle which they used every time they wanted to get inside the house. Like a sort of security measure, family members had their own pitched melody that was easily identifi-able and each of us could distinguish who was who.

When most children were tucked up in bed having a nice bedtime story read to them, I was probably running around the neighbourhood until all hours of the morning. I can't ever recall having a bedtime story read to me as a small boy. It simply wasn't part of my upbringing. I was an extremely energetic little kid who lived life to the full. Carntyne provided me with so much streetwise knowledge, which I feel became invaluable in an existence where criminality was prevalent. Sometimes I would wait until my grandparents both fell asleep, then I'd go out into the night on my bicycle and ride about until all hours. I would often sellotape a torch to the front of my handlebars and just ride through the dark streets for hours on end. This was great fun and I felt on top of the world, but for a five- or six-year-old boy it was going just a bit too far. There was no control over me when Nessie and Hector were drunk. At times I was locked out the whole night, and on these instances I would have to curl up by myself on the first landing in the close, where it was always freezing cold.

The local gang, the Goucho, ran a free membership so long as you were from Carntyne itself. Even as a wee boy I understood the meaning of being part of a gang. It was very important, as it gave me a sense of identity, a feeling that I belonged to something. Ultimately, it gave me a feeling of power, and all I wanted to do was be like the older boys. I was always extremely sociable and thrived on going about in large groups. Most nights there would be plenty of activity, fighting the nearest rival gang, the Powery from Haghill. A common place to confront the Powery was on the top of a steep hill we called the Bing that separated the two neighbourhoods: the fighting was all about who could dominate the top of that hill.

This constant fighting resulted regularly in severe injuries. I can remember one tragic incident where the older brother of my pal, John Kinnaird, and one of his mates, caught someone from the Powery gang. This took place up on the railway line. They brutally killed the boy with hatchets and pick shafts. The journalists and press at the time made a big thing about it.

As kids we would talk about the Black Maria, the black Sherpa van the police drove slowly around the area. I was a bit too small to know what the inside of one looked like, but I clearly remember stories of those who did and they weren't at all pleasant. So, from an early age I was taught that the police were the enemy. This was drummed into me. In Carntyne there were rules of conduct and a code of silence that everyone in the district understood. It seemed everyone viewed the police with hostility, typical of an underprivileged neighbourhood, and this in many ways bonded the whole community together. That's one thing I can say about the Manson family – there were no stoolpigeons amongst us and we always stood for what we believed in. Nowadays that connection amongst communities in Glasgow has long gone.

It was always a right treat for me and all my wee pals on the street when my uncle Billy and his friends drove up to the close in their fancy E-Type Jags and Jensen Interceptors. Sometimes as many as three or four cars would pull up outside in the street. Burly men with long hair and sideburns, usually in dark suits with flared trousers and platform shoes, would step from the vehicles, pick me up and swing me about as if I was their own. This meant that I became the centre of attention amongst the kids who were hanging around staring in awe.

Quickly a big crowd would appear to find out what was going on. With dirty smiling faces, my pals and I waited for my uncle Billy and his friends to emerge from my grandparents' house, having finished what they were doing, and jump back into their cars. As the excitement amongst the crowd reached ecstatic proportions, and just before the cars started to pull away, the windows would go down and then all you would hear, above anything else, was the clatter of dozens of loose coins pelting off the pavement. This is what we called a 'scramble' and for every kid in the street it was a mad free-for-all. Other times my uncle Billy would bring his camera, the old self-timer type, and he would take snaps of my granny, granda and me together. Wherever these photos have gone, I've no idea.

Sometimes Billy would take the three of us to Largs or somewhere else along the Ayrshire coast, to go out in the boats fishing. There's no doubt he was very good to us and would spoil us with gifts all the time.

The uncle after whom I am named was born on 20 March 1939. He was the mastermind of an expertly planned jailbreak from top-security Perth Prison on 9 December 1979. He astonished the police and prison authorities with the speed and precision with which he carried out such a highly sophisticated escape. Billy and one of his pals sawed through their cell bars, scaled the wall and got onto the roof. They used homemade rope to descend to the yard, then escape over a surrounding fence. A high-powered vehicle was waiting to take them to freedom. Billy's old pal, legendary Arthur Thompson, who dominated the organised crime scene in Glasgow from the 1950s onwards, and whose son I was later accused of killing, played a vital role in assisting him during the escape, especially after he got away.

Billy was serving a twelve-year sentence at the time, having been found guilty at the High Court in Glasgow on 13 January 1978 of robbing the Orient bingo hall, and threatening staff with a sawn-off shotgun and a meat cleaver. Billy always strenuously denied ever being involved in this hold-up, and he went to extraordinary lengths to prove it. He claimed that Strathclyde police officers, acting through malice and gratification of personal desires, conceived and orchestrated a plot to pervert and corrupt the course of justice. He also claimed the coppers seriously assaulted him in the back of a police van and committed perjury at his trial.

He raised a £30,000 action against then Chief Constable Patrick Hamill and in a 40-page High Court writ he asked the court to declare that the incompetence, neglect and maladministration of the police in abusing the legal process had caused the High Court to be deprived of fairness and equity. Billy claimed that the coppers bundled him into the back of a police van simply because he was in the area where the robbery had been committed, and that on the way to Tobago Street Police Station he was punched, kicked and beaten with batons until he was black-and-blue and had a fractured nose. He also said that the police took money from a plastic carrier bag found near the scene of the robbery and smeared it with his blood and fingerprints.

It wasn't just Billy who claimed he was innocent. His lawyer, the respected Glasgow professor Peter Watson, examined the case thoroughly and as a result went out of his way to secure a Royal Pardon. He said at the time: 'Billy Manson is a well-known figure in the Glasgow underworld, but in the past he has always admitted his crime. When he is "done" for something, he doesn't complain. This is the first time he has protested his innocence. I've no doubt in my mind that he is in fact innocent.'

When Glasgow and North Argyll Legal Aid Committee had rejected Billy's application for legal aid, Arthur Thompson paid £750 towards his civil case when a judge asked him to lodge the money against future expenses. On 22 January 1980, six weeks after Billy escaped from Perth, two police officers who were investigating a completely different matter arrested him in the Garrowhill area of Glasgow. Billy happened to be walking nearby when the call came in and the police thought they'd pull him anyway. Billy tried to do a runner, but the police caught him and hauled him back to the police station, where they quickly discovered he was the most wanted man in the country. A nice and unexpected result for the two uniformed bobbies.

The following day Billy was taken to court handcuffed to two members of the Serious Crime Squad and during a private hearing various charges were put to him. Sheriff Archibald Bell QC sent Billy back to prison to complete his twelve-year sentence, as well as sentencing him to a further three years for escaping.

Billy served his time in tough Peterhead Prison. He refused to wear the prison uniform, wearing instead a pair of overalls, on the chest of which he embroidered the words 'I Am Innocent'. He went on hunger strikes to bring attention to his plight and he also refused parole at every opportunity, as this would have been, in his view, a declaration of guilt. He served out his full sentence at Peterhead and was finally released in 1989.

In 1964, Billy had also escaped from Barlinnie Prison in Glasgow and managed to elude the law by living as a fugitive for 18 months. He was once described as one of the most dangerous villains in Britain and at one stage senior police chiefs throughout the UK held top-level conferences about him, his associates and his activities.

He also possessed a talent very few of us could match: the ability to turn a block of wood into a masterpiece of craftsmanship. He specialised in carving models of old Spanish galleons and other ships it was simply amazing what he could achieve using his hands. He could quite easily have made a career for himself using the skills he possessed as a carpenter. It saddens me when I think about what he could have done with himself.

His story is quite remarkable. In his heyday he drove the best of cars and wore the best tailored suits. He was also adventurous and occasionally he would drive to Brands Hatch to race fast cars around the track, or he would take flying lessons in a light aircraft. There's no doubt he led a luxurious lifestyle, but what major villain didn't back in the 1960s and 70s?

On 12 November 1997 Billy was found dead in his flat in Maryhill. His death certificate states the cause of death was an overdose of co-proxamol, a particularly dangerous painkiller which, before it was withdrawn from the market in 2007, was the second most frequent means of suicide using prescribed drugs in the UK. Billy was using co-proxamol for the back pain he suffered and for ongoing ailments connected to an attempt on his life. Co-proxamol was a drug he'd been prescribed by his doctor, but I believe Billy was taking a few more than he ought to have been. His friend Walter Norval – known by the serious crime squad as 'the Glasgow Godfather', and the notorious leader of the XYY gang – assured me that Billy was using light drugs for recreational purposes but during the latter stages of his life he became a bit more dependent on them. Years in prison had taken their toll on his mental state, and his friends were reporting a change for the worse. According to Norval, Billy was losing the plot and was beginning to cut himself off socially.

Crime writer and ghost writer to Paul Ferris, the late Reg McKay, made wild claims in one of his books, *McGraw*, suggesting that Billy Manson died after being forced to swallow a huge quantity of co-proxamol tablets. It wouldn't surprise me if this malicious rumour had been instigated by Ferris himself, but it is complete and utter nonsense, as the Toxicology and Post-mortem reports indicate no signs of forced ingestion. In addition, witnesses present when the police had to gain entry to Billy's flat after he hadn't been seen for several days stated that the door was locked and bolted from the inside. And footage from CCTV cameras in the vicinity showed no suspicious comings and goings from Billy's flat.

Recently a member of the Manson family wrote to the Crown Office and asked them to look into the shocking allegation. Prosecutors are now examining the claims and a cold-case team could conduct an inquiry. This is welcome news to the Mansons, who are quietly confident that any inquiry will show how ludicrous the claims in *McGraw* are.

In Carntyne there was always plenty of exciting stuff for us youngsters to get up to. It's not like today, when kids are spoiled with laptop computers and mobile smartphones, or else spending time chatting to their mates on Facebook. As kids we would venture outdoors and sometimes walk for miles in search of things to do.

The greyhound-racing track, which was literally just a good stone's throw from where I lived in Penicuik Street, was a favourite haunt for us wee ones. It was one of the largest tracks in Scotland, always an extremely busy place full of activity. The reverberations from the loudspeakers echoed right across the neighbourhood. In order to get really close to the track we would first need to cross a live railway line. This was a very dangerous and stupid thing to do, but I suppose it all added to the excitement and fun of it all. Having crossed the railway line, actually dodging trains at times, we made our way towards a small hole we'd cut in the fence. From there we watched the greyhounds chasing the dummy rabbit around the track. This was a magical time. Thousands of men would be shouting encouragement for their greyhounds to win, while the commentator screamed over the speaker system as the dogs passed the finishing line. As a result of the huge floodlights, the whole stadium shone with this brilliant white light against the night sky. It was fantastic – there isn't a kid in the world that wouldn't have relished a couple of hours being entertained like that.

Next to the greyhound track there was a coal depot, or 'coaly', as it was better known. In the evening when the coal men went home, my wee pals and I would cross the live railway line again, climb up a steep embankment and there right in front of us were mountains of coal. There was a slight problem, however: guarding the coal was a massive Alsatian dog chained to a post.

The only way it was possible to get to the goods was for one of us to distract the dog while the rest of us filled plastic carrier bags with as much coal as we could carry. Luckily the Alsatian never broke loose. At times this was a nice little earner because we would sell plastic bags full of coal all around the neighbourhood, and there was that much of it nobody seemed to notice any had gone.

Another favourite pastime was heading to the other end of Carntyne to look for what we called 'lucky didgies' or 'raiding the middens'. This would involve going to the so-called toffee-nosed part of Carntyne, where people lived much better than those down in the lower end. The houses were nicer, with lovely gardens and fancy cars parked in the driveways. We would target the rubbish bins outside the properties and more often than not we would come across all sorts of goodies to take back home with us. It's amazing what well-heeled folk chucked away and every deprived kid who went on a lucky didgie escapade loved it.

Another childhood memory is the Big, Black Hand. This was something my grandparents dreamt up to frighten me when I'd been bad. As a very young child, I was so terrified of it that sometimes I couldn't get to sleep at night. When I was naughty, my grandmother would grab me and make me stand in front of the coal fire in the living room. My grandfather would stand in the kitchen, out of sight, and silently open the small compartment in the kitchen wall which gave him access to the back of the coal fire. This type of set-up is what we called a back-to-back grate. The compartment was meant to be a way of cleaning the chimney. I would be screaming, 'Please Nana, please Nana, naaaaw!' and tears would be running down my face. I couldn't bear to watch, but she made sure I looked straight ahead into the fire. She would say to me: 'Right, the Big, Black Hand is going to get you because you've been bad,' and then a hand, which Hector covered in soot from the chimney, would slowly appear from the fire, accompanied by a bogieman sound. I was petrified, and I could never quite understand how this black hand appeared. It took me a long time to figure out what Hector had been up to in the kitchen.

With an irresistible urge to fulfil my ever-growing imagination, sometimes I would walk to Duke Street, which was a good saunter from where I lived. This was a busy shopping thoroughfare in a slightly more affluent area of the East End, nearer to the city centre. I liked to hang around there, mostly on my skiving-school days.

I became obsessed with an air rifle that stood out in the window display of a shop on Duke Street. This shop sold fishing tackle, knives and hunting gear, and I would stand and stare at the rifle for long periods, oblivious to the throng of shoppers as they went about their everyday business. I had decided that I had to have that air rifle, and I had been nicking money from my gran's purse to pay for it. When I had enough stashed away for the gun, I skipped back to the shop, knowing that there was no way the shopkeeper would sell me the weapon. I waited outside the shop for the first half-decent-looking person to come along and, pointing to the air rifle in the window, I asked him to help me get it.

'Mister, gonny go in and buy me that gun?' I asked him.

'Aye, nae bother, son,' he replied without a moment's hesitation. I handed him the money. He got me the gun, as well as pellets and darts to go with it.

I took off back home carrying the air rifle, which was as big as I was, and heavy too. Penicuik Street was a good twenty-minute walk from Duke Street shops and when I got home my grandparents were sitting on the sofa, blazing drunk. They were unaware that I had been dodging school and were oblivious to the fact that I quickly got up to mischief with the air rifle, firing pellets at pigeons on the neighbouring rooftops.

But it wasn't long before I was picking out bigger targets. From a good vantage point one day I could see a young boy I knew called Gilchrist, who was playing on the grass verge about 30 yards away. The Gilchrists lived on the other side of the street from my grandparents and Hector had never got on with them. I might have been young, but I knew what was what around the neighbourhood. I took aim and fired, hitting him in the thigh. What a shot! But the screams he made were loud, too loud. I panicked and ran through the back court, up the close and into my grandparent's house, stashing the weapon under some bedding in a wicker basket.

It wasn't long before two uniformed police came banging on the door. Now I was in trouble. Someone must've seen me running away, or the Gilchrist parents must have worked out who was responsible. I was the little baddie in the street and the finger of blame was always pointed in my direction first. The police came into the house and quickly found the gun. I received a slap on the wrist, but that's all. I was far too young to be charged with a crime. My grandparents I'm sure took the flak, but they would have had a chuckle to themselves afterwards.

I was taught to steal from a very early age. My grandparents encouraged me to shoplift in all the big stores and supermarkets. I had to hold a plastic carrier bag and when I was told to open the bag Hector would normally put a chicken or packets of meat inside. I cannot remember ever being caught and we did this regularly – at least whenever we went to Parkhead or the city centre.

On one of these outings I remember my grandparents taking me to one of their favourite haunts called Paddy's Market – or the Briggaite, as it was much better known – situated at the Saltmarket near Glasgow Cross. The Briggait was a popular place amongst the city's most destitute, and you could pick up almost anything there, such as cheap second-hand clothes and even used dentures – it had the lot! When I saw one of the traders busy gabbing to another a few stalls away, I managed to slip a bunch of the then fashionable snake belts into the plastic carrier bag I had in my hand. It was probably the first time I'd stolen something without encouragement; later that same day all the kids from my street were running about sporting a colourful snake belt!

I'll never forget how I got my first bicycle. Your first bike as a kid is always a big deal, although I waited quite a long time for mine. The popular kid's bike back then was a red-coloured Tomahawk. It was a smaller version of the classic chopper and it had all the same characteristics. I'd always wanted one of these bikes and was forever asking my granny to get me one. My bike did come eventually, by way of my granda pinching a woman's rent book stuffed with £20 notes. As my grandparents and I were waiting in the queue to pay their rent in the Parkhead rent office, Hector noticed a woman in front of us who had a wad of cash inside her rent book. Hector quickly pulled me aside, pointed out the woman, and instructed me to fall over in the exit doorway as soon as she approached.

The rent office in Parkhead was only up the road from Carntyne. It was a very busy place, with maybe five or six different queues snaking all the way outside onto the pavement sometimes. I have this vivid image of the inside of the rent office with clouds of cigarette smoke hanging in the air. With people coming and going and everyone chatting away, it was the ideal setting for Hector to dip the woman's bag. Nessie had already made her way to the exit swing doors and I quickly followed her to get myself into position. As the woman approached the doorway, I did as I was told and fell over to block her path. It was a team effort and my granda wasted no time in dipping the prize, with Nessie giving him that extra bit of cover. It was all over very fast and the woman didn't notice a thing. My granny grabbed my hand and we made our way out of the building. Hector hailed a conveniently passing black taxi and the three of us set off home. During the short journey back to Carntyne, Hector pulled out a bundle of £20 notes. Nessie turned to me and said: 'Now you can get your Tomahawk bike tomorrow.' I was over the moon.

Chapter Two

In the Clutches of a Stranger

My mother appeared one day, right out of the blue. There was no warning of any kind; she just turned up at my grandparents' door and demanded that I leave with her. She was unwavering and totally adamant that she was taking me back into her care. She had no thoughts for how this would inevitably affect me and it made no difference when I courageously protested against it.

There was absolutely nothing my grandparents or I could do to prevent it. My mother's mission that day was, in a wicked sense, to kidnap me and remove me from the environment I had grown up in. What a nasty thing to do. What was she thinking? One thing is certain: my feelings weren't taken into account. To say I was confused by this would be an understatement. I was horrified. Here was this woman, my real mother – who I looked upon as a complete stranger – suddenly appearing at my grandparents' and demanding the unthinkable.

Following her arrival, a massive argument ensued in the sitting room. I recall everyone shouting and screaming at each other, but in the end there could be only one outcome. My mother grabbed me by the arm and dragged me to her Morris 1100 parked outside. I kicked and yelled out while looking at my grandparents, as if expecting them to release me from my mother's grip. But she was stronger than I was and she was in a heightened state herself, so it wasn't too difficult for her to forcibly take me from the house and chuck me into her car.

The shouting and bawling continued right up until the point that I was thrown head first into the back of the car and the door was slammed shut in my face. Locked inside with no escape, I could see my granny crying outside at the close entrance. I felt so frightened and I was crying my heart out. For the first time I knew what it felt like to be held against my will. As my mother started the engine, all I could do was kneel on the back seat with my face pressing against the back window. With blurry eyes, clouding my vision I banged on the glass. It was horrible: I was now in the clutches of a stranger, and it broke my heart having to watch my grandparents fade into the distance.

Although I was only a small boy, I wasn't prepared to let this woman get away with snatching me from the only place I ever knew to be home. For three years, I ran away from my mother at every opportunity. I would steal money when I could and get a bus or even a taxi back to Carntyne. At first, my mother took me to live in Blackhill, which bordered Carntyne in the north-east of Glasgow. Developed as a council housing estate in the 1930s, it had become known as one of the roughest areas of the city, notorious for deprivation, chronic housing and drug-related problems. The western side of Blackhill, near Riddrie, was the more desirable part of the area because the accommodation there was considered a cut above the rest – the houses were of the 'cottage flat' type, with back and front gardens, and the streets were much better kept.

We went to live in Craigendmuir Street in 1975, a typical three-storey, slate-roofed tenement block built of reconstituted stone. This was the not–so-desirable part of the area. My mother had a boyfriend at this time, a chap called Alex Gibb. Alex was a very tall, imposing figure who stood at well over six feet. He was an electrician by trade and held down a decent job working for an electricity company. He had been going out with my mother for a few years before I came to Craigendmuir Street. I remember him treating me very well; he was always spoiling me with loads of presents, the sort of thing you'd expect a man in his position to do with his partner's wee boy. Because my mother had a twelve-year on/off relationship with Alex Gibb, naturally my wee pals called me 'Gibby', a nickname that would stick later in my life, and one that I became well known by in certain circles.

Like any kid my age, it didn't take me long to adjust to my new surroundings. I quickly settled in to the Blackhill way of life, which was similar to Carntyne, as there were loads of kids my size and age running wild in the streets. We children learned to make use of the pavements and back courts. We would play 'dreepy' – hanging down and then letting yourself fall from massive walls and gable ends – jump around in puddles when it rained or play 'jorries' (marbles).

I have a deep scar on the palm of my left hand, which is as visible today as it was after it first happened. I picked this up while playing in the big metal rubbish bins that stood in the back courts of Craigendmuir Street and the surrounding area. I'd managed to climb up onto the top of one of these huge bins but quickly found myself falling inside. After a quick rummage about I jumped out instead of climbing back down the way I had got up. As I made contact with the solid concrete, I fell forward and automatically put my hands out in front of me to prevent me tumbling over. My left hand slammed down right on top of the neck of a broken milk bottle. Ouch! I was rushed to hospital, where I had five stitches inserted into the deep gash in my hand. It kept me from climbing the rubbish bins for a while.

I believe my mother did at times try her best to bond with me. She could be extremely charming and loving towards me, but only when she was absolutely sober and level-headed. As soon as she started to take large quantities of alcohol she would change into a horrible, evil woman who showed nothing but hatred and violence towards me: a scar far worse than the one I picked up jumping from the rubbish bin, albeit of the mental type, was heading my way.

It started as a quiet evening. I was at home with her and Alex Gibb in the house at Craigendmuir Street. Alex and my mother suddenly had a colossal argument. They had both been drinking heavily that day and the alcohol certainly fuelled the dispute. Alex got to the point where he'd had enough of the shouting and screaming so he put his jacket on and left for the pub. I went out and followed him along the road until he reached the local boozer. When he went inside, I about-turned and made my way back home.

My mother was bitterly furious by this stage. She was pacing up and down the sitting room in a blind rage. She had locked the front door and removed the keys, and, realising I was locked inside alone with her, I watched her every move. Ranting and raving, she grabbed a knife from the kitchen, one with a long machete-type blade, and began walking back and forth with it in her grasp saying 'I'm going to kill him' and 'Just wait till he comes back.' She had a look of pure evil in her eyes and I knew that I had to alert Alex to the danger that awaited him.

My only way out of the house was to climb through the window, and I didn't hang around. I shot back along the road to the pub, where I could see Alex inside, drinking. I waited for him to come out. I recall it was a warm night and it was beginning to get dark, and I wasn't wearing a top. It's strange how these little things stay with you. When Alex did eventually leave the pub, he was staggering, now even more intoxicated than he had been before. I tried telling him that my mother had a big knife in the house and that he'd better not go back as she was going to stab him with it.

I tried everything I could to persuade him not to go back, but it did no good. He took no notice of what I was saying. I even pulled at his arm and his trouser legs, but to no avail. He just shoved me away and, slurring his speech, told me to shut up. I ran along the road ahead of him and climbed back into the house through the open window. My mother was still holding the knife and I pleaded with her to stop. We could now see Alex approaching the entrance of the close and as he got nearer my mother stood right behind the front door clutching the knife. I scrambled out of the window again and ran into the close after him.

Alex kept his house keys on a chain and I could see him struggling, trying to get the keys out of his trouser pocket. Again I yanked on his trouser legs and I begged him not to open the door, but again he pushed me away. He would never have realised the danger he was in. Not even in his wildest dreams would he have suspected anything like what was about to happen to him.

After a couple of failed attempts at finding the keyhole he managed to undo the lock and pushed the door open. As he withdrew his key from the lock my mother appeared and without warning she plunged the knife right into his stomach with such force that the tip of the blade exited his back. I watched Alex fall back into the close with the knife rammed right through him to the hilt. My screams echoed and amplified throughout the close. There was blood everywhere and, hearing the commotion, neighbours began to appear from their houses. I recall an ambulance arriving and the police turning up, blue lights flashing all over the close. I remember Alex being stretchered away with the handle of the knife still sticking out of his stomach.

Alex remained in hospital on the critical list for quite some time. I don't know how he survived or how my mother evaded prosecution for this savage attack on a person she supposedly loved. Other than me, just a small boy, there were no witnesses to the stabbing and the police were powerless to charge her. Alex never gave a statement to the police against her, not that he was in any fit state to do so. My mother was also a terrific actress when she wanted to be, so it wouldn't have been too difficult for her to make up some dramatic story to fool the police.

Another time, when we later moved to Possilpark, I saw her slitting a woman's throat. The victim's name was Ellen Forrester. A fight had broken out between them in the kitchen of my mother's house. Back then, we had a coal bunker in the kitchen and my mother held Ellen over this bunker while she grabbed a kitchen knife and cut her throat. The woman received 60 stitches and could easily have died. To add insult to injury, my mother subsequently nicknamed her 'Bunker-nut'!

My mother also bit off one of her boyfriend's ears. If that wasn't bad enough, she kept it in the fridge for weeks.

I sometimes wish that she had received a life sentence, because her health took such a hammering with all the alcohol abuse over the years. A long sentence would have straightened her out for sure, and perhaps she'd still be alive today.

Because of my infrequent attendance at school, and the extent of neglect I experienced as a child, the Social Work Department and the Royal Scottish Society for the Prevention of Cruelty to Children (RSSPCC) played a significant part in my early childhood.

My mother made the situation a lot worse by subjecting me to further abuse and manipulation. Another incident that had a huge impact on my life came in early 1978, and I guess its outcome was inevitable; it was just a matter of time. In a report of 22 February 1978, a good couple of years after my mother had taken me from my grandparents, and which clearly shows the incompetence and complications that engulfed her life at this time, Inspector Eric Cranston of the RSSPCC wrote:

Phone call received from Const. Anderson, Saracen Police Station who complained that the child, William Lobban, had come into the police station in a most distressed state. He had not had a meal all day, and he claimed that his mother had given him a hammering, although he was not marked.

His mother had gone out drinking, and the police had later collected her in a pub and took her home. She appeared to have a good drink in her. The const. described the kitchen in the house as being 'Manky'. The only food seen had been half a dozen eggs and two carrots. A tin of beer was in the fridge.

The child was thought to be illegitimate and the mother was alleged to be a prostitute. It was also alleged by the child that she often hammered him and made him go to the off-licences for a drink for her. On these occasions he had to hang about until he could find a grown-up who was prepared to go in and purchase it for him.

The boy did not want to go home with his mother, but to be returned to the M.G.M [maternal grandmother], Mrs Manson, 32 Penicuik Street, Carntyne. The M.G.M. had brought him up until he was 7 years old, when the mother had demanded to take him back. At the time of this call, both mother and child were back at the police station, and although the mother had sobered up considerably, she had indicated that she would again hammer the boy when she got him home, and it was thought likely that she would indeed do so.

The police were not happy with the situation, but doubted if there was much they could do at this time, although they were concerned for the boy. I agreed to call at the police station to see them, and Emerg. S.W.D. provided me with a local authority car.

At the station, I spoke with Sergeant Fraser, Const. Anderson having gone off shift. The mother was seen to be sitting in the main foyer and was sitting grinning, obviously taking the whole thing as a big joke.

William on the other hand, was sitting alone in an interview room looking cowed and dejected. Sergeant Fraser went over all that the Const. had reported, but added that the mother had apparently tried to commit suicide on a number of occasions. On the last occasion she tried to slash her wrists in front of William.

Along with Sgt. Fraser I first of all interviewed the child, he said that all he had to eat all day had been a cup of tea and a jam piece which a neighbour had given him about 10.30 am. His mother had just returned home that day after a few days in hospital having hurt herself in an accident. He said that she had gone out drinking about 5.30 pm that night.

We then interviewed the mother in a separate interview room. To start with she was still all grinning and very cocky. She denied having gone out drinking before 8.30 pm and insisted at this time she had only gone out to look for William who had been out playing. During her search she had run into a friend who had insisted on buying her a drink. She claimed she had only been drinking for about half an hour. I put it to her that this did not appear consistent with the police description of her condition. She replied that she had just been putting this on to fool around. I suggested it was not a very intelligent way to behave in a police station, but she declared that it had only been a nervous reaction as she was a very nervous type of person. Her whole attitude, however, was very sly and her story did not ring true.

I suggested that perhaps until things cooled down it might be better if William was taken to stay the night with the M.G.M., but she insisted that was the last place she would allow him to go. She stated William only liked staying there because both her parents were heavy drinkers and he could do anything he wanted. I put it to the mother that I would take her and the child home as I would wish to examine the house. I also warned her that she must not beat the child again, as a colleague would visit again the next day to try and sort out the position. At this, her attitude changed and she said that as far as she cared I could take William into care, just so long as he would not return to the M.G.Ps.

We went back and discussed this with William who still wanted to go to the grandparents, but understanding the position, agreed to go to a Children's Home meantime until things were sorted out. He persisted with his plea to be returned to the grandparents as he did not wish to stay with his mother, but I told him that this was something which would have to be sorted out by a Children's Panel.

The mother returned home on her own while I took the boy to John Street Emergency S.W. Bar, then on to Lochaber Children's Home. I assured the House Father that a colleague would be following this up today with the mother and that the home would be contacted since at this time the child was only accepted on the basis of a single night care.

I remember sitting in the back of a big, black chauffeur-driven car as it pulled away from Saracen Police Station and began making its way through the dark, empty streets of Glasgow towards Lochaber Children's Home in Kelvingrove.

The social work inspector sat beside me in the car, and he tried to reassure me that everything would be fine and that I shouldn't worry. His words offered a bit of comfort, but I was still scared and nervous, and I didn't know what to expect. This was the first time I'd been placed in care and it was a big deal to me. I had just turned 10 years old.

We arrived at a huge sandstone building in the middle of what looked like a very posh area. There were tall trees all around the place, there was a slight eerie quietness as well, and the social work inspector walked me up to the front door. There to greet us was the night duty officer, who welcomed us in and he told me to stand in the porch area while paperwork and details of my case were established.

After a few minutes the social work inspector left. I was on my own and it was all down to me now. The night duty officer, a man by the name of Mr McCewan, who had permed frizzy hair and matching frizzy beard, showed me downstairs and took me to an ablutions area. He instructed me to take off all my clothes and to get myself into the shower. Nervously I removed my filthy clobber, stepped into the hot sprays of water and tensely began washing myself. He approached me with a big tub of delousing cream for my hair and body.

'Dip your hand in there and rub that stuff all over yourself . . . and make sure you do it properly,' he said.

He stood there watching while I did as he asked.

'Right, get some more on,' he said, making me repeat the process.

After a lengthy shower and a thorough delousing I was now glowing with health from head to toe. I remember peering at my reflection in the mirror above a sink and couldn't help but notice a sparkle in my eyes. My cheeks, too, were gleaming, a warm rosy colour. There was a set of folded pyjamas sitting on top of a chair, which Mr McCewan told me to put on.

My fate it seemed was sealed at Lochaber Children's Home: I'd be staying there for the foreseeable future and there wasn't a thing I could do about it. Any chance there was of me going back to stay with my grandparents, or to my mother, for that matter, was totally out of the question.

I had been playing truant and had missed far too much of my schooling. My home circumstances were far from adequate, and the neglect I suffered was way beyond the boundaries of responsible parenting. The state had a grip of my life now. I didn't know that this was the start of what would become a progressive path towards a life of crime, punishment and reprehensible behaviour.

It was during my time at Lochaber that the other kids introduced me to solvent abuse. Getting high or glue sniffing was already in existence when I arrived at the children's home, and the staff most certainly knew about it. It wasn't a huge problem, but it did go on. I suppose many kids will want to experiment with solvents of some sort, especially where the peer pressure is high, and the ideal environment for this is in a place such as a children's home where disobedience is collective. Kids will inevitably pick up any bad habits their peer group displays. It wasn't something that happened every day, but I recall the long, hot summer evenings being the time when glue sniffing was most rampant. When there was a glue-sniffing session taking place at Lochaber, it could sometimes involve up to half a dozen kids. We would just disappear and head to a spot we had selected under a bridge, not too far from Lochaber itself. Sniffing glue would become a major problem for me when I finally went back to live with my mother in Possilpark. I had just dabbled at Lochaber, but it became more frequent when I moved from there.

In fact I would go on to have a nightmare experience involving glue-sniffing at Saracen Police Station. I was being held in a detention room while awaiting return to a List-D school when the Police Sergeant found a half-pint of Evo-stik glue in my jacket pocket. He poured it over my head and I could feel it burning my scalp. I remember screaming the place down, and other officers putting my head under the cold tap in the hope it might help. It didn't, and the next morning I woke up looking like Sid Vicious from the Sex Pistols.

Lochaber certainly gave me a sense of stability for a while, there's no doubt about that. The staff always made sure I was properly clothed and you wanted for nothing. My natural inclination to 'take without the owner's consent' was forever present though, and one night, when everyone was sleeping, I devised an elaborate plan to nick the night duty officer's wallet.

My thieving tendencies went even further on 17 June 1978, just a few months after arriving at Lochaber; I stole a quantity of lead flashing from the roof. I committed this theft while acting along with other kids from the home. I don't know what we were thinking. Some of the older boys may have thought we could perhaps take the lead to a scrapyard in exchange for cash – otherwise what point would there have been in taking it in the first place?

I climbed up a drainpipe to get onto the roof. Dangerous as it was, I ripped the lead from its holdings, causing all sorts of damage to the roof in the process. There was a load of it, but there was also a problem – the only feasible way of getting the lead to the ground was to fling it down from the roof. With the roof being possibly 60 feet high, you can imagine the thud the lead made when it smashed into the ground below. Inevitably a staff member heard it. I was caught red-handed.

The staff called the police and I faced a charge of theft. Because of my age I was put in front of a Children's Panel, which was based at a building called Mackenzie House, 400 Argyle Street, in the city centre. A hearing was set for 2 pm on Wednesday, 30 August 1978. When I finally appeared at the Children's Panel, they decided that, as this was my first period in Lochaber, I should be given another chance and they sent me back to live with my mother. My uncle Robert was about to finish doing time at Perth Prison. He was writing to the Children's Panel and taking an interest in my well-being, and this offered some form of stability within the family when he got out.

I suppose I did have some good times living with my mother. One in particular springs to mind. It was the summer and I and all my wee pals from Sunnylaw Street were treated to a day at the seaside somewhere down the Ayrshire coast. My mother had an old yellow Dodge BT van at the time and we sat on cushions in the back of the van. It was a great trip out and everyone loved it. Clearly my mother was on the ball that day, and she could be positive when she put her mind to it.

I also enjoyed travelling around with her when she worked for Pelosi's, a family-run business based in the West End of Glasgow. They specialised in supplying cigarette vending machines, and my mother would travel around Scotland in a Transit van full of fags, stopping at pubs, restaurants and even Calderpark Zoo, just outside Glasgow, stocking up the machines. She took me along with her to all these different places and, to be honest, it was a right treat and something I always enjoyed.

First thing in the morning I would go along with her to Pelosi's office and there would be maybe ten or twelve people all busy sitting at a large table sorting out all the different brands of cigarettes. The workers made a small slit at the edge of the fag packet and then inserted coins to make up the change when someone bought them from the machine. This was big business.

My mother would load up her van for the day, and with her work schedule she would set off to different places up and down the country. I loved this part of it because it gave me the opportunity to travel about as a youngster when probably I should have been at school. Better still was the fact I was allowed to play all the fancy fruit machines which stood in every pub we went to. While my mother was emptying the vending machines of cash and replenishing them with fresh packets of cigarettes, I would be playing the fruit machines to my heart's content.

The fact that my mother was an attractive young woman only helped make my life a lot easier since all the male staff normally spoilt me with bottles of Coke and even gave me coins to play the games. Once or twice I hit the jackpot – I couldn't get enough of that noise when the machine continuously spat out the ten- and fifty-pence pieces.

The thrill of it all was, however, short-lived. My mother was eventually sacked from her job when one day the Transit van and its entire stock of cigarettes disappeared. It was actually one of my uncles and his mates who robbed the van of its contents – a nice earner back then – but it was my mother who put the work their way and who set the whole thing up.

Reports indicate that my mother was receiving counselling and care under various doctors, so the authorities knew of her problems. As far as the alcohol is concerned, I believe she started off with a drinking problem that she controlled, to an extent. It wasn't until later in her life that she became an out-and-out alcoholic. It is now common knowledge that alcoholism is an illness. If only my mother had sought help with the ailment then, her life might have been far better, but she never did. Instead, she just wasted away and in the end it destroyed her.

Alex Gibb accepted my mother back into his life after what she did to him – he must have been right off his nut to take her back, or maybe he was terrified, like everyone else who got close to her. Whatever the case, my mother and he secured a lovely basement flat in Kelvinside Gardens, a very posh and trendy part of the West End of Glasgow.

The flat, where my mother took me to live, was small, more like a large bedsit than a proper flat, and I slept on a fold-down sofa bed in the lounge. Kelvinside Gardens had a different feel to the housing estates where I had grown up. It was certainly much quieter and all the kids had nice bikes and better clothes.

The street was leafy and was opposite a public park, and the houses were of the old Victorian style. This was a far cry from what I had become used to and definitely a step up from the concrete jungle of Blackhill and Carntyne.

On the same street, just up the road from the flat, there stood a primary school called St Charles. I enrolled in this school and have a vivid memory of it. I absolutely detested it because one of the teachers put me on the spot and severely humiliated me in front of all the other kids in the classroom. I suppose I stood out at the school for different reasons. No doubt my dialect was different from all the other kids, mine being more typically based on housing scheme slang. I felt like a fish out of water and I became introverted and withdrawn for a time. This wasn't me; I wasn't my usual outgoing, troublesome self.

One day in the middle of a reading session I remember the schoolteacher shouted out my name and asked me to stand up. I recall a feeling of extreme discomfort and anxiety sweep over me as the teacher asked me to read an extract from the picture book I now had in my hand.

As all the other children looked on expectantly, I cringed and just stood there frozen to the spot in total silence. I was stuck for words; everyone was observing me, waiting patiently for me to say something, and nothing came out of my mouth. It felt like minutes had passed while I stood there, yet still I couldn't utter a single word.

I could feel my face burning with embarrassment and I didn't know what to do. I stuttered a few times and tried my best but I just couldn't read from the book. With a lump in my throat and my cheeks going bright red, I could feel tears begin to run down my face. There was no one coming to my aid. This was the most horrible experience for me as a kid and one I'll never forget. I'm sure that this terrible feeling of public embarrassment affected me later, and goes a long way to explain why, when I would feel threatened and uncomfortable, I would just lash out at other people.

Playing truant at my previous school had caught up with me for sure, and what should have been a relatively simple reading task turned out to be an intense, daunting experience, and one that has stayed with me. I just wished the classroom floor would open up and swallow me whole. It was the worst feeling ever.

I didn't stay in Kelvinside Gardens long enough for the place to leave a serious impression on my life. I recall spending a Christmas there because I actually received a Christmas present for once! I woke to find a massive box which contained dozens of miniature plastic Indians of all shapes and sizes – a box of miniature Indians, can you believe it?

But, as before, and invariably, I ended up back at my grand-parents', which by now had become a bit of a dumping ground. It seemed that when my mother's private life broke down it was convenient for her to take me back to Carntyne to get rid of me.

Her relationship with Alex Gibb was now on the verge of total collapse. It was always stormy and full of ups and downs at the best of times. I guess Alex tried his best and it just goes to show how far he was prepared to take his love, or fear, for the woman who heavily abused him.

By this time we were living in Sunnylaw Street in Possilpark. My mother had several boyfriends during my time growing up there, though Alex was still on the scene to begin with. Some of them were OK, but only a couple held some sort of significance with me. She seemed to abuse the men in her life and I know trusting them was definitely an issue with her. What made things much worse for her was that Alex Gibb ran off with one of her so-called best mates and got married to her. She just couldn't handle that. My biological father had run off with another woman, so it's possible she never trusted men after that.

One of her earlier boyfriends after Gibb was a chap called Ian Dinnie, who was born and bred in Possilpark. I remember this guy well and I liked him; he was a nice person. I would have put him in his early thirties, of medium build, with a receding hairline.

My mother was still a young woman herself, in her late twen-ties and good-looking, so boyfriends weren't hard for her to find. She could have had any guy she wanted in Possilpark. When I think about Ian Dinnie, I would probably have to say he was one of the best guys my mother ever went out with. Level-headed, he certainly had a lot of respect in the local community. I can see in hindsight that he and my mother really liked one another it was obvious they had a good thing going.

One night my mother and I were in the house on our own. We were playing cards and killing time until Ian came to see her. He had made arrangements to pop up to the house sometime after the pub that evening. They had only been going out for a couple of months at that stage. As the hours ticked by my mother became agitated. There was still no sign of Ian. It was now well after midnight and we both hung out of the window, resting our arms on the window ledge, my mother hoping that Ian would walk around the corner at any moment, but still he never showed. It was beginning to look as if he had let her down and I could tell she wasn't too happy about it. She could not understand why he would do that. We both sat up for hours that night, waiting for him to turn up but he never did.

The next morning two police in uniform came knocking on the front door. When my mother answered, they told her that Ian had been stabbed to death just across the street, approximately 50 yards away. My mother just burst into tears.

It turned out that Ian had left the Hawthorn Bar, which was on Bardowie Street, just a five-minute walk from the house. On his way to see my mother, he heard a woman screaming for help up in a top-floor house just opposite from where we lived. Like the decent person he was he went up the close to investigate the screams and to lend a hand to the woman crying out. Doing so cost him his life. It was a domestic situation where some man was beating up his missus. When Ian intervened and confronted the man at his door, the lunatic stabbed him with a butcher's knife before slamming the door in his face. Ian then staggered back down the stairs but collapsed in the garden just outside the close. He lay unnoticed throughout the night until a passer-by found him in the morning.

Chapter Three

Robert Manson Freed

My uncle Robert got out of Perth Prison in 1978 after serving ten years behind bars. He started his sentence in 1968, the year of my birth, along with his best friend, Rab Duncan. They received 12 years each for the armed hold-up of Italian ice-cream factory owner Gerald Capaldi. Another man had also taken part in the hold-up, but he got lucky and was never brought to justice.

Capaldi's ice-cream factory was situated in Coxhill Street in Springburn, just off Pinkston Road in north Glasgow. On the day of the robbery, in October 1967, Robert, Rab and the third man, wielding two loaded sawn-off shotguns, confronted the Italian boss and four of his employees. They ordered the workers to line up against a wall and told the owner to open the safe. Very foolishly, Capaldi refused to cooperate and this resulted in him being blasted with a shotgun. In hospital he had more than 100 shotgun pellets removed from his body and arms.

The subsequent court case made legal history, as it was the first time a Sheriff Court had dealt with a trial of this gravity, although when the trial concluded the case was referred to the High Court for sentencing.

After they were sent down, they found themselves involved in heavy gangland warfare within tough Peterhead nick. Peterhead, sometimes better known as 'The Napper', was unquestionably the toughest jail in Scotland back in the late 60s and right through to the mid-80s. It was a very dangerous prison in which to serve time, especially for prisoners from Glasgow.

This was the Jimmy Boyle era, when the prison screws thought nothing of inflicting violence and brutality on any convict who stepped out of line, the sort of brutality which was highlighted by Boyle in his book (later made into a film) *A Sense of Freedom*. Not only did prisoners have to deal with the rough treatment of prison guards, they also had to stay one step ahead of the Glasgow gangland culture which existed in every hall and which resulted in daily confrontations between antagonistic and ruthless prisoners.

The gangland philosophy in this prison came to a head, and was properly exposed, when my uncle Robert's pal Rab was stabbed to death. Just five minutes after prisoners were let out for their evening recreation on 23 October 1969, a square go (a fight without any weapons) had been arranged to take place inside Cell 12 between Rab and a prisoner called William 'The Thug' Bennett. My uncle Robert had stabbed Bennett some time before this confrontation, but during a trial just two weeks beforehand Robert had lodged a special defence of impeachment, which involved his friend Rab Duncan saying that it was actually he who had stabbed Bennett.

In the end it was Rab who agreed to fight Bennett in the cell as a way of straightening things out, but Bennett pulled a knife he had hidden tied around his neck and stabbed Duncan to death in a frenzied attack. Realising what had happened, my uncle Robert ran into the cell to assist his pal and attacked Bennett. The screws raised the alarm and medical staff rushed to the cell. Rab Duncan was found sprawled across the bed and was pronounced dead at the scene. He had been stabbed several times: he hadn't stood a chance.

At a lengthy trial which started on 20 January 1970 at the High Court in Aberdeen, 49 witnesses, including 15 prisoners, were cited by the Crown. Bennett spoke about a 'reign of terror' at Peterhead, and claimed the Manson brothers and Rab Duncan were the leaders of a gang. A dagger and two knives were among the list of productions in the case. A jury of seven men and eight women found William Bennett, who was 28 years old at the time, guilty of murdering Rab Duncan in Cell 12. Lord Wheatley sentenced Bennett to life, with a recommendation that he serve at least 20 years.

My uncle Robert, who was only 23 years old, was called to give evidence on the first day of the trial. Lord Wheatley sentenced him to a further three years for committing perjury and for contempt of court, adding that this would run consecutively with his 12-year term. Later, Robert would get this extra sentence reduced by a year at the High Court of Appeal. Robert maintained the contempt sentence was incompetent and contrary to natural justice. Lord Emslie, Lord Justice General, presiding, said that the court had with some considerable hesitation concluded that Robert's sentence for contempt was excessive. Because Robert's additional sentence was for perjury and contempt of court he served that part of his time as a Civil Prisoner, minus the year he had knocked off. This gave him many more privileges and he completed that part of his sentence at Perth nick.

Robert was in his early 30s when he came out of jail, and he went to live at my mother's in Possilpark. I remember taking to him straight away. He had a magnetic personality and he would become a father figure to me. He was about 5 feet 8 or so and had a full head of jet-black, shoulder-length hair, which he kept looking sharp at all times. He had the typical Glasgow hard-man facial features: a strong chiselled expression along with a fearsome presence. Always immaculately turned out, he looked very dapper in the sharp suits and dress clothes he wore. He didn't have a problem wearing a pair of red suede shoes; he was very flamboyant and could carry it off.

Robert really helped me settle down in my mother's house. He appeared in my life when I was wildly running back and forth from my mother's to my grandparents', and at a time when the Children's Panel had become the focus of my confused little world. If Robert hadn't come to live with us at that point, I'm quite sure I would have continued to run wild in the streets. Robert would also stand up for me against my mother and he was able to reduce the amount of beatings she dished out to me on a regular basis.

A pal of Robert's, San Duncan – Rab Duncan's brother – would come to see him, along with a team of bikers on big, powerful motorcycles. We lived in the 'square' at Sunnylaw Street, a cul-de-sac, and San and his biker friends would take my wee pals and me for a spin around the block on the back of their bikes. All you could hear was the revving of half a dozen powerful motorbikes; they would do wheelies up and down the street. My uncle Billy was also very much into bikes and he was involved with the notorious Blue Angels biker gang. When my mother had parties at Sunnylaw Street, Robert would bring his girlfriend, Christine Gallacher, to stay the night and this would be the only time I saw him drinking alcohol. As a rule he wasn't a drinker, but there were exceptions when he felt relaxed in the right company. Robert could be the life and soul of any party. Bacardi and Coke was his favoured tipple, and when the drinks were flowing he would always bring out his harmonica. Robert could play this instrument effortlessly. These sessions could go on throughout the night and the merrymakers would take it in turns to sing a song.

My mother was a lovely singer and she would teach me to harmonise with her. She liked to sing 'Tenderly', a beautiful ballad. I still remember the words to this day. She took great pride in telling anyone about how she beat Lulu in a talent competition at the Lindella Club in Glasgow just before she went into the big time and became famous.

Christine, Robert's girlfriend, who must have been about 18 at the time, would sometimes come back to my mother's to take me shopping in the city centre. I loved these outings with her because she would spoil me with plenty of gifts, and she would even buy me clothes. I loved Christine's company; she was like the big sister I never had.

One night I was sitting in the house with my mother and Uncle Robert when we heard all sorts of noise coming from the street outside. A few of the lads from the square could be seen standing around one of the parked cars and beside them Dusty, a dog that my pals and I would encourage to catch rats around the rubbish bins, was barking like mad.

It soon became clear that Dusty had caught a neighbour's cat and the poor thing had managed to escape, half dead, underneath a parked car. Dusty didn't belong to anyone; he was a street dog and his instinct was to kill anything smaller than himself. Robert loved cats, and when he heard what was going on he went berserk. He went into the kitchen, grabbed a kitchen knife and ran downstairs. He got hold of Dusty by the scruff of the neck and began stabbing him.

My mother and I watched from the window. Half of Sunnylaw Street must have seen it as well. I could really see the hatred in Robert's face. He must have stabbed Dusty five or six times before throwing the dog to the ground. Dusty howled and limped off along the road. Robert then got the cat from beneath the car and brought it back up to the house, but life was clearly draining from its body.

In the morning, the cat was barely alive and Robert ordered me to take it to the nearest vet, which was located in Woodside, about a 20-minute walk from the house. I wrapped my green snorkel parka round the cat and set off but just as I arrived at the vet's door the cat let out a deep breath and died in my arms. I left it outside the door underneath a hedge – I didn't even bother going in with its body. I slowly walked back home, terrified of what I was going to tell my uncle Robert.

As time went on I saw Robert less and less. He was spending more time with Christine, and eventually he went to live with her in Castlemilk, in the south side of Glasgow.

Robert was also busy building his business in scrap cars. He had a scrapyard called Plaza Car Spares in Butterfield Place over at Eglinton Toll, just off Pollokshaws Road. Sometimes I went over to Castlemilk to stay for a few days and Robert would often take me to Plaza Car Spares to show me the ropes of how scrap cars worked as a business. I was still a bit too young to take it all in, but I loved going there. He had a caravan he used as an office and people would be coming and going all day.

I suffered because of Robert going to live in Castlemilk, as gradually things started to worsen at my mother's house. Sometimes when she was steaming drunk she would drag me from my bed, often when I was wearing just a pair of underpants, and chuck me out into the freezing close. At times I would have to sit for hours on the cold stairs outside, shivering and traumatised.

If she ran out of cigarettes, she would tell me to go and find fag butts up the other closes, and I was told not to come back unless I got some. I found out later in life that my mother and her sister, my aunt Patsy, had had to do the same thing when they were kids. It was a chore nicknamed 'pearl diving'.

Eventually I wised up to my mother's booze-filled misdemeanours and I figured out ways of avoiding her when she was in this drunken state. I would build myself a den somewhere hidden in the house, beneath a table or under the bed, as this was the only way I could get to sleep. There was hardly ever any food in the cupboards, as my mother preferred getting meals from the local chip shop or the Chinese takeaway – I can't remember her ever cooking a meal for me, not once. I was afraid to take my pals up to the house because of the awful state of the place. The RSSPCC and Social Work were never far off. Inevitably, they came back into my life and it wasn't long before I was facing more Children's Panel hearings, which resulted in me being sent back into care.

Chapter Four

Larchgrove, Kerelaw and the Mayfair Café

Like countless other young Glaswegian boys before me, I found myself heading to Larchgrove Remand Centre – The Grove.

The Grove housed the city's young tearaways and toe-rags – the rejects of an impoverished society – while preparing them for the important next stage of their lives. The Children's Panel sent me there for three weeks in 1979, initially with the aim of letting staff and social workers assess my needs and work out a plan for my future care. I was 11 years old.

The Grove was divided into three main units – Arran, Jackson and Bute – and could hold up to 70 boys between the ages of 11 and 16, but at times it held youngsters as young as eight. Each unit had dormitories of half-a-dozen beds, a recreation room, a television room and two ablution rooms for showering, washing and using the toilet. Each also had its own distinguishable colours embroidered onto the cuffs and neckline of the brown uniform jerseys. Arran was blue, Jackson was yellow, and Bute was red. Grey trousers and black plimsolls were also mandatory.

Adjacent to Bute unit was a vast dining hall where all three divisions assembled at mealtimes to eat. This was the only time all three units came together. There were rules in place and the staff took it very seriously if you were daft enough to break them. Each dinner table sat four boys and you were required to sit in total silence with your arms folded as you waited to collect your food. The staff made it clear that there was to be no speaking before, during or after meals. Like jail warders, they would stand eagle-eyed, watching everyone's every move.

The punishment for talking during mealtimes was scrubbing the floors with a brush and a pail of water. This was a daunting and arduous task, especially for a young boy. If you were unfortunate enough to be caught talking, you'd be given a patch of floor to scrub in the entrance hall, nicknamed the 'Magic Square', where you'd get down on your hands and knees with a wooden scrubbing brush. This form of punishment was most dreaded and could take a whole hour to finish.

The education block had its place upstairs from the main offices and entrance hall. During the day the boys would attend a wide range of classes, but these lessons didn't have a serious impact on most of the kids. They weren't at Larchgrove long enough for it to be productive.

Near the entrance hall, next to the main offices, was the much feared 'pokey', or solitary confinement cell. This was the most secure room in Larchgrove, the mere mention of which was enough to send shivers down every boy's spine. Stories circulated about how bad it really was; it was every young boy's worst nightmare. There was no bed, toilet or window. It was just a stone floor, and the light in the cell was so bright it almost blinded you. I should know, I was flung in there often enough.

The pokey was often used as a punishment cell by the night watchman when the kids were being rowdy. The night watchman, or 'watchy', as we called him, was tolerant to an extent, but the golden rule was not to leave the dormitory at night under any circumstances. The watchy would set traps by placing an empty tin ashtray against the dormitory door, which would make a loud clunking noise on the stone floor if the door was opened.

The watchy had a very difficult job, there is no question of that, but it didn't entitle him to be cruel towards the children, dragging you from your bed by the arm and frog-marching you down to the pokey because he had flipped his lid due to the children being too disruptive. More often than not I would be singled out as the main instigator of trouble and the watchy would drag me to the pokey and leave me there for up to six hours at a time, only returning to let me out just before the early shift staff members came in for work.

Jackson Unit was the best unit in the Grove, as it was where the more troublesome youngsters seemed to end up. Every morning when the staff came on duty, the noise they made would have woken the dead. One staff member would clunk two teapot lids together and another would shout out: 'Come on, lads . . . get your hands off your cocks and on with your socks.'

After breakfast, all the boys sat in the television room waiting for their morning ciggy. These days most people would be horrified and cringe at the thought of this routine, but back in 1979 and into the early 1980s a staff member would fetch what was called 'the cigarette drawer' from the office. In the drawer, there would be a variety of cigarette brands in packs of tens and twenties with your name scribbled onto the packet, but you only had them if your family or visitors handed them in for you. There was no age restriction on smoking. If you had cigarettes, you could smoke, it was as simple as that.

Picking out one packet at a time, a staff member would shout out your name, open up the fag packet, take out a fag and toss it to you, and this routine he repeated until every boy who had fags got a smoke. This happened after every meal and in the evening time just before your bed. I was only 11 years old when I arrived in Larchgrove for the first time, and there were boys who were younger than I was; it made no difference: the staff allowed, and in a sense encouraged, us all to smoke. After your morning fag, it was off to get the buckets and scrubbing brushes. Every morning the kids were expected to get onto their hands and knees to scrub the floors. The showers, toilets and urinals all got their turn. The staff would hover about next to you and you had to work hard. This vigorous cleaning routine took place every morning, seven days a week.

Visiting time at the Grove was usually in the evening. When my mother came to see me, without fail she would turn up half drunk. Visits were extremely strict and boys would be strip-searched immediately after their visitors left the building. These searches included having to bend over for an inspection between your bum cheeks. I don't know what the staff expected to find, but it wasn't right; it was totally humiliating, even for boys so young.

It was very difficult to smuggle anything into Jackson Unit. Boys were forever trying to sneak in extra cigarettes to smoke in the dormitory at night, but they always got caught. My mother was always trying out different methods designed to outwit the staff, but they were on the ball and knew exactly what to look for. Sometimes she would make a tiny slit in the bottom of a packet of crisps and slip two or three homemade fags inside. It was a decent enough job, but the staff at the Grove had seen it all before and knew all the tricks. This foolishness invariably led to a stint on the Magic Square, as well as a good talking to from the staff.

The purpose of my initial three-week admission to the Grove was to enable an assessment of my care needs, and for the next three years I was in and out of the Grove on numerous occasions. It was around this time that I met John 'Ponny' Shannon and his brother, Alex. As 12-year-olds Ponny and I would go into Glasgow city centre and hang around the railway stations and the bus stations dipping women's purses, or 'cats' as we called them, from their bags or jacket pockets. I would put my jacket on but leave one of the sleeves empty so that I had a free but hidden hand. We were that small and innocent-looking that no-one would suspect us and we could get really close to our target without being suspected.

We were that good we could get five or six purses every day, making hundreds of pounds, which we would spend on clothes, hats, shoes, or other new designer gear of the time. But I was caught one day dipping a woman's cat in Glasgow Central Station, having helped her onto a train with her trolley. I ran to the toilets with her purse, took the £40 that was inside and dumped the empty purse in a bin. The railway police stopped me in the station and suspected me of pick-pocketing due to the amount of cash I had on me. They took me back to my mother's house in Possil and told her what I had been doing. Without a moment's hesitation she said, 'That wee bastard has taken that from my book money,' and she gave me a slap in front of the police. I got away with dipping the purse but my mother took the £40!

These exploits, together with other antisocial behaviour and constant skiving from school, was naturally of concern, and finally in 1982 a report by the head of The Grove recommended that I should be placed in care.

Accordingly, I was admitted to Kerelaw List-D School on 16 February 1982, five days before my 13th birthday. This institution was tucked away in the seaside town of Stevenston in North Ayrshire, about 28 miles from Glasgow.

By the time I got there, I was still dabbling in solvent abuse, practising persistent truancy and I had an unremitting pattern of stealing. The bad habits I had picked up during my spells in Larchgrove had instilled in me an anti-authority persona, and Kerelaw seemed a natural progression towards a life of getting into trouble. But Kerelaw was a new and different ball game, too. I was no longer in the familiar realms of Glasgow, where I knew my boundaries and limits, and I had no choice but to go along with the residential supervision orders that the Children's Panel hearings were handing out to me.

The dormitories were on the top floor. During the two years I lived there, dormitories were very much in use, although this practice was phased out soon after I left. There were single rooms available, but they weren't as popular as shared rooms: it was always better to be in a dormitory setting, as you could enjoy the night-time shenanigans and the banter between your pals. Being on your own wasn't much fun, and the boys who occupied these single rooms were usually the weaker ones, who were introverted and shy.

Kerelaw also had a sort of solitary cell, just like the pokey at Larchgrove, with bars on the window and a red-painted concrete floor. It was exactly like the inside of a police station cell and I found myself languishing in it for hours on end.

On one occasion one of the lads brought some blue Indian ink back to the dorm with him after a weekend on home leave. What a big mistake! The kids in the dormitory decided to tattoo each other and I foolishly joined in as the ink made the rounds. I was more than happy to tattoo myself. The five in my dormitory thought it was a good idea to have identical tattoos and, using sewing needles to prick our skin, we got the words 'Love' and 'Hate' tattooed on our fingers. 'Love' was spelled out across the four fingers of one hand and 'Hate' on the other, and then we went on to tattoo the name of our local gang on our forearms. I got the letters YPF tattooed on mine – this stood for the 'Young

Posso Fleet', a gang in Possilpark. By the end of the session, every kid in the dormitory looked like he'd just come out of a tattooing studio.

Understandably the staff were not at all happy when they found out what we had done, but at that time it gave us great pleasure and it defiantly put the finger up to authority. A few years down the line I would come to detest these ugly tattoos, especially the Love and Hate on my fingers. When my uncle Robert saw the state of my hands, he went right off his head and assured me that one day I would seriously regret doing what I had done. He told me I was now a marked person, one the cops could easily identify. He was dead right, as the first thing the police did whenever I was lifted was to check my hands. The tattoos would become so embarrassing for me that I even went as far as buying special make-up just so that I could cover them up. In the end, I found the tattoos so demeaning that I paid over £1,000 to have them removed by laser.

At weekends most of the kids would go back to their families. A minibus drove from Kerelaw to Glasgow each Friday and dropped them off, and on Sunday night the same minibus would take everyone back. I never qualified for these weekend leaves, mainly because of my bad behaviour and poor home conditions, and so it was at this stage that I started to abscond again.

I remained in Kerelaw for about 18 months, and my frequent absconding marred most of my time there. Sometimes I'd be on the run for weeks at a time. There was no security to prevent kids from doing a runner. If you wanted to go, it wasn't that difficult. You just had to pick your time carefully, and once I started I couldn't stop. I would run away at every opportunity. I would steal a car from the town of Stevenston, or somewhere nearby on the Ayrshire coast, and choose a destination according to who was absconding with me. Kilmarnock was a favourite destination of mine, as there was always plenty to get up to. I had a friend there, who lived with his mother. I had met him during one of my exploits on the run. He was a couple of years older than me, but we got on really well and as soon as I told him that I had nowhere to live and that I was sleeping rough on the street, he was only too happy to help out.

His mother was a nice old woman who always wore an apron around her waist, and I got the impression that she was more like his granny than his actual mother. There was, of course, no way she would let me stay overnight, and this was made crystal clear to me and my friend, but as soon as she went off to her bed, he would open his bedroom window and I would climb in to sleep for the night.

I slept in a small spare room, with no bed or furniture, and just old clothes scattered on the floor for a mattress. This room was freezing cold and I would put on jumpers, shirts – anything that would fit me – just to keep myself warm. The fact that I could have had a nice warm bed back in Kerelaw didn't even enter my mind.

Not far from the house was a yard with ice-cream vans coming and going. It was obvious that the vans belonged to the adjacent Mayfair Café, and I watched them park up at the end of the night in the adjoining garage. I knew that if I could get into that garage during the night there would be rich pickings in those vans. The café was on Innellan Drive, just off Western Road, next to plenty of houses and not far from the town centre. I figured that I could transport the haul back to the spare room, so we made a plan to wait until my pal's mother was fast asleep and then act.

As night fell, we set off along the road towards the Mayfair Café. We managed to climb up onto the roof of the garage at the back of the premises and I prised open a small skylight window made of thickened plastic. As luck would have it, I could see an ice-cream van parked directly underneath me. I wasted no time in dropping down onto the van roof. I told my friend to wait on the rooftop and keep lookout for cops or anything else that looked suspicious.

I could make out four vans in total, and as I went round them I found that they were unlocked. I had the premises to myself and I knew I was on to a winner. I quickly came across a cashbox full of notes, and the first van was full to the brim with confectionery and thousands of cigarettes. We were going to need some sort of transport to shift it all.

It was time to nip back up onto the roof for a chat with my pal.

I suggested that we go and steal a car so that we could come back and clear the vans of their entire stock of cigarettes. Stealing cars back in the early 80s was very simple. A house key would have started most cars back then, the ignition hole was that wide.

It was 1 am when we sauntered the short distance to South Dean Road and spotted a Ford Escort. I unlocked the door, got myself inside, put down the handbrake and let the car freewheel along the road a bit so that the owner wouldn't hear his motor starting. I got to work on the ignition and as soon as it started I drove, like a novice, the few blocks back to the garage and parked the car at the back of the premises. We then began stripping the vans of all of their fags and other treats, until something spooked us in the process and we had to leave many of the goods behind but we got a good haul.

I was lifted by the Kilmarnock police a few days later and charged with breaking into the garage and stealing the Ford Escort. I also stole in the region of 13,000 cigarettes; someone in a pub later shopped us, as we tried to sell some of the fags. The police got my description, and it didn't take them long to link the stolen car, the garage break-in and, of course, that I was on the run from Kerelaw List-D School. I was sent back, but within hours I was on the run again.

I spent most of the period from 21 January to 21 July 1983 on the run, staying with my uncle Robert at the house he shared with his common-law wife, Christine, and their baby daughter, Mandy, in the south of Glasgow. It was only a sudden tragedy within the Manson family that forced me to hand myself back in to Kerelaw. This terrible event would break my heart and send me spinning out of control. My life would never be the same again.

Chapter Five

The Murder of Robert Manson

Robert Manson, a bit of a loner, was feared throughout the Glasgow underworld. Like his older brother Billy, Robert possessed an evil streak and had cold, death-like eyes. He was a one-off, a *real* Glaswegian gangster of a long-gone era, a proper hard man. Some would argue that he was arrogant to the point of annoyance, a nutcase who was unpredictable and a liability, but Robert Manson didn't give a monkey's for anyone – no matter their reputation. It made no difference to him. This was a weakness and it led to his destruction. He was the architect of his own demise; the victim of his own undoing. The fact that he was too spirited and too fearless turned out to be his downfall.

In the five years or so that I spent around him I think I got to know him pretty well, even though I was only a youngster. For most of that time he was a father figure to me, always trying his best to keep me right. Robert had two very different sides to his character, and I saw a more tender and loving side; he was the proud father of his young baby daughter. He was intelligent and really switched on. He had a great sense of humour and was a naturally gifted artist, the life and soul of any social gathering, but there's no getting away from the awful truth that he had been born into a criminal family at a time in Glasgow when merely surviving was very tough, an everyday struggle.

In the late 60s and 70s, villains played by the rules and there was real honour amongst thieves, unlike today where it seems anything goes. The old Glasgow gangster has long gone, rubbed out by the greedy drug dealers and cardboard cut-outs of today, who have injected a different kind of fear and panic into the hearts of Glasgow people.

The best part of Robert's short life was spent locked up in jail; he lost all of his twenties to incarceration. On his release, he vowed never to end up back inside. He swore that the 12-year sentence he had served for armed robbery and attempted murder was more than enough, especially after he got a further three years added on for perverting the course of justice in his pal's murder trial. He viewed jail as a waste of life – he was dead right about that.

Robert met the love of his life, and the future mother to his beautiful daughter, in an upmarket baddies' haunt called the Square Peg in Glasgow's St Enoch Square in the heart of the city. Christine was 14 years younger than him and she was an absolute ringer for Jennifer Rush with the song 'The Power of Love' back in the 1980s. Their relationship started as a casual friendship: they would meet up at various pubs around the city centre where Robert was acquainted with most of the pub landlords, then after a few months hanging out together as friends they realised that they had fallen madly in love with each other and became bonded as one.

The morning of Friday, 22 April 1983 was a peaceful one, nice and quiet, and Robert played around with wee Mandy as normal. There was an air of excitement within the home. A family wedding was due to take place the following day and this had been playing on their minds for some time. Robert hadn't been to a proper wedding in many years, if in fact he'd ever been to one, full stop.

He left their Castlemilk house early to deal with some matters connected to his scrapyard business, appearing back late that same afternoon. On his return, he told Christine he'd met an old friend during his travels. This friend was going to help him find new and secure premises for his scrapyard business, and Robert had arranged to meet up with him again later that same day.

Robert had talked about moving his scrapyard to new premises in the weeks leading up to this meeting, and Christine was well aware of how keen he was to do this. There was no need for Christine to worry; she trusted Roberts's judgement, and if he'd already made arrangements to meet up with someone he knew and had met earlier in the day there was no need for her to worry at all. Why should she?

Christine prepared some food and they sat down with Mandy for a bite to eat. Robert then had a wash and a shave, and got himself ready to go out. It wasn't unusual for Robert to be smartly dressed in a suit, shirt and tie, as he preferred being well-presented; it's the outfit he felt most comfortable wearing.

He left the house at around 7 pm, well turned out in a clean white shirt and silvery-grey suit, and as it was a cold, crisp spring day he wore his three-quarter-length camel-hair overcoat – or 'gangster coat', as I call it. They kissed goodbye and, at that point Christine had no reason to suspect that this would be the last time she would ever see Robert alive.

He never told her exactly where he was going. He was making his way to a small pub on London Road called the New Monaco Bar. This was a lively pub right on the corner of London Road and Arcadia Street, not far from Bridgeton Cross. Popular for its live music nights in the 70s and 80s, it attracted local musicians as well as up-and-coming bands who played the pub circuit and who were out to make a name for themselves.

However, the clientele of the New Monaco were often associated with the darker side of Glasgow. It had acquired a fierce reputation as being a bit of a 'heavy' boozer, where some of Glasgow's major villains hung out.

Witness reports state that Robert was in the pub for the whole evening and that he stayed back after hours for late drinks, eventually leaving at around 1am. Robert was not a drinker as such, although he did enjoy the odd Bacardi, if the mood took his fancy. Bar staff working that night say that Robert had at least a few Bacardi and Cokes over the course of the evening, more than enough to send his head spinning, and as a result he wouldn't have been as alert and on-the-ball as normal.

Why he stayed in the pub for so long is unknown, but I suspect that someone stalled him, deliberately kept him busy and talking all night. Robert knew he had a wedding to attend in the morning and he had assured Christine he wouldn't stay out too long. Yet something far more important held him back, and cost him his life.

As it got late, Christine was getting worried. When she saw that it was after one in the morning and he wasn't home, she knew that something was wrong. She knew Robert would not have purposely stayed out that late. Just after 4 am a car pulled up outside the house. In that moment her gut instinct told her that there was bad news coming. There was a knock at the door. Christine opened it and the look on the faces of the police standing there told a story in itself. The police broke the shattering news that Robert had been the victim of a fatal shooting, blasted in the face with a shotgun, sometime between 1.10 am and 1.30 am.

That night I was camping out with my cousins Frank and Gary Manson on a steep mound just opposite my older cousin Carole's house in Barlia Drive, Castlemilk. Carole came rushing up to the tent, screaming and shouting, 'Robert's been shot! Robert's been shot!' I had just turned 15 years old, still only a youngster, with no real sense of the severity of what had actually happened. I was on the run from Kerelaw and I had been living in the Castlemilk area for some time. With Robert gone my shelter and safety in Castlemilk was gone too.

A marked police car carrying three police officers had driven past the New Monaco Bar at the junction of London Road and Arcadia Street at around 1.10 that morning, and the driver, Constable Brian McGroarty, said in a witness report that all he saw at that time was four passers-by. Twenty minutes later when he and his two colleagues drove back along the same route they found a well-dressed man lying face down at the side of the pavement just yards from the bar. The constable noticed that the man still had his hands in his overcoat pockets. He and his two colleagues assumed that, because of the location and the constant traffic at that spot, they had come across the victim of a hit-and-run driver.

Constable Malcolm Chisholm of the Police Identification Bureau said that when Robert's dead body was finally turned over he could tell from the wound on the right cheek, as well as the powder burns and blackening on his face, that he had been shot at close range. He said that some time later they discovered a plastic carrier bag containing a cartridge belt lying on some waste ground nearby. There were 21 cartridges still in the belt, but four of the loops were empty. Over the course of the subsequent murder investigation no spent cartridges were ever found.

Dr Raymond O'Hare of the Royal Alexandra Infirmary in Paisley carried out a post-mortem examination and concluded that Roberts's death was due to a shotgun wound to the face, which penetrated the base of the skull. He concluded from the powder burns and the gunshot wound that whoever shot Robert did so from only 'a few inches', and he stressed that Robert's death would have been instantaneous. At least Robert had not suffered.

I've often asked myself why Robert didn't see what was coming and distance himself from harm's way. He would have been tipsy, and the fact that his hands were still in his pockets suggests to me that maybe he was bluffing his way out of a situation. It's the sort of move I've performed myself and it's designed to make people think that you're carrying a weapon.

It didn't take the murder squad long to establish exactly what Robert's movements were on the night he was killed. Two names that kept coming up were those of Henry Mochan, a 35-year-old jeweller and antiques dealer from Busby, just outside Glasgow, and Francis Jackson, a 40-year-old mechanic from Dennistoun in Glasgow. Mochan and Jackson were also partners in a garage business they owned in Tobago Street, just along the road from where Robert was shot dead. Witnesses confirmed that both Mochan and Jackson were drinking in the lounge of the New Monaco Bar that night.

The murder squad, led by Detective Superintendent John Inglis, began focusing its attention on Mochan and Jackson, and after bringing them in for questioning, the investigation team decided that they had enough evidence to charge them with Robert's murder. The Procurator Fiscal, who ultimately believed there was more than sufficient evidence to take both Mochan and Jackson to trial, duly set a date for the hearing at the High Court in Glasgow: 23 August 1983. Mochan called upon the services of leading Glasgow lawyer Joseph Beltrami, a real legal wizard. Jackson opted for William Dunlop, an equally competent solicitor with a desire to win cases. At the trial Mochan and

Jackson both lodged a special defence of alibi, claiming that they were together in their jointly-owned taxi repair garage in nearby Tobago Street at the time of the murder.

The main thrust of evidence against Mochan and Jackson came from an 18-year-old youth by the name of Colin Carolyi, who was in the lounge of the New Monaco Bar until closing time on the night of the shooting. He told the High Court in Glasgow that he saw Mochan, his brother and Jackson (whom he knew), along with Robert Manson, drinking in the lounge, adding that Mochan and his brother left around midnight, and Jackson shortly before 1 a.m. Jackson returned for a 'quick double brandy' shortly after. When Carolyi left the bar, he and several other witnesses noticed a taxi with one of its lights out. Going over to bring this to the driver's attention, he noticed a figure crouched in the back, which he recognised as Mochan. Roger Craik, prosecuting, then asked Carolyi: 'How certain are you of the identification?' to which he replied: 'He was with Jackson all night and I recognised his hair. I am certain.'

A firearms expert by the name of John Robertson, an Inspector from Strathclyde's Police Identification Bureau, told the jury: 'In my opinion the murder weapon was a 12-bore shotgun and it could have been fired from the open window of a taxi or car. In my estimation there was some 12 inches between the face and the gun muzzle, no less than 9 inches and no more than 14 inches.'

Another witness by the name of Louis Robinson told the court that while he was on his way home after a night out he heard a 'crack like a gun' coming from behind him. Mr Robinson said he was waving, trying to attract the attention of a taxicab parked at the Bridgeton Cross taxi rank at around 1.10 a.m. when he heard the noise. He said, 'I turned and saw a taxi without lights moving away from a spot of about 30 yards behind me and what I thought was a bundle of rubbish lying at the side of the pavement put out by the shops.'

The trial at the High Court in Glasgow took a bit of a twist when three anonymous letters appeared in open court claiming Robert lost his life because of protection rackets and his involvement and knowledge of the importation of drugs, allegations strongly refuted and contested by the Manson family and people who knew him. The letters, which turned up two days after Robert was murdered, went on to outline how heroin made its way into the country from Toronto by merchant seamen and was going through 'the Italian market in Glasgow'. They claimed that Robert's real killers were not on trial and other people were responsible.

The anonymous letters also spoke of the fact Robert had served a 12-year prison sentence for armed robbery and attempting to murder a man by shooting him.

Detective Superintendent John Inglis told the court there was a 'conspiracy of silence' amongst witnesses of the last movements of Robert Manson. Some of the witnesses had complained that the police threatened them with detention during many hours of questioning. Jamie Barnes, front man of rock band Cochise, who were playing there that night, was one of them. Barnes said he was 'paralysed with drink' by the time he was taken home and didn't remember seeing anyone as he left the bar at closing time yet he was asked to attend London Road Police Station. He said when he got there two detectives told him they had witnesses who had seen him with Robert and Mochan outside the pub at closing time. Barnes stated that the detectives wanted him to say that Robert and Mochan were in a 'heated argument' and, if he refused, they threatened to lock him up for obstruction. He refused to change his story and then the police allowed him to go home.

Robert's murder trial ended on 7 September 1983, just 15 days after it had started. Lord Murray, the sitting judge, deliberated over the legal arguments overnight and decided that there was no case to answer because of insufficient evidence and a lack of corroboration. He instructed the jury to find both Mochan and Jackson not guilty.

Strathclyde Police kept Robert's body for nearly three weeks so that they could conduct their post-mortem and forensic examinations. This was a tough time for the family, especially Robert's brothers, Vincent and Billy, who, at the time, were incarcerated and excluded from attending the funeral because they were deemed a high security risk. No one got a chance to say a proper farewell to Robert. The coffin lid remained screwed down tight so that no one could see the brutal damage caused to his face by the 12-bore shotgun blast. My mother insisted that I be a pallbearer at the funeral, despite the fact I had just turned 15. I recall looking around me as I carried the coffin, taking everything in, listening to my mother howl with emotion clouded by alcohol, and still I never once shed a tear for the person I had looked up to and respected since the age of 10. It's not that I didn't want to cry, I simply couldn't.

I was far too young to comprehend all that was going on around me, but within a few short years that changed.

But first I would have to see out the rest of my youth.

Chapter Six

The Balmore Bar

Breaking into shops and other businesses had become a bit of a speciality for me and my pals, and one of the most memorable and best-planned break-ins I ever masterminded – at only 15 years old – took place at a boozer called the Balmore Bar.

The pub wasn't the easiest of places to break into. Surrounded by shops, it was situated in a very busy part of Saracen Cross in Possilpark, right on the corner of Saracen Street and Balmore Road. Saracen Street is a bustling thoroughfare throughout the day. It also forms part of the A879 and is a busy distributor and commuter road for the north of the city and beyond. By night, things are much quieter, though there is plenty of police activity, as the local nick is just a stone's throw away from the pub. It simply wasn't feasible to consider breaking into the bar under normal circumstances; it was far too dangerous, and in all likelihood you would have been caught. But an incredible opportunity caught my eye.

A few shops along from the Balmore Bar was a general store that sold everything from toothpaste to cigarettes; it was the typical corner shop of the early 80s, with games machines as well, such as Space Invaders and, one of my favourites, Galaxian. These machines were a big hit with many local kids, and the shop was definitely the number one hangout for my wee pals and me.

I was such a regular visitor that I got to know the owner quite well and it got to the stage that I did whatever I wanted in his store. I would even help serve behind the counter whenever it took my fancy – and not once did I attempt to fiddle the till. I had a bit of respect for this shopkeeper.

While standing outside the shop one day I noticed that the apartment above had no curtains or blinds on the windows. This could mean only one thing – it was unoccupied. I knew I had stumbled on something that offered a fantastic opportunity for 'tanning' (i.e. thieving). Finding an empty flat above a shop premises was like finding a hole in the roof of the shop itself, – breaking into businesses that way became one of my trademarks. I used to tour about looking for empty flats above shops, travelling all over Glasgow sometimes, and as soon as I found somewhere suitable it was then easy for me to gain access via the ceiling by ripping up the floorboards and kicking a hole down through into the shop itself.

I'd come to the conclusion that from the empty flat above the corner shop it would be possible to reach the cellar of the Balmore Bar, where huge quantities of alcohol were kept. This would require a lot of very hard graft, as it would involve not only staging a break-in to the shop from the upstairs flat, but also tunnelling from underneath the shop through the cellars of several adjoining buildings until we got to the Balmore. But I had a feeling it could be done. I had already accomplished the technique of tunnelling through brick walls using a brace-and-bit, a jemmy and plenty of sweat and guts. But there was a slight snag – without the shopkeeper's approval it was pointless even contemplating such an enormous turn. I knew he normally pulled down the steel shutter at about 6 p.m., and I wasted no time in going in just as he closed up. I got straight to the point with him and it worked.

I persuaded him to cooperate with my plans, making it clear he would be able to make a healthy insurance claim on anything he wished to report stolen or damaged, for that matter. All I had to do now was have a talk with one of my partners, a big guy called Wullie Dixon, to find out if he would give me a hand in tunnelling through into the Balmore Bar cellar. Wullie was an imposing figure for a boy only a year or two older than I was, and we knew each other purely through tanning and grafting other premises together. He had hands the size of shovels and I had seen him rip out corrugated iron shutters using them – he was as strong as an ox.

Dixon turned out to be one of the best shop-breakers in Possil-park. He was an instrumental asset on any break-in because he would rip through all the hard graft in no time. We carried out dozens of break-ins together, but the Balmore Bar was the most cunning and inventive we ever accomplished. It didn't take much persuasion to entice the big fella into the job. He jumped at the chance, knowing we were on to a winner.

Another pal I brought in on the action was young Ponny Shannon. Ponny wasn't the best at getting his hands dirty; he much preferred keeping lookout, or 'edgy' as we called it. He and I had of course been grafting partners long before Big Dixon came on the scene, but through time the three of us became a shop-breaking trio that worked well together.

We carefully planned our next move for the Balmore Bar break-in, going over every detail. The back of the shop wasn't the biggest of spaces but there was enough room in it for us to be able to stockpile the booze from the bar cellar. Using the tools of the trade, we set about ripping up some of the floorboards so that we could get down into the basement to have a look.

While we worked away in the back of the store with the door shut, the shop owner carried on serving his customers as if everything was normal. It didn't take us long to make a sizable hole in the shop floor, and with a torch in my hand I got down into the shop basement for a better look, followed by my two pals. Piles of rubble, stone and other builders' debris was scattered over the basement floor, and visibility was extremely limited. Dampness and a vile stench clung to our faces, but in the shop basement we could actually hear the faint sound coming from the games machines upstairs. Having sussed out what wall we had to tunnel through, we used the brace and bit to drill holes in the cement between the bricks. We then rammed the jemmy into the loose cement and prised out the bricks one by one.

Time was an important factor now. It was Friday after-noon and we had to wait until the Sunday morning, when the Balmore Bar was closed, before we could break through into the cellar where we knew the booze would be waiting. It was vital that we were in a position to knock through into the cellar wall by Saturday night. That way we would have all day Sunday and right into the early hours of the morning to clear our haul before the Monday morning, when the bar staff would raise the alarm. We would need as much time as possible to move all of the alcohol from the pub cellar, and up into the back of the shop.

We finally got to work on the last wall, which we hoped would take us into the pub cellar. The three of us had grafted our butts off by this stage – we had been hard at it for well over 16 hours. But we knew we were close to breaking through, and the excitement of what might be behind the final wall was more than sufficient to keep us inspired. The first brick in that final wall came loose. We quickly prised it out, and I put the torch through the small hole and glanced inside. Straight ahead I saw what looked like some sort of cage, but I wasn't sure what it was. I gave Big Dixon the honour of being the first to put his arm inside the small opening.

'I feel something,' he said. 'Wait a second . . . I've got a bottle in my hand.'

I had butterflies in my stomach. We could hear bottles rattling together. Then Big Dixon retracted his arm from the hole grasping a full litre bottle of Famous Grouse whisky.

'Yes, ya beauty!' I shouted with excitement and the three of us jumped up and down and swung our arms around each other. We were fortunate enough to have broken straight through into the caged section of the cellar where the expensive spirits were stored under lock and key. We quickly set about making the hole much wider.

'I've never saw as much drink as this in all my life,' reported Big Dixon, having gone through first. 'The whole cellar is full to the brim with whisky, vodka, Bacardi – you name it, it's all there.'

I popped through to have a look for myself. There were boxes of spirits stacked on top of each other as high as the ceiling. There were litre bottles, 70-cl bottles and then there were the two and a half litre bottles you would normally find hanging upside down in the optics behind the bar. There were spirits of every kind piled high in each corner. My first reaction was: 'How are we going to shift this lot?'

Our first task was to carry as much booze as possible back to the shop. It was now early on Sunday morning and by this time we were expecting the owner to come and open up. A couple of the holes we'd made were too small to take full boxes of spirits through, so we had to backtrack and make the openings a bit wider. We were soon on our way to transferring full boxes of spirits along the underground route and up into the back store of the shop. Ponny and I stacked the boxes anywhere we could, and as soon as we were satisfied we had enough we began shifting the cargo back towards the shop.

The shopkeeper had a white Escort van parked outside on Saracen Street, and we began carrying the boxes out into the van. This was dodgy, considering it was now broad daylight and Saracen Police Station was just around the corner. Ponny Shannon stood across the road, keeping the edgy for the coppers or anybody else who looked suspect. Big Dixon and I began transferring the boxes from the back shop out into the van. All day we did this, in and out, in and out, and in the end we took four full vanloads away – and there was still drink left over. It was a laborious mission, but we relocated a fair whack of the booze to a safe house close to where my mother lived. Then we hit a snag – there's always a snag. The spare room we were using as a stash was soon packed full of drink: we had run out of space.

Big Dixon suggested that someone he knew might be able to lend a hand, so we raced over to where he lived, not too far away. He was so convinced his acquaintance would help us that we thought we had better fetch another vanload of alcohol to take along with us. Things were beginning to get messy and a bit slack, and I could sense we were heading for trouble. The problem was that we simply had too much drink and we didn't know what to do with it all. Dixon's pal lived in a top-floor flat in a three-storey block in Keppochill Road, which links Possilpark and Springburn. It turned out to be a good move and, as a bonus, Big Dixon's pal helped us carry thousands of pounds worth of spirits up the stairs and into his loft. With the pressure off, we headed back to the shop to deal with the loose bottles we had left behind.

The operation was now going well again, but then came

another twist. Ponny was again keeping the edgy across the road while Big Dixon and I finished clearing up inside the shop. Most of the drink left on the premises was by now the single bottles we had moved into the back store at the beginning of the job. We rounded them up and put them into a large trolley similar to a hospital laundry basket and we were good to go. We had just finished clearing up when, all of a sudden, Ponny kicked the steel shutter of the shop and screamed through: 'Edgy! A copper is coming over. I think it's Half-Pint.'

Half-Pint was the nickname of the local beat bobby; he was the last policeman on earth we wanted on our case. He hated me, and I'd had a number of run-ins with him for different crimes. The shopkeeper, Big Dixon and I looked at each other in complete disbelief. Had someone seen something? Perhaps Half-Pint had been watching us. We had no time to think about it. I grabbed a sweeping brush, as if to clean the floor, and I tossed a jacket over the drink that lay exposed inside the trolley. Big Dixon made a dash for the back store and just in time got himself out of sight. Without warning, the steel shutter at the front of the shop lifted with a resounding clatter.

'Hello there, sir. Is everything OK in here?' Half-Pint asked.

He had Ponny by the arm and the two of them came right inside the shop.

'Yes . . . yes, Officer, everything's just fine. Is there a problem at all?' replied the shopkeeper nervously.

He was now standing at his till, making out that he was cashing up for the day. I continued sweeping the floor and kept my head down.

'I caught this young tearaway messing about with your shutter and I thought he was trying to break in,' said Half-Pint.

'No, no, Officer, everything's fine. As you can see, this young man is helping me sweep up before I go home, and the lad you have there is one of his pals, I think. He's probably waiting for him to come out, that's all.' Half-Pint let Ponny's arm go but then told him to go wait outside. I could sense he thought something wasn't quite right.

'So you're about to close the shop then, are you?'

'Yes, that's right. I'm just going home now.'

'OK, then. I won't hold you back any longer . . . Just doing my job.'

The copper had one final glance about the premises – it was obvious he had a suspicion. He just couldn't put his finger on it. If he had looked in the back store, he would not only have clocked Big Dixon, but also the massive hole in the floor. It was a close shave and one that would come back to haunt us. For the time being, we had to pull up our socks and quickly deal with the remainder of the booze still lying in the shop – and we also had to go upstairs to the empty flat above to kick the ceiling in, as I'd arranged with the shopkeeper.

I wheeled the trolley out to the van and began loading the last of the bottles in the back while half-expecting the copper to reappear at any second. We drove to the safe house once more, but this time I had to plead with the householder to let us drop off this load on the condition that we would come back later to take it away. I was pushing my luck by imposing myself on these people, but we went back a long way. Their eldest son was a very good pal of mine. Before we left the shop we went over everything with a fine-tooth comb, making sure we didn't leave any trace of fingerprints or other incriminating evidence.

Later that night, as soon as it got dark, Big Dixon and I went back to the flat above the shop. Together we ripped up a few floorboards and easily booted a hole in the ceiling below, making sure we made it wide enough for boxes of spirits to go through. Happy with the opening we had created, we left the empty apartment and closed the door behind us. This was crucial to the success of the break-in, as it had to look as if this was where the robbers got into the shop.

It made sense, but realistically it was a bit far-fetched, especially with the amount of alcohol we stole. That was the least of my worries – for now, anyway. Providing the shopkeeper stuck to our arrangement and kept quiet, there wouldn't be a problem; it was as simple as that.

That night we went back to the safe house to start removing some of the booze, then we began selling some of the bottles around the doors in the neighbourhood – big blunder. We started in Sunnylaw Street, knocking on front doors and carrying plastic bags full of litre bottles of whisky and vodka. Within no time we had a pocket full of cash, and at the sight of money we wanted more. People were asking us for different makes and types of spirit and we were being obliging in getting them what they wanted. It was there, why not? For hours, we sold bottles of drink all over Possil for a fraction of the normal price, and these sales never really even put a dent in our stock.

We required a serious buyer to take the rest from us in bulk, but we were a bit young and inexperienced to deal with over £13,000's worth of spirits. We didn't really have a clue what to do with that much alcohol, and we never made allowances for moving this much on. I guess we didn't realise we would get away with such a large amount. We put out some feelers to a few people who we thought might be in a position to help us – pub owners and suchlike – but in the meantime all we could do was carry on selling single bottles door to door. At least that way we wouldn't run short of cash.

The following day the shopkeeper had the daunting task of calling the cops to report the break-in, as he would have done under normal circumstances. Whatever happened, and quite how he did it, was way beyond me, but he stuck to the arrangement I'd made with him. My guess is that he called the police from his shop as soon as he opened up for business. The cops would have turned up and seen for themselves the devastation to his ceiling and his floor.

It wouldn't have taken the police long before they came across the underground passageways leading straight to the Balmore Bar cellar. I believe, to begin with, the CID wouldn't have suspected that the shopkeeper was in any way involved. But sometime later that day the inevitable happened. My so-called safe house became the setting for mayehm: coppers' vans and police motors lined the street. The game was up. As soon as Half-Pint found out about the break-in and theft, he knew that seeing me sweeping the floor in the shop the day before was just too much of a coincidence. A warrant went out for my arrest and the police were looking for me everywhere. I was still an absconder from Kerelaw List-D School. The cops got most of the booze back, although I think Big Dixon's connection managed to get rid of a fair bit of it and probably ended up with more money than the rest of us.

In the end, I was put down as the ringleader and when I was caught I received 12 months under a special conviction as a young prisoner – a CYP. I received my sentence at Glasgow Sheriff Court five days before my 16th birthday. I was sent to Longriggend Remand Centre for Young Offenders, which, due to my age, was the only prison in Scotland that could accept me. I was placed in the CYP section, known as the 'Schoolboys'. Big Wullie Dixon received a six-month sentence in a Young Offenders and Ponny Shannon got only three months in Glenochil Detention Centre.

The shopkeeper was placed on remand in Barlinnie Prison, suspected of being involved in the robbery, and lost his white van, which was impounded by the police. After pleading not guilty – part of his defence was that I had threatened him with a knife against his throat – he faced a sheriff and jury trial at Glasgow Sheriff Court. And then, after giving a statement against us, he cheekily called me as a defence witness. The jury found him not guilty and he got his white van back. I was returned to prison to complete my sentence, and ended up serving the whole 12 months.

Chapter Seven

'Long' and Polmont

On 16 February 1984, I was sent to Longriggend – or 'Long', as it was known. Long was a notorious remand centre for young offenders, located not too far from the town of Airdrie in North Lanarkshire. In its heyday Longriggend was capable of housing up to 300 young prisoners and I am sure that most of the major villains in Scotland, and Glasgow, in particular, went through its gates at some point during their teenage criminal careers. This was a step up from the laid-back List-D School setting that I was accustomed to, but I knew I would have to stay alert at all times. At the age of 15 I had no fear of what was in front of me. Prisoners in the Schoolboys' section were kept apart from the rest of the jail population most of the time, but I was only kept in that section for the first five days of my sentence, before I turned 16.

During my five-day stint in the Schoolboys I met a prisoner by the name of Paul Ferris, who was housed in a section called the Dog Leg. Our acquaintance began quite innocently as we shared an interest in table tennis. It was common knowledge amongst inmates at Longriggend that Ferris was connected and well in with the big names, but to look at him you wouldn't have thought so. He was short and thin and didn't give off a presence as a tough guy. But, as I later found out, looks can be deceiving: you should never judge a book by its cover.

At this stage of his criminal career he was one of crime boss Arthur Thompson's most loyal enforcers. Ferris and I became friends, and in the future were close associates, but eventually it all turned sour: he betrayed me and tried to fit me up for the murder of Thompson's son, Arthur Junior, as his own personal feud with his former boss spiralled out of control. Ferris wrote about this, and the events that led up to it, in his book *Vendetta – The Ferris Conspiracy*, though much of what he describes bears little resemblance to events as they actually happened.

Ferris was in Longriggend on charges of attempted murder and possession of a gun. This was a botched attempt at shooting a guy called William Gibson because he had failed to take the rap for guns found in a car. Instead, Gibson's innocent cousin got shot in the thigh. The case had drawn a lot of attention because Billy, the youngest son of Arthur Thompson, had been a part of it. Naturally the inmates at Longriggend were fascinated with Ferris because of his association with these big players. Our first encounters at Longriggend would pave the way for future chance meetings within the prison system, as well as outside in Glasgow gangland where it mattered most.

As soon as I turned 16 the prison authorities wasted no time in shifting me straight over to the young offenders part of the jail.

I became quite pally with a big guy called Wullie Robertson. Wullie was from Govan in the south side of Glasgow and he stood at least six foot tall. His most discernible feature was his burnt face and neck. When he was a wee boy, he had received 90-degree burns when an aerosol can blew up in his face as he was standing next to a bonfire on Guy Fawkes night. His permanent disfigurement did not seem to bother him in the slightest, even though he resembled Freddie Kruger from *Nightmare on Elm Street*.

Wullie was on remand for the attempted murder of a fellow prisoner in the kitchens at Polmont Young Offenders Institution near Falkirk. He was nearing the end of his Borstal training in Polmont when he speared another boy with a 12-inch cooking pin. What had started as just a bit of bad blood between Wullie and this other young guy almost ended in the other boy losing his life, as the medics fought hard to save him.

By April 1984 there was still no word of a permanent prison placement for me to serve out my sentence. I was a convicted prisoner and Longriggend was essentially a remand centre. My situation became more complicated when CID officers came into the prison to question me over a serious assault on another prisoner.

The word going about the hall was that one of the inmates on the bottom landing was a rapist. It doesn't take prisoners long to find out who is who and what sort of crimes you have committed. Like private dicks, they will get the truth on any prisoner who has a question mark hanging over his head. In jail there is nowhere to hide. If a prisoner tries to conceal a dodgy charge, then it's just a matter of time until he's exposed.

There was no doubt in my mind that the prisoner in question was in fact a dodgy character who was on remand for a serious sex offence, so I decided to teach him a lesson.

Apart from the obvious disgust at knowing this guy was a sex case, there was also the element of building a solid reputation for myself. I was just starting out in the prison system, and it was important the other prisoners knew exactly where I was coming from, and there was no better way for me to show off my strength of character and audacity.

An opportunity presented itself when the guy in question appeared on my section wanting to borrow cleaning materials to take back downstairs. He was up and down like a yoyo most days, asking to borrow stuff, so he was used to seeing my face and would not have considered me a threat. I signalled him into the cleaning cupboard so that he could get what he wanted. I made sure there were no guards hanging around. I could see them sitting in their office drinking a cuppa. The coast was clear, so I followed him inside the cleaning store and banged the door shut behind me. He froze on the spot and looked at me with fear in his eyes. My back was to the closed door, so he wasn't going anywhere.

I picked up an old 10kg metal floor buffer that was lying on a shelf and with no compunction began smashing him in the face with all my strength. I could hear the bones in his jaw crack with every wallop. Blood began spurting from his nose and mouth, and I could tell I had caused him more than enough injury. I opened the cupboard door to let him out, and told him to get back downstairs and keep quiet. With wobbly knees, he staggered back downstairs. I quickly wiped the metal floor buffer clean and chucked it back on the shelf, but the amount of blood was a giveaway. It was everywhere; in fact, a claret trail ran along the corridor and back downstairs in the direction in which he had gone. I felt I had made my point, but I knew it wouldn't take long for the guards to figure out what had happened, so I made my way back to my cell, cleaned myself up as best I could and waited for the inevitable.

Sure enough the deafening sound of the prison alarm screamed through the hall. Guards began closing the cell doors. The word about the hall was that a prisoner had been severely assaulted. A bit later in the day, just after the prison authorities had carried out their preliminary inquiries, the prison governor placed me in solitary confinement under Rule 36 (locked up in your cell 23 hours a day) until such time as further inquiries had taken place.

When the CID came to the prison to interview me, of course I denied everything and refused to answer any questions, just saying 'No comment'. The cops told me I would be charged and that the prisoner who I assaulted was in quite a bad state, with a broken jaw and half of his teeth missing. The Scottish Home and Health Department decided I should go to a Young Offenders Institution. So almost immediately I found myself back on the move, this time to HM Young Offenders Institute Polmont.

Everything was moving so fast I had no time to think about what was happening to me. I was bundled into the back of a prison minibus and driven straight to Polmont, near Falkirk, about 32 miles from Glasgow.

The prison was the largest of its kind in Scotland and the biggest YOI in Britain, designed to hold approximately 450 inmates between the ages of 16 and 21. It was also home to the famous Officers Training College (OTC). In the OTC newly recruited prison guards would complete their officers training course. At the time Polmont was going through a period of change from being a Borstal to becoming a Young Offenders Institute.

Borstal training had been officially abolished in Scotland in 1983, so by the time I arrived in Polmont, in early May 1984, many Borstal inmates were still finishing off their sentences, which could be anything up to two years. Borstal boys wore blue pinstripe shirts and convicted prisoners wore red pinstripe shirts, so it was easy to differentiate between the two. Every new arrival into Polmont would go straight to the admissions hall (known as the 'Aly-caly') for an induction process. The admissions hall was massive, with galleries which were typical of the older Victorian prisons.

Polmont had four wings in addition to the Aly-caly: North, South, East and West, and it also boasted, would you believe, an indoor swimming pool. The Aly-caly had a punitively hard-hitting regime designed to soften you up for when the time came to move on to one of the four wings. A corridor called 'the Mile' went from the Aly-caly to the other end of the jail. A line of guards stood along the Mile and prisoners were forbidden to talk as they shuffled along it. If you were caught gabbing, you would be locked up and placed on Governor's Report, no questions asked. Cells had to be kept spotlessly clean at all times and it was compulsory to make a bed block every morning. Shaving every morning was another required task; if you refused, it meant a sure trip to see the governor.

Whether it was going downstairs for your food, or outside for exercise, there was a daily routine. Inmates had to stand at their cell doors with their hands on the door handles. Then, simultaneously, and on the command of one of the prison guards, who stood on the bottom landing shouting at the top of his voice, 'Shut cell doors!' over a hundred young offenders pulled their doors closed with a thunderous bang.

Polmont still had a chief officer in place, a long-gone officer's rank within the prison system, and you could spot him by the little red emblem on the front of his hat, along with the myriad pips on the shoulder of his tunic. The chief officer was ranked just below the governor, but was considered more powerful and influential amongst his staff. He was the main man, commanded respect, and he held all the cards.

Polmont also had jail matrons, hardy old women who did not suffer fools and who were known for their austerity and firmness of attitude. They were as tough as old boots and wouldn't take any nonsense from fresh-faced juveniles with a chip on their shoulder. Even the screws thought twice about backchat. The matrons helped with the general running of the wing and had a fair bit of influence from all quarters of the prison.

I hold a mixture of good and not so good recollections of Polmont. The first six months of my stay was marred by frequent noncompliance, constant fighting and a lack of respect for prison management. I was never out of the segregation cell. I was only 16 years old, young and irresponsible, and I didn't have a care in the world. On top of that, and like so many other young Glaswegians, I had this burning ambition to make a name for myself.

When I first arrived in South Wing, the question on my lips was: Who is the Top Man? Every wing in Polmont had a top man, the hardest prisoner on the wing. The top man on South Wing was a guy called Brian 'Dopey' Cochrane, from Foxbar in Paisley. Dopey was a big lad with dark hair, about 19 years old, and he was a Borstal boy who didn't have long to serve until the end of his term.

After Dopey was discharged in mid-1984, to my deep sadness I never got the chance to hook up with him again. On 27 March 1995, just a little more than a decade later, he was shot dead as he sat in his car on Glenlora Drive, Nitshill, Glasgow. Apparently, he had been executed on the orders of a notorious Glasgow gangland figure by the name of Stewart 'Specky' Boyd, who was later killed himself when the sporty Audi TT he was driving in Spain mysteriously blew up, killing him and his other passengers outright.

Big Dopey was not the only pal I made in Polmont to meet a violent death. The year before Dopey was murdered, another pal of mine, James 'Jama' Boyle, son of Jimmy Boyle, was also the victim of a grisly demise. Jama worked with me in the joinery workshop at Polmont and we got on well together. He was a right character, with a heart of gold. He liked nothing better than having a good laugh and we were always fooling around together. Other prisoners didn't like him because of his father, but at no time did he try to use his old man's name to intimidate anyone. What you saw was what you got. On 15 May 1994, Jama was stabbed through the heart with a potato peeler. His killer received an eight-year sentence for culpable homicide. Jama was only 28 years old when he was killed.

I recall sitting in the joinery workshop, enjoying my break with the other lads, when Radio Clyde broadcast the news that my pal Wullie Robertson from Longriggend had been killed. We looked at each other in shock. It later emerged that someone had rammed a sword right through his stomach outside a chip shop in Govan on the south side of Glasgow. Poor Wullie managed to stagger as far as his mother's house before he collapsed and died near the close. He was just 21 years old.

South Wing could be a very unforgiving environment for young offenders in the early 80s, and those from outside of Glasgow were the worst hit. This was the unpleasant truth and, in my experience, it is the same all the way through the prison system in Scotland. There might have been the odd prisoner from Edinburgh who broke the mould, but they were very few and far between. The truth is prisoners from Glasgow have always run the show in the Scottish jails. It's the way it's always been.

In South Wing at Polmont the young offenders had no morals and were the world's worst for pressurising their peers. Fear, intimidation and oppression for many of the young prisoners from outside of Glasgow must have been unbearable at times. I was guilty of exploitation of this class of prisoner and although it is downright inexcusable, I was only 16 at the time and I was merely carrying on a well-established tradition. I had a big pal called Stretch who was about six foot four, from Saltcoats in Ayrshire. I came up with a plan that involved getting big Stretch to stand in the washroom area and wait for me to send an unsuspecting young offender in to see him. I would handpick someone who was not from Glasgow and tell them my pal wanted a word with them. As soon as the selected inmate went into the toilet, Stretch would grab them by the scruff of the neck, lift them off their feet and then demand a quarter ounce of tobacco the next canteen day. Depending on who it was, that quarter ounce could go up to a half ounce without any scruple whatsoever. It was horrible and nasty, but it was the way of life inside one of Scotland's toughest jails for young offenders. Three-quarters of the prisoners in South Wing were paying out tobacco and toiletries as 'protection' on a weekly basis. That is just the way it was.

I did my first six months in Polmont the hard way, there's no doubt about it. At that time, I was always fighting or getting up to all sorts of mischief. I felt I had something to prove, and my sights were set firmly on the Top Man's crown: this definitely accounted for the vast majority of my Governor's Reports and the number of times I got myself locked up in solitary confinement. I certainly built up a formidable reputation for a wee 16 year old from Glasgow. The guards would call me the 'jawbreaker' because of the amount of prisoners' jaws I fractured over a six-month period. Not that they were complaining, because the way they saw it, I was battering all the loudmouths and troublemakers and it suited them just fine. It all came at a cost though.

I spent my fair share in solitary confinement, sometimes for weeks on end, at the hands of Crazy Joe, the senior screw in charge of the block. I can even remember the governor giving me the ultimate punishment when he had my mattress removed overnight. I was the only inmate in Polmont at that time to lose their mattress for 24 hours. It was considered a harsh punishment and very rarely handed out. In the end, the South Wing management went for the appeasement approach, and after working in the pantry in South Wing for a few months I was then given a fantastic job working over at the Officers Training College.

At no time in Polmont did I receive any form of rehabilitation or preparation for release back into the community. This was a major responsibility for the prison department, and they failed miserably when it came to helping me settle back into the outside world. With this in mind, it is hardly surprising that I ended up going straight back to crime.

I was discharged on 16 February 1985, a year to the day after I had been sentenced.

Chapter Eight

Back on the Streets

The night before I was released from Polmont, I didn't get a wink of sleep. Prisoners call it 'gate fever', and it certainly lived up to that name!

Now a free spirit, all I envisaged doing was hitting the streets to pick up where I had left off. I felt virtuous and victorious knowing I had just put a 12-month sentence behind me, and I suppose I had a much greater swagger. I'd had a chip on my shoulder to begin with, but the way I saw it I had done the crime and done the time, and in the process had managed to keep my head held high. With no rehabilitation or job to go back out to, I felt I had no choice but to return to the only life I knew . . . law-breaking. Rehabilitation wouldn't have done me any good anyway. Criminality was in my blood and it had established itself as the main driving force in my life.

On release my social worker, Penny McCallum, went out of her way to make sure I got my own flat. Having my own place was very important to me, and I had been dreaming of this for quite some time. Penny had been my social worker ever since the Social Work Department took over from the Royal Scottish Society for Protection of Cruelty to Children (RSSPCC), and we got on extremely well together. Penny was a first-class social worker and helped me get through many difficult times.

I longed for independent living, as there was no way I was going back to stay with my mother. She had not changed a bit whilst I was in jail. She was still drinking heavily and her house in Possilpark looked dilapidated and was in a complete mess.

Penny found me a one-bedroom flat in a high-rise block in Wester Common, Possilpark, five minutes' walk from where my mother lived. It was perfect. It had a small living room, a tiny kitchen, a bedroom and a bathroom. The flat was empty and had cold concrete floors when I first moved in, but within a fortnight of getting the keys, my social worker had wangled a cheque for about £1,300 to help me furnish the place. The cash didn't go far, as I bought a brown seven-piece corner unit sofa for the lounge at a cost of a grand and the remainder went towards an expensive wine-red Axminster carpet.

In my younger days I was very fashion conscious and I wanted the very best of everything. The more expensive and luxurious something was, the more of a thrill I got from having it. It didn't take me too long to lavishly furnish the rest of the place top to bottom with the spoils of crime. I had the flat kitted out well and it looked very classy. That high-rise flat was my little pride and joy, and for 18 months it offered me a real sense of stability. Being in and out of care, List-D Schools and approved schools from an early age had instilled in me a real sense of discipline and cleanliness, so keeping my flat spotless wasn't an issue for me.

For money, I was doing the occasional turn, and one enterprise was particularly lucrative. I was stealing telephones from British Telecom compounds all over the country. I had a contact, a fence, who would take any amount of these telephones – brand-new and boxed – that I could get my hands on. He had a stall at the Barras market, a place I knew well from my childhood days selling razor blades with old Hector, my granda. My contact was a bit of a crank who also dabbled in selling sex toys of every type imaginable. It didn't bother me what he did in his spare time because he was well off; he had a few bob, and if I took a thousand telephones to him he would take the lot from me at a tenner a shot, no questions asked.

Another area I began specialising in was fraud. I would go out of my way to obtain stolen driving licences by whatever means I could, and when I managed to get my hands on a suitable one, I would sit down and practise the signature until I had it copied to perfection. With the hot driving licence, I could get cars from practically any hire company in Scotland. Unlike today, when hire companies have more vigorous identity checks, which require photographic ID, in the 80s you would hand over your licence and select a car of your choice. It was as simple as that. I would use the car for my own personal use and then would move it on for an agreed price. Sometimes I would just break the car and sell the wheels and parts to taxi drivers. There was never a shortage of buyers.

Although I remember most of my time at Possilpark in a positive light – I had my freedom and my own place – it was while living there that one of the most significant events in my life occurred.

One night, around two in the morning, while I was lying fast asleep in bed, I woke up with the buzzing of my intercom going crazy. I got up from my kip to find out who it could be at that time in the morning.

'Who is it?' I asked through the intercom.

'It's the police.' What did they want at this hour? I knew I didn't have any outstanding warrants, so it left me a bit confused.

'What is it you're after?' I asked.

'Willy, can you open the door and let me in, because I need to speak with you in person, not over the intercom.'

I quickly nipped through to my bedroom to glance out of the window. My flat looked out into the forecourt and I could see exactly who was standing at the main entrance. Sure as hell, there was a copper down there on his own, and I noticed he was holding his hat.

'What's the problem, officer? What's going on?' I shouted down.

'I have some bad news in relation to your grandmother. Will you let me in, and I'll come up and tell you what's happening? Don't worry, Willy, I'm not here to arrest you for anything.'

The copper got the lift up to the second floor. I invited him in and I stood in the small hallway dressed in just a pair of shorts.

'Right, Willy, we just received a telephone call at the police station from the Royal Infirmary. Apparently, your grandmother has been taken there and it seems she has put you down as her next of kin.'

I couldn't believe what I was hearing.

'How is she? What time was she taken to the Royal?'

'We don't know, Willy. We just received the phone call and I'm here to let you know. If I were you, I would get down there as fast as you can.'

This cop knew me from previous run-ins with the law in Possilpark, but he seemed very calm and genuinely moved about the matter. I thanked him for letting me know as he made his way back towards the lift. I had an old two-tone Ford Escort Mark 1 parked outside, so when I knew the copper had gone I got dressed as quickly as possible, jumped in and drove the few hundred yards to my mother's house to let her know the bad news.

I woke her up from a drunken sleep and told her to get herself ready, as we had to go to the Royal Infirmary. Still half-drunk, she managed to get herself together, downstairs and into the car, but it was a struggle. I must have gone through every red light there was on the way there.

When we arrived, I parked my car, and my mother and I made our way to the reception area. The hospital was still busy, even though it was probably three in the morning. In A&E, I explained that I was here to see my grandmother, Esther Manson, and that I was her next of kin. When we got to the ward, my mother was in a right state. She was crying and moaning because she didn't have any cigarettes. My grandmother was dying and my mother was more interested in a fag. One of the female nurses was waiting to greet us as we arrived at the ward: 'Well Mr Lobban, it's not looking too good, I'm afraid. Your grandmother came in with gallstones. She is sedated at the moment, but I must warn you she won't make it through the night.'

At hearing this, my mother began roaring and crying again. I felt a touch embarrassed at this point because she was still harping on about needing a cigarette. The nurse then took me into a private room where my grandmother lay motionless in bed. As I observed her lying there in a deep, sleep-like state, she looked calm, peaceful and very much at ease.

'Will she not wake up at all?' I asked the nurse.

'I'm afraid not,' she said, before adding, 'I do have a piece of jewellery belonging to your grandmother. I took it from her finger; this is it here.'

The nurse handed me a small, shiny white metal ring. I remembered giving it to my grandmother when I was only about six or seven years old. I found it in the street while out playing with my pals and, as she had kept it all those years, it had clearly meant a great deal to her. I sat and held her hand for a while and then my mother started shouting and wailing for a fag again. The nurses could obviously tell she had a drink in her. I felt so ashamed. I asked the nurse I had been dealing with where the nearest shop was so that I could nip away and grab some fags for my mother to shut her up. The nurse told me I should find a paper shop open not far from the hospital, and she gave me directions on how to get there.

I sprinted to my car, jumped in and drove the short distance to the shop. I was in luck – it had just opened – so I ran in and paid for 20 fags and a lighter. I quickly made my way back to the Infirmary car park. I ran back to the ward as fast as I could. I had only been gone for maybe 15 minutes, but the nurse was waiting at the top of the stairs for me and I could see she was crying. 'I'm so sorry, Mr Lobban, your grandmother passed away just a few minutes ago.'

I was utterly distraught: the surge of emotion that washed over me brought home to me just how close I had been to her. In the end I hadn't been there for her in her final moments, and all because my mother couldn't get by without her tobacco fix.

The odd thing is that I'm convinced I sensed the moment of her death. Coming back from my trip to get cigarettes, I was reversing into a parking space when suddenly the car jolted backwards into a metal bench, smashing the nearside rear brake and indicator light. I have always been a good driver, and there is no reasonable explanation as to why I suddenly lost control at that moment. To this day I'm sure that was the moment she passed away.

I went back into the room where my grandmother lay, and I sat holding her hand for a while longer before leaving to take my mother home.

I continued robbing telephones from British Telecom compounds. I always worked with the same people – Wullie Dixon, Ponny

Shannon and an old Polish man who was rock-solid, reliable, and who would drive for us in his Transit van whenever we called upon his services.

Our strategy was always the same: drive to a particular area of the country and find out where the BT compounds were located. As soon as night fell, we would cut a hole in the fence with a set of bolt cutters. Some of these compounds had security guards, so we had to be very selective and mind what we were doing. As soon as we had a goer, it was straight down to business. Our driver would sit in a built-up area, where he was less likely to stand out, and as soon as we were ready, one of us would have to go and get him to drive round to the compound: there were no mobile telephones back then. There might be as many as 50 BT vans parked up overnight in these places, and in the back of each van there would be box upon box of phones in all sorts of different colours, models, shapes and sizes. Sometimes we would come across ornamental phones in the shape of Micky Mouse and Donald Duck. These types of telephones were more expensive and in high demand so we would get a far better price for them. Most of the vans would be unlocked, but even if they were, no van was impregnable; there was always a way in.

One evening we travelled to do a job in Ayr. Our Polish driver parked his Transit in a street nearby while big Wullie Dixon, Ponny and I got to work on the fence using the bolt cutters. This particular compound was one of the biggest we had come across and there were over 60 vans parked up inside. We quickly set about emptying each and every one of its contents.

Everything was ticking along nicely when we heard a noise, then footsteps, and then came the light of a security guard's torch. We managed to climb 30 feet up onto the roof of one of the adjoining buildings, and this gave us a bit of breathing space to find out exactly what was going on. Down below we could just make out two security guards with torches standing next to our massive stockpile of phones. Then the coppers turned up in force, their flashing blue lights illuminating the night sky around us.

We hadn't been detected at this point. It seemed the police were more interested in checking out the BT vans and surrounding area as opposed to the flat of the roof where we lay, inconspicuously quiet. But as we waited, listening to the hubbub going on below, Ponny decided to wolf-whistle, giving away our location. I was seething with indignation, and his excuse for whistling was pathetic. He felt we were done anyway and it was only a matter of time before the cops turned their attention to the roof. I strongly disagreed. We were on the roof and out of sight long before the police turned up, and the security guards didn't have a clue, so we were obviously hidden and out of reach and had a good chance of escaping arrest. A police dog had arrived at the scene and it certainly never seemed to have picked up any sort of scent. Embarrassingly, once Ponny had drawn attention to us, we had to climb down from the roof. Big Wullie Dixon received a mauling as he climbed down, the dog tearing his flesh so severely it drew blood from his calf and thigh.

The police took us to Ayr Police Station and charged the three of us with opening a lockfast place and attempting to steal £12,000 worth of telephones (that's over £30,000 in today's value). The following morning after appearing at Ayr Sheriff Court, it was off to Longriggend Remand Centre for the three of us. Incredibly, I made bail after my mother applied to the High Court claiming I was still under 18, which meant I was still legally under her jurisdiction as a parent. A perfect manoeuvre on her part, it has to be said. Big Wullie Dixon and Ponny Shannon had to spend Christmas in Longriggend and were released a couple of weeks later.

A court date was set for 8 May 1986, and the three of us pled guilty. During the hearing, the prosecution made a fundamental error in disclosing the exact value of the telephones involved and, as a result of their slip-up, the Sheriff had to let the three of us off with a token fine of £40. This was a great result for me, considering I had served a 12-month sentence for grand theft the year before.

During the 18 months I lived in the high flats at Wester Common, I can honestly say I had some of the best times of my life. I didn't have a care in the world, and it was probably the first time I had experienced some sort of stability.

The teenage love of my life was a lassie called Liz Young, a real stunner. She had long blondish hair and the perfect figure, and she always wore tight miniskirts that accentuated her beautiful long legs. Within a couple of months of first meeting Liz, she had moved in with me. We were in love, and it was during this period that I managed to keep my nose clean and stay well out of trouble.

For the first time in my life, I didn't have the police at my door. I now knew what it felt like to not be in trouble with the law. I might not have been doing as well financially as I could have been, but it didn't matter because I was happy. I felt content. It was out of the love and respect I had for Liz that I steered well clear of criminal activities.

My little world took a nose dive when I had to give up my apartment. All the solid work and effort I had put in to avoiding run-ins with the law turned out to be in vain. It all happened when Ponny appeared back on the scene. He had disappeared for a time, sort of faded into the background as soon as he knew Liz Young and I were involved in a serious relationship, especially when he knew that she had moved in with me. While Liz and I were savouring the quiet life and simply plodding along, Ponny had been away secretly building bridges with one of the biggest drug dealers in the north of Glasgow. I knew nothing about Ponny's activities because, to be honest, I couldn't have cared less. I was quite content doing my own thing. Then one evening when Liz and I were having a quiet night in watching the telly, I heard a knock on the door. It was Ponny, and I could tell he was there to impress me and that he was bouncing on a high.

He was looking smart in a brand new tracksuit and trainers, and he showed me a wad of cash that would have choked a horse. I knew him only too well. The older brother of a pal of ours had climbed the ladder within the control-and-supply-of-drugs scene and was now raking it in big time. This person had Italian origins but had grown up in Glasgow. He was a very shrewd character, I'll give him that, and he knew exactly how to pull Ponny's strings.

After numerous attempts at trying his best to persuade me to join him selling heroin on the streets of Possilpark, about a fortnight later I finally succumbed; all because the temptation of loads of money, expensive clothes and fancy cars proved far too much for me resist. Within a month, the pressures of selling drugs and not being there for her had taken its toll on my relationship with Liz. We parted and she moved out. Greed, power and absolute selfishness had taken me over, and before I knew what was happening I found myself caught up in a rancorous, evil tide that would wipe out many young drug addicts from Possilpark and beyond.

It was the mid-80s and the use of heroin in the district was in its infancy. But like an infectious disease, it quickly gobbled up everyone in its path, and then it began to eat away at the very fabric of a once proud and spirited community. I was sensible enough not to take the drug. I had seen the effects on those who did take it; pals of mine I went to school with were suddenly dropping down dead like flies. Those the drug didn't kill were walking about like zombies, their hair falling out and such like. A girl I fancied at school ended up looking like a walking corpse, ugly and horrible.

The drug scene in Possilpark reached epidemic proportions, and the money I was coining in, albeit off the backs of people I knew, ran into thousands of pounds every day. At its peak, I had that much money I honestly didn't know what to do with it. Everybody had a choice in life, and mine was making money, hiring fancy cars and going out to the pubs and clubs to live it up and enjoy myself. It's not as if there were other opportunities presenting themselves to me.

After only a couple of months, Ponny and I had cornered the market in and around the Possilpark area, and because we had access to the best gear in the north of Glasgow we had people coming from all over the city to buy from us. But we didn't always have it our own way, and selling smack did have its drawbacks. One occasion that springs to mind is when a nutter whose name I'll leave out was so strung out and in need of a fix he grabbed Ponny in the middle of the street in broad daylight, put a blade to his throat so hard that it drew blood, and then demanded a sorter to clear his head. This guy was sweating because of withdrawal. I'll never forget the look of fear on Ponny's face. I had to run as fast as I could to one of our stashes to get some gear to take back to this guy, as there was no doubt in my mind about what he would've done had I left him roasting. I went back and passed him a handful of gear, and he released Ponny in one piece, albeit badly shaken.

Money kept pouring in and the lifestyle was amazing, but I knew it was only a matter of time before the Drug Squad got on to me. Little did I know that they had actually been watching me for a while. It all came to a head when, one evening, I was in my flat ironing my trousers. With no warning whatsoever, my front door came crashing in and Drug Squad officers piled in with a sniffer dog and a toolkit for unscrewing light switches, getting behind worktops and other places I never even knew it was possible to hide stuff. The only really incriminating evidence in the flat was £250 in cash that was sitting on top of the corner unit of my sofa. I was quite lucky because just ten minutes before there had been enough drugs in the flat to amount to me receiving a 12-year sentence, for sure.

For about two hours the officers turned my flat upside down, and after they were finished they left the place in an absolute mess. What scared me the most was when the leader of the pack, a small bearded copper, with long curly fair hair and glasses, took me by the arm and walked me straight into the kitchen. Once we were out of earshot of his companions he opened his jacket and took out a clear bag of powder that looked very much like heroin. Being careful not to let his colleagues see what he was doing, he said to me: 'You think you're clever don't you? I'm working and I get paid, but I don't have a nice flat like yours. I can't afford a fancy car like the one you've got parked outside. Don't think for a minute that you're fooling anyone just because we've not found what we came for.'

As he held up the bag of powder and waved it about a couple of times, he continued: 'See this, Willy boy? If I've got to come back here to search your flat ever again, then this bag of smack won't be coming out of my pocket, it'll be coming out from under your couch! Do you understand what I'm saying to you, son?'

I nodded my head to let him know I knew what he meant. He then put the bag of powder back in his pocket and signalled to his men that the show was over.

The Drug Squad had just given me a real fright, and they were a right mean and nasty-looking bunch, too. It made no difference that I had no drugs in the flat – I still got the message loud and clear. When I stood listening to that copper telling me he would set me up, I knew he wasn't messing about. If I continued selling drugs, the next time they appeared I was going straight to the jail. That really put the frighteners up me – it was enough for me to pack it in immediately. I collected all the money I had, gave my mother most of the furniture from my flat and within a fortnight I had moved out and gone to Hawick to live with my half-uncle, Archie. I missed the flat and the comfortable lifestyle, but it was not the end of the world.

And, in fact, my life was about to take yet another twist when Old Mother Fate did her stuff and put me on the same path as one of the best armed robbers of our generation, a master criminal from the East End of Glasgow by the name of Michael Healy.

Chapter Nine

Cops and Robbers

I went to Hawick with a view to staying there for a few weeks, just to give myself enough time to consider my next move. One thing is for sure, selling heroin again was right out of the question. There was no chance I was stepping back into that rotten scene; the Drug Squad would've swooped on me in no time. But as things stood, I was now homeless and the money I'd saved up from my time supplying heroin wasn't going to last me forever, so I soon found myself heading back to the only place I knew I could make money – Glasgow.

As much as Hawick is a lovely part of Scotland, there were very few opportunities there for a criminal like me, with serious ambitions to get to the top. Back home, I fell in with a group of villains who I knew operated mainly in the city centre. These guys were like celebrity criminals, emulating Scottish football players in their lifestyle and hanging out in the same nightclubs and bars.

Laurence 'Lorny' Barclay and Frank 'Tosh' McIntosh were two players who knew the city-centre circuit well, and over time I became good friends with them. We would go to the Cotton Club, a small trendy nightclub on a steep hill just off Sauchiehall Street; the Italian restaurant La Costiera on West Regent Street; and the ex-Celtic star Charlie Nicholas's pub, Nobody's Inn, on Howard Street.

Also on Howard Street was a sauna and massage parlour called Angels that we would hang out in, owned by another villain well known on the scene called Frank Carberry. Carberry was a bit of a wild one who wore lots of 'tom' (i.e. jewellery, from the rhyming slang 'tomfoolery', jewellery).

Lorny Barclay reminded me of George Best. He had the same long black hair and beard, and he was always impeccably dressed. He had the gift of the gab and a way with the ladies. With his gregarious, ostentatious personality, he was full on and had bags of magnetism – or, as he would put it, he was on a VHF (Very High Frequency) level above everyone else. Lorny lived in Castlemilk along with his older brother, who was also a crook.

Tosh was from Shettleston in the East End and was as equally flamboyant as Lorny, with film-star looks. People were forever saying to him that he resembled Sylvester Stallone. On the downside, Tosh was a mad stabber and always carried a blade of some sort. He had such a nasty streak that I was always worried he'd do someone in whenever we went out on the town together. He had stabbed people in my company before for absolutely no reason. Tosh lived by the sword and, in the end, died by it, when someone struck him over the head with a hatchet, killing him stone dead. This happened well after my time of knowing him, but I wasn't surprised when I heard what had happened.

It was toward the end of 1986 that I became involved with this lot, and it was through them I met Michael Healy, a Glaswegian from Ruchazie in the city's East End. From what I'd heard about Healy, I couldn't wait to meet him. He sounded just like the sort of person I wanted to work with. Tosh drove me to Inveraray where Healy was staying. Healy was a six-footer with a thin physique and straight, shoulder-length fair hair. I could tell just by listening to him that he was clever and more than capable of handling himself. I pulled Healy aside after just an hour of meeting him and, when Tosh couldn't hear us, I suggested that we drop Tosh because I didn't believe he was properly cut out for the heavy stuff.

Healy agreed with me and that was it; we connected immediately. We had a profound understanding of where we wanted to go, and from that moment on we would play Tosh along just so that he felt he was a part of the game.

Michael Healy would become a very good friend of mine, and we stayed friends right up until the point we hit a situation that was way out of our control and which destroyed our friendship, but I'll get to that later.

When I first met him, Healy had carried out loads of mini-hold-ups, taking cashboxes – which usually contained anything between £10,000 and £50,000 – from security guards as they carried them to banks, building societies or post offices. Healy was a competent armed robber, and his niche was these relatively small jobs, but he always had his eye on something bigger – something that would set him up for life.

Around this time complications were beginning to develop with cashbox robberies. Some boxes were being rigged with metal spikes that shot out from their sides if the guard dropped them. Others sprayed red or blue dye over the money inside, making it almost impossible to move on, and others again would set off a deafening screamer. I didn't rate security box robberies highly at all.

Healy had been monitoring the movements of a red, reinforced Royal Mail van for a few weeks before I met him, and by the time I came on the scene he had decided this was going to be his next job. He had followed this particular van from its depot near George Square in the heart of Glasgow and tailed it as it dropped off cash to no less than nine different post offices all over the south side of the city. These vans could contain hundreds of thousands of pounds, and normally there were three post office co-workers assigned to managing cash deliveries. Unlike the heavily armoured security vans whose guards wear protective helmets and clothing, there was nothing stopping someone from swiping the cash from the post office van as soon as the delivery guard opened the door. Ponny and Tam Shannon had been accused of robbing a Post Office van of £109,000 but were cleared due to lack of evidence, so I knew there were rich pickings to be had.

The most important component in the success of any robbery is surprise. The more you can take the person(s) you're about to rob off guard, the better chance of success you have. One of Healy's tactics was to dress up as a woman in order to surprise his victims. He was a bit of an odd sight in drag, but it was a great disguise nonetheless.

When I first sat and watched him apply the foundation, powder, make-up and lipstick, I couldn't believe how convincingly he could pass himself off as a woman. For hours he would sit in front of a vanity mirror slowly smearing on the cosmetics he kept in a special overnight bag. I couldn't help but think that he actually enjoyed dressing up. With his real hair tied back in a hairnet, he'd put on an eye-catching, shoulder-length wavy wig followed by a long skirt, woman's shoes, overcoat and handbag, big hoop earrings and a pair of hexagonal-shaped glasses to finish the job. When he stood back and asked me for my reaction, I told him that he resembled an old social worker nearing retirement. He would have given Dame Edna a run for her money.

Big Healy was so confident and brazen with his disguise as a woman that sometimes we would go about our business with him fully dressed up for the occasion. I recall one day as we were sitting at a set of traffic lights a police car pulled right up alongside us on the nearside. Healy was in the passenger seat so the coppers would've glanced over and seen what appeared to be a woman sitting in the car. We were carrying guns that day and what a nerve-racking moment that turned out to be. This was typical of Healy's self-composure under extreme pressure; he was a real cool customer.

Healy introduced me to one of his pals and fellow robbers, a guy called Michael Carroll. Micky Carroll had been working with Healy for some time, but it was Micky's Cockney girlfriend who I was taken with the most. She was called Samantha, a real stunner, with the looks of a model, but as dangerous as a black widow spider. Still only in her early 20s, she was just as much involved in the robbery game as the rest of us. Carroll and Healy had met her and a friend when they were abroad in Spain. I was impressed with this lassie . . . very impressed.

Midway through writing this book, I heard the tragic news that Micky Carroll had died after a long-running battle with a serious illness. He was only in his 40s. Micky was a top-drawer guy and we worked together a lot. One of the fondest memories I have of him is when we went to the aid of an entrepreneur who owned a chain of health clubs and gyms in Glasgow. The story goes that someone who worked for the entrepreneur had been ripping him off big time over a number of years and had left the company to set himself up in a chic, designer-clothes shop business. Understandably, the entrepreneur was furious and wanted him severely sorted out. That's where Micky Carroll and I came in.

During a meeting in one of his swanky gyms, the entrepreneur said that he didn't care how we punished his ex-employee so long as we did something. I told the gym owner not to worry; his ex-employee would be regretting his actions by the end of the day.

Straight after this meeting, Micky and I went and got two massive tins of gloss paint and made our way down to the fancy clothes boutique to brighten up the place. We knew that the swindler had no insurance cover on his stock, so we waited until there were no customers before entering and we emptied the contents over all the outfits on display. It was a complete mess and we must have destroyed thousands of pounds worth of designer clothes.

There was no shortage of guns in Healy's camp. I already had my own six-shot, pump-action shotgun, capable of firing six 12-bore cartridges as opposed to the standard five. This shotgun was my first owned weapon and I'd sawn the barrel off as soon as I'd got it. Someone I knew had broken into a gun shop just outside Glasgow and had stolen loads of guns and ammunition. As a gift, this guy gave me the opportunity to choose one of half-a-dozen shotguns lined up against his living-room wall. By the time I shortened the barrel it sat comfortably under a jacket, being a mere 16 inches long. Carroll carried his own handgun while Healy preferred the armed robber's favourite – a double-barrelled shotgun.

We were good to go with this post office van heist, but first I wanted to find the best getaway route from where the robbery would take place, as I had been nominated the getaway driver, as well as participating in the actual robbery. I remember driving round every street in the area to ensure that we had the quickest and most effective escape route in place immediately after the hold-up.

There were four of us taking part in this robbery – Healy, Carroll, Samantha and me – and we each had our roles down to a T. We knew that when the post office van manoeuvred into position at the back of the Post Office, the first thing that the two post office workers in the front of the van would see would be Healy and Samantha standing chatting to each other. That is where the element of surprise would come into play.

Micky Carroll and I would be in a stolen car parked just yards from where the van was going to stop, and it was arranged so that only I could be seen sitting in the car should anyone happen to look over. Carroll would be lying across the back seats clutching his handgun and a massive holdall, and it was his job to get himself into the back of the van as soon as he got the green light.

We were relying on the post office workers in the van opening the door as normal to drop off the money. They were extremely observant at all times, and it was an important part of their job to be so. But there would be no need for them to be alarmed since they would simply think that they were looking at two women talking to each other. They would never have imagined that one of the women would pull back her overcoat to reveal a double-barrelled shotgun.

The night before the heist we went out and stole a car from just outside Glasgow. It was a Ford Orion Ghia, a top-of-the-range fast vehicle of the time. We parked it in a safe place overnight, and everything was now in place. Healy already had a ringer (a car with a false number plate) on the go and we planned using this vehicle as a second car. It was all go, and we were very confident that we could pull this robbery off. There was really nothing more we could've done in terms of being organised; weeks of hard work and planning had gone into this job.

We timed things so that we would be arriving at the van's drop-off location just before ten o'clock in the morning. Micky Carroll had managed to tune the FM radio in the car to the frequency of the police, and now and again we would get some hissing information coming over the channel.

We had just arrived at the spot where we planned to wait for the post office van when the four of us looked at each other in total disbelief as we heard a police message come over the radio:

'Be on the lookout for a Ford Orion Ghia . . . registration number . . . stolen from . . .'

Great. Here we were sitting in the thing. All it would've taken was for a squad car to pass by and, with all the firepower we had in the vehicle, I didn't relish the probable outcome. Weighing up the situation, we realised it wasn't worth the risk and it was time to go. With the post office van about to show I put my foot down and drove away feeling well and truly annoyed. We all were! Now we would have to wait until the following week before we got another crack of the whip.

We struggled to get a different stolen car in time for the post office van heist the following week. Time was now against us and through desperation, as well as the thought of having to wait yet another seven days until another opportunity came round, we went to see Lorny Barclay and ask him if he could organise a suitable car for us. Lorny would never get involved in the heavy, hands-on stuff such as armed robberies. He was more an organiser: he could sort out just about anything you wanted him to, providing it was within reason and you gave him a few quid for doing it.

I knew that Lorny had a green Ford Escort Ghia parked in a lock-up, as I had borrowed this car from him on a previous occasion. The motor had false registration plates and it was effectively a ringer, perfect for our needs. I arranged to get the keys from him and, with no questions asked, I assured Lorny that after I was finished with the car I'd set it alight to ensure no incriminating evidence was left behind. Before we used this motor we gave it a right good wipe down too, inside and out, as we didn't want to leave our fingerprints.

On the last Thursday of August 1987, we set out on a carbon copy of what we'd done the week before. We arrived at the location just before ten o'clock in the morning and we quickly got ourselves into place. Healy and his partner stood chatting away while Micky Carroll and I waited anxiously just yards away in the green Ford Escort. All we were waiting for now was for the van to turn up. It felt like we'd been waiting for ages when I finally saw a van approaching. But it wasn't the usual red, square-type van that appeared.

'There's a van coming,' I said to Micky, who was lying on the back seat. Then Healy looked over at me and raised his shoulders slightly, as if to ask 'What do we do here?'

A snap decision had to be made. I wasn't happy about the van – its shape, size, in fact anything about it – and so I vehemently shook my head, gesturing a no-no.

'It's the wrong van . . . it's definitely not the money van,' I said to Micky. Healy and his girlfriend got themselves back into the car and once again we drove away with an intense feeling of angry disappointment.

It all felt a bit too much at this point. For the second week running, we'd hit a snag, a big snag. It would have been mad to hold up the van and find it was a mail delivery instead. We couldn't take that chance. We drove back to a safe house to give ourselves time to rethink our strategy, and there I remembered that a Group 4 Security guard uplifted the money from a rent office in Rutherglen on the last Thursday afternoon of every month. Coincidently, that day was the last Thursday of the month and, although it popped into the picture at such short notice, I thought that this was far too good an opportunity to let slip by. It was a straightforward bit of work we knew existed, even if there might not be much cash involved.

At the back of the Rutherglen rent office on King Street there was a conveniently placed back door leading into the building. People could enter this back door, coming and going as they pleased in order to pay their rent, but most of the time it was extremely quiet. Just inside the back door you came to a set of part-glazed swing doors. Through the doors' panes of glass it was possible to see the security guard walking in and out of a side door, and this is where he would collect the rent office money for that month. The security guard made various trips in and out of the building and I knew that the first run was normally a dummy one. Previous holdups had taught me never to make a move on the first trip, as you could bet your bottom dollar it was a mock run. I'd been caught out that way before.

Samantha sat in the waiting room of the rent office at the front of the building, keeping her eyes open for the arrival of the security guard. I sat in the green Ford Escort at the back of the building on King Street. It wasn't long before she came out to tell me that the Group 4 Security van had pulled up on Main Street, and that the guard had entered the building and was now on his first run. I quickly got myself into position behind the glass-panelled doors and waited for him to come out of that side door for the second time. I was still smartly dressed in the suit I was wearing from earlier in the day, and I also had a stocking pulled down over my face for that old-school armed robber look. When I saw the security guard come out from the side door, I burst through the swing doors and made sure he saw the shotgun. 'Drop the money and move back!' I shouted and, without hesitation, the security guard did as I asked.

I picked up the bag, which we later discovered contained £10,000, and I sprinted back to the car that was parked outside. King Street was a relatively quiet, one-way system so I decided to drive at speed against the flow of traffic. The getaway was going well up until the point where I tried to take a right turn onto Queen Street. Two people in a Mini Metro, a man and woman who had just finished work, happened to be driving along Queen Street at speed, so a heavy collision was inevitable. Their car clipped the back end of my motor, sending the two vehicles spinning out of control until we ended up facing each other with stalled engines. It got worse because I had already taken my stocking off, which meant there were now two reliable witnesses who had had a good look at me.

I quickly started the engine again and I managed to get away from the scene, but it was ugly and I'd drawn a lot of attention to the car. I made sure I drove a few miles right out of Rutherglen and I eventually parked up in a quiet little street in the middle of a housing estate. Not once had I passed a police car. No sirens either; it had all gone to plan apart from the car crash.

I told Samantha to put the bag of money up the front of her jacket to make it look as if she was pregnant, and she really looked the part. We still had to get right out of the vicinity so we chapped on someone's door and asked the occupant, an elderly man in his 70s, to phone us a taxi because my wife was having birth pains and we had to get her to hospital.

The old man showed great hospitality by offering Samantha a

chair in his hallway and while she sat there she clutched the ten grand and began making wailing noises as if she was going into labour. This was another of this girl's attributes: she was a good actor. We were so short of cash that day that I had to dip into the bag of money we'd taken to pay the taxi fare!

Later that night I went back with Micky Carroll to torch the getaway car, and to our relief it was still parked where I'd left it. We were getting slack and things were a bit too messy. We wanted to eliminate any chance of the police finding anything that would implicate us in the hold-up. Ideally, we shouldn't have heard anything else about the rent office robbery, but that wasn't to be the case.

Police reports of the time stated that certain members of the public had called to say that there was a car burning in their street. The fire services raced to the scene but by the time they got there all that was left of the car was a burnt-out shell. The police forensics department got hold of the car, and guess what, – despite our careful attempts to wipe it down they found a fingerprint on the inside of one of the false registration plates. This fingerprint belonged to none other than Lorny Barclay, the guy I got the car from.

At six in the morning the following day, the police went to kick in Barclay's door, while he and his bird were in bed asleep. They dragged him from his kip, took him to the police station, and put it to him that he was in a lot of trouble. The police informed him that they had found his fingerprint on the inside of a registration plate belonging to a green Ford Escort Ghia used in the £10,000 robbery in Rutherglen. Then they told him that he would be going to jail unless he came clean and started cooperating. Barclay knew the coppers weren't winding him up, as it was he who had changed the plates on the car. He knew he was in a sticky situation.

I had assured Barclay before he gave me the car that I would wipe it down to the best of my ability, but that didn't stretch to cleaning the inside of a false registration plate. He should've worn a pair of gloves. The bottom line was that the police had Lorny Barclay right by the balls and they knew he was going to tell them everything they wanted to hear.

There was no way Barclay was taking this heat by himself, so he opened up and grassed big Healy and me. He told the coppers that he gave me the car but that he never knew what I was going to do with it. The two people who smashed into me with their Mini Metro as I left the scene ended up identifying me as the driver of the getaway car, and this became the main piece of evidence that got me six years in jail.

The police didn't apprehend me straight away. I disappeared down south for a while and avoided capture for nearly three months. But in November 1987, Strathclyde CID caught up with big Healy and me in a flat in Cranhill in the East End of Glasgow, bringing an end to our armed robbery spree. The police made us stand in an identification parade for five different armed robberies that had taken place all over Glasgow and the only witnesses to have picked me out were the two people who had seen me as I was driving away from the rent office job.

Healy and I went on indictment for the Rutherglen hold-up, and because I was only 19 years old I was sent back to Longriggend Remand Centre for 110 days. I knew I was in serious trouble, but I was still only a youngster starting out in the big playing field, so I took it all in my stride. The coppers charged Healy with two armed robberies: a post office job for thirty grand, and the rent office one in Rutherglen. Somehow Healy's fingerprint mysteriously ended up in the inside of the security case. Come on! As if Healy would be daft enough to leave his dabs on a security box! It would never happen in a million years. What's more, a forensic fingerprint specialist would agree in court that it was possible to transfer a fingerprint from one place to another by means of sticky tape. Whatever happened, it didn't prevent Healy from receiving a 10-year sentence.

The next time Healy and I would see each other would be in the cells at Paisley High Court when we both went on trial. Our hearing wouldn't commence until February 1988, which meant spending yet another Christmas and New Year behind bars.

Chapter Ten

Locked up with the Big Boys

From an early age, I always gave the police a false date of birth. Like many young people I wanted to appear older than I was, and it certainly gave me more credibility as an aspiring criminal. Now I had the Deputy Procurator Fiscal questioning exactly how old I was in the Glasgow Sheriff Court.

'I have two different dates of birth for the accused, Mr Lobban, Your Honour . . . and I would respectfully ask that this hearing be adjourned until I can establish what the correct date of birth is.'

The Sheriff peered at me above his spectacles and addressed me in a stern voice: 'Please stand up, Mr Lobban. Now, tell me, how old are you?'

I looked straight at the Sheriff and, unwaveringly, gave him my answer.

'I'm twenty, Your Honour.'

'And what is your correct date of birth, please, Mr Lobban?'

'It's the 21st of February 1967, Your Honour.'

'Very well. Please continue with the hearing.'

I had just told the court that I was a year older than I actually was. I glanced over at the Deputy Fiscal and it was evident that he wasn't at all pleased, but the Sheriff's word was final. I'd been given the opportunity to plead either guilty or not guilty during this preliminary hearing at the Sheriff Court in Glasgow. I pled not guilty, even though I knew the cards were stacked against me. In fairness, the Sheriff should not have allowed the proceedings to go ahead at all, especially as the Procurator Fiscal had asked for an adjournment in order to check out my true date of birth. For the record, my correct year of birth is 1968, not 1967.

I was on my way to Longriggend Remand Centre near Airdrie as a 19 year old, and I would remain there for 110 days, while the police carried out their full investigation into the rent office robbery. The last time I'd been in Longriggend was when I was a 15-year-old school kid. I was still only a kid at 19, just a bit wiser, that's all. I knew deep down that by the time my case went to trial I would be in deep trouble, but there is always that small part of you that thinks with the help of a good Queen's Counsel, it's possible to clinch at least a not proven verdict. There was also an unwritten rule that I adhered to at that age, which was never to admit to anything, regardless of the cost. As blinkered a view as it was, it was my conviction and I stuck to it like a limpet.

When I first landed back in Longriggend, it took me a while to get my head around the fact that Lorny Barclay had betrayed me and thrown me, to the wolves just to save his own skin. It was a massive shock for me as I'd never put him down as someone who'd turn so easily. It was also a wake-up call for what lay ahead in the big bad criminal world, because on my journey through the ranks of law-breaking I'd come across many more stool-pigeons just like him.

Not long after arriving in Longriggend I found myself at loggerheads with a Principal Officer who remembered me from my previous stint in the jail. This PO disliked me with a passion and he would go out of his way to make my life hell. First, he put me on closed visits for no apparent reason and then he slung me in the silent cell because I tried to smash the heavy reinforced window that separates you from your visitors with a fire extinguisher. When I was carried to the silent cell, a prison guard had his fingers in my nostrils and he pulled my nose back that hard it felt as if it would tear from my face. The pain was unbearable. I decided to go on a dirty protest because of the ill treatment I was receiving, not just from the PO but from most of the other guards as well.

A dirty protest is exactly what it says; it's dirty and disgusting. It really is the most degrading and humiliating undertaking prisoners can involve themselves in, but, there again, you have to ask yourself: what drives a person to resort to this sort of deplorable behaviour? For ten days I ate, slept and did the toilet in the silent cell without leaving it once. I didn't shave or change my clothes; the cell was in a right mess, with urine and faeces everywhere. After a few days, my sense of smell became accustomed to the strong stench of filth and rotten bits of food left in the corner of the cell.

Most of the guards would use handkerchiefs over their noses to block out the reek when they opened the cell door to feed me, and the pained expressions on their faces showed how repulsed they felt. For health and safety reasons, I shouldn't have been left in such hazardous conditions for so long, but I was.

On 23 February 1988 at the High Court in Paisley, Lord Sutherland sentenced me to six years for my part in the rent office raid. Michael Healy received a not proven verdict for the same crime, but Lord Sutherland got him on the post office robbery, as the police had somehow found Healy's fingerprints on the inside of a security box. The trial, which lasted about ten days, became a bit of a shambles, as I had to sit through the separate trial of big Healy for the post office raid. I remember that Healy and I laughed all the way through both trials, poking fun at witnesses and drawing immeasurable and unnecessary attention to ourselves sitting in the dock. We showed nothing but contempt for the court and its proceedings. I suppose we didn't care because we felt we were going to the jail at the end of it all anyway.

The significance of my real date of birth popped back into play when the courts sentenced me as a 21 year old, despite me having in reality turned 20 years old just two days before-hand. By rights, the courts should've sent me straight to a young offenders institution to begin my six-year sentence, but instead I was sent to Barlinnie, along with Healy. This scandal for the prison system – and it was a scandal – would go unnoticed for nine whole months: by the time the prison authorities discov-ered my real age and noted that I had slipped through the net for all that time, it was too late, the damage had been done. To my knowledge, no prisoner under 21 years had ever evaded detection for so long, serving their time in a maximum-security prison as an adult. It was certainly a first in Scotland, that much I do know.

During February 1988 the prison officers at Barlinnie were on strike and were still trying to recover from the horrific prison riots of the year before. If I remember correctly, prisoners arriving from court weren't being processed in the prison reception until just before midnight, and in some cases into the early hours in the morning. Queues of jail buses and vans shipping prisoners from court had to wait their turn because of the lack of staff on duty. The whole nick was in turmoil: never before had Barlinnie experienced anything like it. Warrants that should've been checked properly weren't checked at all, and because of this my true age went undetected.

If it hadn't been for the strike at Barlinnie, there is no way I would've been able to continue serving my time as an adult. The reception staff would've uncovered the error of the court. I expected the prison authorities to realise the mistake at any time, but it never happened.

Like every other convicted adult in Barlinnie, I attended a two-week assessment course, at the end of it which, I'd been selected to go to HMP Maximum Security Shotts, along with Healy. No young offenders for me; it was off to rub shoulders with some of the most violent criminals in the Scottish prison system I couldn't believe my luck. This was another huge blunder by the authorities. I'd taken a massive leap forward in the prison system and, so as far as I was concerned, it was all good.

In 1988, Shotts was definitely a prisoner's prison. It was easy to smuggle almost anything in when visitors came. The guards just let you get on with it; there was no discipline whatsoever. I remember seeing prisoners walking back to the hall with guitars, banjos and other instruments they had just picked up at a visit, and these items went totally unchecked.

There were a handful of prisoners selected for a strip search, but the searches were more like pat-downs, a bit of a joke, really. This meant the rest of the prisoners walked right on back to the hall with whatever they had stuffed down their strides. Drugs swamped the jail. I recall seeing lumps of marijuana in nine-bar

(9 oz.) form lying on the top of worktops inside the cells. Prisoners would sit around as nice as you like, freely smoking joints.

Inmates could apply to have their own curtains and bedding; in fact, you could even ask for a fur rug for the floor! I had matching curtains and a quilt set with a fancy black-and-red stripe, and I had the white fur rug as well!

Downstairs from me, on the bottom landing, was a prisoner called Gerry Rae, and this guy had the whole hall petrified. Rae was like the daddy of the jail, so to speak. Apart from being a raging homosexual who had a penchant for young boys, he was an evil man who should've been labelled a beast and locked up in Carstairs state mental hospital. Rae wasn't the tallest of people and he was overweight, covered in acne; he had horrible greasy skin and hair. Like a lethargic fat slob, he sat in the security of his own cell with the curtains drawn at all times. No one could just wander into his cell without first knocking at the door, and fellow prisoners and guards considered him so dangerous that no one dared say a bad word about him, at least not to his face.

I saw in the summer at Shotts, and if it was a scorching sunny day outside most prisoners would take advantage of the nice weather by heading outdoors. But not Rae. During these hot sunny days, you would find him sitting inside his dimly-lit, smoke-filled cell with the curtains closed. The guy really was an absolute freak and I'd heard a rumour that he'd hit one of my uncles, Vincent Manson, over the head with a hammer in one of the workshops in Perth Prison.

I also crossed paths with Paul Ferris. He was in the same section as Rae doing time for possession of a shotgun and all sorts of other shenanigans involving a bent copper. We got on fairly well together and I suppose our capacity as associates intensified once more through our shared passion for table tennis. Ferris, like everyone else, was terrified of Gerry Rae.

I recall one day swiping a large tin of fruit from the kitchens, where I worked. It was one of those huge tins, quite a luxury in jail, but theft was a sacking offence, if caught, so I sneaked it past the guards and smuggled it back to Ferris's cell for us to eat in a bit of peace and quiet. We'd barely opened up the tin and tasted one of the nice juicy pears when Gerry Rae walked in and stared right through us as if we'd done something wrong. We were like two kids being caught with our fingers in the cookie jar, as Rae fumed: 'What's going on here? . . . So, that's the way it is, then?' He then promptly left the cell. Still munching away at the mouth-watering pears, I think we managed a half-smile.

'I better go and give Gerry some to keep him happy,' Ferris said, and he went straight over to Rae's cell and gave him the whole tin. I can't say I was too happy since that tin of fruit was for Ferris and me, and I had risked being booted out of the 'cooks' (kitchens) in getting it, but that's the effect Rae had on everyone, Ferris included.

I can't say I was sorry when, in October 1999, Rae was found dead by a gang of kids slumped at the wheel of his white Vauxhall, the victim of a suspected heroin overdose. Much has been written about his grisly demise. There was speculation that there had been a conspiracy to murder him after he successfully raised a civil action against the Chief Constable of Strathclyde Police, in which he claimed Drugs Squad officers had severely beaten him during a raid at his home. As far as I'm concerned, it was a fitting demise for a horrible man who, in my opinion, brought much pain and suffering to countless young boys. Was he murdered? Who knows.

As a 20 year old thrust into the deep end amongst some of Scotland's most hardened criminals, I became a big attraction for the likes of Ferris, Rae and others. Ferris would see in me someone who, like him, was young and up-and-coming, and it didn't take long before he pitched his stall with a fanciful invitation for me to come on board with him. Rae, on the other hand, saw in me a young, baby-faced kid who he thought would capitulate under the stress of the pecking order and put up with his pugnacious sexual innuendos and harassment. Little did he know he had something else coming.

Big Healy came rushing into my cell one day – I don't think I'd seen him so ecstatic and excited. 'You'll never believe what I've managed to get my hands on,' he said, producing a butcher's meat cleaver from under his white uniform.

As he passed it to me, my eyes were transfixed by the massive bulk of Sheffield steel. It was a proper meat cleaver, and it had a piece of cord through the tip of the handle to give the user a better grip. It wasn't in the best of condition, and it was obvious that it hadn't been used for quite some time. There was corrosion all over the thick blade, but this didn't detract from its formidable appearance.

'I got it from inside a steel filing cabinet in the back store in the cookhouse, but it wasn't easy . . . look at the state my arm is in.'

Michael pulled back his sleeve to reveal a scraped, bleeding, black-and-blue forearm; it was in a right state.

He went on: 'The door on the filing cabinet was locked, so I pulled it back as much as I could, without actually breaking the lock, then I squeezed my arm in as far as I could and luckily I was able to grab it.'

I'd seen many weapons in jail, ranging from homemade chibs to actual lock-back blades, but never before had I seen anything like this. This was the real McCoy, an actual butcher's clever used for cutting cows' heads off, and here it was inside a maximum-security prison. And the best bit about it was no one knew, not even the guards, because no one in the kitchens would've missed it. With a little bit of elbow grease, a green pad and some soap and water, it didn't take me long before I had the thick blade looking as good as new. This terrifying weapon gave us a powerful upper hand amongst potential enemies in the jail, and if ever there came a time when our backs were against the wall and we required its services, then pity help whoever was unfortunate enough to be on the receiving end.

In the summer of 1988 Ferris had come to the end of his three-year sentence and, like most cons who were due for release, he followed the custom of going round and saying cheerios to pals. There was no cold bath or boot polishing for him, although he did come up to my cell for his going-away chat. We spoke for a while and I remember saying to him: 'Look, Paul, all I want is for people to respect me . . . never to mess me about.'

I was trying to make the point that I wasn't anyone's fool. Ferris turned to me and said: 'I need people like you to work with, people with bottle who can stand up for themselves.'

I was flattered, and I liked the guy, so I was prepared to keep an open mind as to where we went from there. All we were doing was building bridges for the future, although I don't think either of us could predict just how dangerous that bridge was going to be if we crossed it. Ferris wrote down a telephone number, handed it to me and asked me to get in touch as soon as I saw the light of day. Using a special number code, I kept the phone number safe in amongst my private letters and I would bring it out when the time was right.

During my stay at Shotts, the prison was generally calm, though certainly lacking in real discipline. I'd arrived at the very beginning of March 1988 and, undetected, I continued to serve my time as an adult right through to the autumn. Cracks were developing by then, signs that the jail was about to explode, but nothing could've prepared anyone for the avalanche of disturbances that swept over the maximum-security prison in such a short space of time.

First, one of the workshops went up when some prisoners began smashing everything in sight. An inmate by the name of Colin Murdoch instigated this incident; it was a well-known fact that he was hell-bent on causing as much havoc in Shotts as he possibly could. From that single incident in the workshop, there followed a spate of smash-ups where inmates in a copycat flurry destroyed the furniture and property in their cells.

The hall I was in wasn't involved in any disturbances at this stage, although all the prisoners knew exactly what was happening over in other parts of the jail. As a security precaution, the management in their wisdom, decided to restrict prisoner movements within the hall by locking the big grille gate at the end of each section. Inmates could still interact, but only within the confines of the landing. At first, this approach seemed to work while the prison management tried desperately to regain control, but as you can imagine the prisoners were becoming more uptight and angry as the hours passed. There was no work to go to and during the first day or so the guards were allowing inmates to sit in each other's cells, sometimes permitting three or four to a cell.

At one point, the guards allowed me to go downstairs to sit

with Healy. Prisoners were even moving mattresses into their pals' cells so that they would be more comfortable. The whole hall was in disarray. The authorities were teetering on the brink of a full-scale catastrophe, as one by one inmates smashed up their cells in different halls. Prisoners were shouting over to us from other halls, telling us what was happening, and it was just a matter of time before my hall went up like the rest of the nick. All it required was someone to trigger it.

A prominent tension gripped the hall and then I could hear the smashing up of cells down below me. The trouble had finally reached my hall and it didn't take long before others joined in. I remember the noise was deafening and, in the end, it was a case of getting involved and doing my bit. Prisoners started shouting to one another and I know that 80 per cent of inmates housed on my landing trashed their cells. It was amazing just how quick the hall lost its equanimity. This was the first time I'd been involved in a disruption of this scale and I began ripping the toilet pan, sink and furniture from their holdings, and water sprayed out all over the cell. I turned my once lovely and clean cell, which I'd taken so much pride in decorating, into an absolute and unrecognisable wreck. Anything that didn't belong to me I trashed with acrimony.

For what seemed like hours, the destruction continued. At the time, the press reported that 50 prisoners were responsible for the destruction caused in the Shotts riot of 1988, but I believe that figure was putting it mildly. Even so, 50 rioting inmates were more than enough to cause the damage which horrified the prison authorities.

I recall lying back in the freezing cold cell with water all over the floor. The windows were made of thickened glass back then, and I'd smashed them. I had also drawn a big black cross on the wall with some paints I had. I've no idea what possessed me to do this, but I remember it started to freak me out.

The days immediately after the upheaval were the worst days a prisoner could face, especially if they'd participated in smashing up their cell. The whole jail went into a heavy lockdown, the only inmates being allowed out of their cells were those who worked in the cookhouse. This lockdown continued for some considerable time and some prisoners found themselves banged up for up to a year or more.

Shotts had been plagued by disorder and frequent unrest since its opening in 1978, so the prison authorities weren't prepared to take any further chances. They'd had enough and it was time to get back control of their jail. Mercilessly, guards wearing full riot gear were instructed to enter one cell at a time and clear it out until it was totally bare. First, the guards dragged the inmates out into the corridor and, with no hesitation, they then began chucking every single piece of property right out the windows.

Any windows that weren't broken the riot squad broke with their batons. Their task was to empty the cells by whatever means necessary. If something didn't fit naturally between the small gaps in the bars, then they simply made it fit. It made no difference if the property belonged to the prisoner, was personal and in good nick – everything went out . . . there was no compassion at all. The riot squad officers caused just as much noise and chaos when they cleaned out the cells as the rioters themselves had at the height of the disturbance.

Outside the cells, piles of smashed furniture, personal property, broken toilet pans and wash-hand basins lay scattered all over the place. I remember that it was dark outside when the riot squad embarked upon this accelerated destruction and some prisoners started lighting fires.

Directly below my window, a huge fire took hold and since there was no glass in the windows it meant prisoners started choking with the smoke blowing into their cells. I couldn't believe my eyes when I saw a senior officer – a hated figure within the jail – actually placing a mattress and other bits of furniture on top of the fire.

Whatever Healy did with the meat cleaver he took from the kitchens, I do not know, but he was looking after it when the hall went into lockdown. What I do know is that search teams turned the jail upside down shortly after the lock-up took effect, and they did come across it during the search process. Seemingly, the cleaver is now kept in a special display cabinet, like some sort of souvenir, somewhere in the Officers Training College at Polmont. I've heard there's a plaque underneath saying, 'This weapon was found in Shotts Prison during the 1988 riot.' Its purpose is to let rookie prison officers see what sorts of weapons can be found in jail. I don't think anything like it has ever been found again. Now the Scottish Prison Department knows exactly where the meat cleaver came from and what the true story is behind it. Luckily, it wasn't found embedded deep inside someone's head, as it could easily have been.

With no movement allowed in the hall, I spent the entire lockdown thinking about whether I should come clean about my real age. Riot squad officers would open the cell door and push meals along the bare floor, the food catching the dust and muck in the process. No one got exercise and that meant being locked up in your cell 24 hours a day in the freezing cold, as there was no glass in the window frames. After a few days living under these extreme conditions, it suddenly dawned on me that I didn't have to suffer the prison authority's vindictiveness or live with the repercussions of the riot, so I thought it was time to tell the governor how old I really was. This is how I went about it.

The number one governor would visit prisoners on the lockdown on a daily basis as part of his morning schedule. When he came into my cell, I was nice and polite on this occasion and I said to him, 'Sir, I have something to confess.'

'And what's that, Lobban?'

'Well, sir . . . I shouldn't be in Shotts Prison because I'm only 20 years old. I don't turn 21 until next February.'

You should have seen the look on his face. He considered what I had just told him and looked at me as if I were mad. He probably thought to himself he'd heard it all before.

'So you're only 20, Lobban, are you?'

'Yes, that's right, sir, and if you don't believe me then why don't you call my lawyer and he'll confirm my date of birth.'

That statement seemed to lend some credibility to what I was saying.

'Just give one of my officers here all the details and we will look into it for you.'

Then the governor trotted off. I knew that if I wanted to be heard properly, to get out of Shotts because of my true age, then

I'd need to press the matter much further than just telling the prison governor.

When I was allotted my next privileged telephone call outside, I phoned my mother and asked her to send a copy of my birth certificate to Shotts. I then called my solicitor, Davie Kinloch, at his office in Glasgow and I instructed him to start the ball rolling in order to get me out of Shotts and back into a Young Offenders Institution. All I had to do now was sit back, albeit in a cold and empty cell, until such time as the prison authorities were satisfied that indeed I was only 20 and therefore should not have been in an adult institution in the first place.

The guards opened my cell door a few days later and informed me that I would be going to Greenock Young Offenders to see out the remainder of my twentieth year. I was jumping for joy. I couldn't believe how fast the governor had acted. In effect, he had to, because it was law. Heading back to a Young Offenders Institution, having spent the greater part of the year in Shotts as an adult, was quite a daunting experience for me, but I was so excited about being free from the wearisomely mind-numbing practice of the lockdown that I couldn't care less.

By the time I landed in Greenock, or Gateside, as it is officially known, I'd reluctantly grown a beard from my spell on lockdown back at Shotts and I looked at least 21. The move to Greenock was a massive transformation for me. I'd just spent most of a year rubbing shoulders with some of Scotland's toughest criminals, yet here I was surrounded by raw teenagers starting out in the game.

Greenock jail has always held a mixture of adults and under-21s, albeit in different parts of the prison. I went straight into A-hall, or 'Ailsa', as it was known. This was a huge hall with four galleries; at full capacity there were over 130 inmates locked up there. There were a further two smaller halls – C and D – each capable of holding up to 60 or so prisoners.

I'd barely been in the jail a few days when a horrific knife attack took place just along the landing from where I was located. This meaningless and tragic incident created a lot of drama within A-hall, with a great deal of police questioning. The victim was an

18 year old from Glasgow called Mark Mulheron. His attacker was a baby-faced lad with blond hair and the appearance of a school kid, a 19 year old called Thomas Gordon, from Dundee.

Mulheron was attacked because he stole a Temgesic tablet that was part of a smuggled parcel of drugs that came into the jail. Tommy Gordon, who worked in the cookhouse, managed to walk out of the kitchen with a large, razor-sharp knife used for cutting vegetables with the sole purpose of ramming it into Mulheron back in A-hall. Unchallenged, he calmly walked up the stairs to the top landing and entered Mulheron's cell. A fight broke out and baby-face Gordon stabbed Mulheron through the side so hard that the blade exited the boy's stomach, slicing a major artery that supplied blood to the lad's lung.

With blood pumping from the wound, Mulheron ran from his cell cursing and swearing: 'Bastards! Bastards!'

Mulheron had that look of shock written all over his face, that faraway look that showed he knew he was in serious trouble. The boy managed to get as far as the top of the stairs, about 15 yards away, and then collapsed on his back right on top of the cold concrete floor. There was so much blood that it left a thick trail behind him and started dripping downstairs onto the inmates who were standing on the bottom floor landing. Mulheron died at the top of the stairs as a result of his stab wound. No one could do anything for him. And all for a single tablet that he apparently stole. What a waste of life and what a senseless killing. Thomas Gordon would go on to receive a life sentence for murder.

Shortly after this horrific killing I managed to get myself a job working as the gym-pass man. This is a well sought-after number, especially in a Young Offenders, and it's there I met two of the best physical training instructors ever to work in the prison system, Ian Cushley and Rab Anderson. These guys knew how to handle inmates and I would see more of them in different jails as I progressed through my sentence.

The day after I turned 21, I was off from Greenock Young Offenders and on to the maximum-security Perth Prison. Perth jail in the late 80s and early 90s was a proper man's jail. Every hall had at least one football team and usually one in reserve. The gym facilities were fantastic, and the circuits and indoor five-a-side football were excellent. The vast majority of cons took great pride in their appearance, and because there was a cobbler's workshop the cons with influence wore fancy brogues complete with segs – small bits of metal on the heels of their shoes.

I progressed to a job in the cookhouse which became my full-time workplace until I left Perth to move to Dungavel semi-open nick. But first I would have to get awarded my C-Category status, and that was no easy feat back then.

I started off as a baker in the kitchens, working the ovens and preparing the dough for the daily bread. Perth jail always made its own bread. There were six of us working in the bakery section, and after we had finished our work for the day we would take chairs into the steam room, which was used to make the dough rise. It was just like having our own sauna.

Any time a lorry came to drop sacks of vegetables and potatoes off at the jail, I'd volunteer to unload and pack them all by myself. Everyone thought I was mad, guards included, but I did it without losing too much puff. At times there might have been a full lorry-load of 165-pound sacks needing carrying from the delivery truck along a long corridor and stacked neatly in the dry store room. I'd go back and forward until every last one of them was stacked neat and tidy. It gave me a satisfying workout and it also gave me a lot of brownie points for extra grub, meat and all the other goodies normally kept out of the reach of inmates. I'd sit in the steam room wearing only a pair of shorts after a delivery and there was no better feeling. What a way to do time!

When it came to food, I always had the best. I'd get the butcher to cut the steaks and then we'd make beef and liver stews. I could eat a full chicken myself, and that was on top of a dozen raw eggs every day. So long as you kept your workplace clean and tidy and didn't slack with the job, then the cook's party was a fantastic number, and it paid well too.

In Perth I also trained for the world record for parallel bar dips. My uncle, Vincent Manson, held the world record at that point and I wanted to break it. When he was in Gartree jail in

Leicestershire, Vincent had smashed the existing record in front of Guinness Book of Records adjudicator Norris McWhirter.

Eric Duff, who was the senior physical training instructor at Perth and the main man behind all the staff training at the jail, suggested that I should have a go at beating Vinnie's world record and assured me that I would get all the support I needed to succeed. He called me into the gym one day and, along with another couple of PTIs, set about finding out how many I could achieve in a full hour. Duff had it all worked out right down to exactly how many dips I'd need to accomplish and in what space of time – the record stood at 1,320 dips in one hour. It was a trial run and my first attempt.

I went on the timetable he'd prepared, doing a set of dips, short rest, then another set, short rest and so on. We did this for 48 minutes and, with 12 minutes in hand I had to do a further 316 dips in order to beat Vinnie's world record. Every dip was officially checked – we had a PTI standing at the dips bar and I had to touch my pectoral muscles off his clenched fist for a dip to count. After this trial run I was hooked, and every day I would train hard with the goal of setting a new world record, though events conspired against me, and despite coming very close, I never achieved this.

I eventually got my Category C status and was transferred to Dungavel Prison. I had served out my time in Perth quietly; I kept out of trouble and was focused on training for the world record. I had been, for a time, a model prisoner.

Chapter Eleven

On My Toes

Almost as soon as I arrived at Dunvagel I made up my mind to escape, and for days the only thing I thought about was gaining my freedom. Nothing was going to stand in my way – nothing.

I needed out, as my mother wasn't keeping too well and I was concerned for her, and for my pal Ponny, who was being threatened by people connected to the well-known McGovern crime clan in Glasgow. He was on the verge of being shot and possibly killed.

The McGovern family were well known and much feared throughout the Glasgow underworld, and they are still a force to be reckoned with today. Like most criminal families, they have been plagued by the Glasgow Curse. They are a large family who specialised in the drug trade and they made their mark in the late '80s when drugs were really taking a grip on the city.

Joe McGovern, the eldest of five brothers, was said to be the real brains behind the family's operations, but I never got to know any of them on a personal level so I can't really say for sure. Then there were Tony, Tommy, Jamie and the youngest, Paul. Paul was sentenced to life imprisonment in 1990 for stabbing to death a man by the name of Thomas Cushley. He was only 16 at the time of the killing. Tony, the second eldest of the McGovern brothers, was shot six times as he sat in his Audi A6 having just left the New Morven Bar in Balornock. He was just 35. His murder remains unsolved. Tommy McGovern stood trial for shooting a rival gang member but was acquitted on all charges. He later received a four-year sentence for firearm and drugs offences. Jamie was seriously disfigured when someone shot him in the face in 1987. He was very lucky to have survived.

While I was in jail doing time, Ponny was outside building up his lucrative drug business. The money might have been good, but along with selling drugs comes obligatory violence and bloodshed, and this was the problem he was now facing. He was bringing attention to himself, and the McGovern family were keen on putting him out of business. At that time, early in 1991, Ponny was nothing more than a mid-level drug dealer with aspirations of climbing the ladder within the drug world. He had been involved in the drug trade as far back as 1985, when we both sold smack on the streets of Possilpark, but unlike me he stuck with it and his business had grown considerably over the years.

Now I had to get out of prison so that I could help Ponny clean up his mess – and it was a serious mess. A battle had broken out between rival factions within the drug world in the north of Glasgow, and the likelihood was that Ponny would end up being murdered. But who in their right mind would do a runner from a prison sentence they had almost finished just to help their pal? Not many, but when you see a childhood pal crying his heart out to you during a visit and he tells you he could possibly be killed, you're put on the spot. I couldn't just sit back and do nothing. This was the loyalty I had for this guy.

I do have serious reservations about this time in my life and the impulsive decisions I made. Was it worth it? Was it hell! In a nutshell, I regret putting myself forward and trying my best to help someone who I believed to be my best pal, as in the end I got no thanks for it at all.

It was early in 1991 when I was given a day pass and let out of Dungavel semi-open jail in order, supposedly, to have my Kerelaw tattoos removed. I was to attend a private clinic for a skin graft on the condition that I returned later that same day. Dungavel near the town of Strathaven in South Lanarkshire, is roughly a 30-minute drive from Glasgow. I had organised a lift from one of my mates the day before, telling him to be outside the prison at a prearranged time. Just before I left Dungavel I went round my pals in the prison and shook their hands, saying my farewells. The senior officer on duty that day walked me to the prison gate, opened it up and said he would see me later. I gave him a wry smile before stepping out into freedom and to an awaiting car just across the road. Dungavel was now a thing of the past.

I had an air of confidence about me that day; I was really bouncing with energy to the point of being arrogant. All those sessions working out in the gym and training for the parallel bar dips record had given me a particular feeling of self-assurance. Armed with such poise, I felt invincible. My driver, Ronnie, knew the score and why he was picking me up, and that I had no intention of going back. Ronnie had somehow managed to keep on the fringe of things, although he wasn't really a crook. I had known him for many years and he was trustworthy, but as far as the big time was concerned he simply wasn't cut out for it. Unlike me, he always avoided being sent to prison.

It didn't take long before Ronnie and I were in Glasgow. We nipped up to see how my mother was doing first. I thought I had better see her before the cops started searching for me. Then we made our way over to Cumbernauld. Ponny had a safe house there where I could live and keep low for a while. When we reached our destination, Ronnie dropped me off, wished me the best of luck and then hastily did a U-turn back to his normal daily life in Glasgow.

My safe house was actually a two-bedroom flat in a block of maisonettes. First impressions are always important, but I could tell right away that this place was inadequate for my needs. I was hoping for somewhere quiet, in a half-decent area. Instead, it looked rough, and there were people constantly coming and going. The flat was sparsely furnished and looked drab.

Worse still was the fact that Ponny's brother Tam and his young son were also living there. This wasn't good. The boy was only ten or twelve, if that, and there were guns in the flat – lots of guns. The young boy's father had already accidently fired a pump-action shotgun while he was sleeping, nearly blowing off his foot, and I didn't like the idea of the youngster living where guns and ammunition were kept.

Parked outside, in a communal car park, was a small blue ringer, a vehicle whose registration plates had been changed. I always preferred having a car of that nature on standby, just in case it was needed in an emergency. It didn't take long before a planning meeting was held between me, Ponny and his brother at the safe house. I wanted to put some sort of strategy together quickly and I was savouring the prospect of the action that would follow.

I wanted as much information as possible on those who posed the greatest threat to Ponny and so we decided to have words with those close to the action. After arming ourselves with handguns we travelled to a bookmaker's in Cumbernauld. We'd been told that three guys we wanted to speak to would be in there betting on horses. They had information we wanted and we were determined to get it. It was late in the afternoon, so we knew the place would be full of punters. This didn't put us off. The betting shop, a William Hill establishment, was situated in a shopping centre – not the ideal location, but this was business, and it was probably the only place where these characters could be easily approached. They would have felt safe inside a busy bookmaker's, especially as it was inside a shopping centre. But for me, this was where they were also vulnerable.

We calmly strode past the crowd of shoppers until we reached the betting shop. Ponny's brother stood just inside the doorway while we moved in to mingle with the large number of punters inside. We were aware of the CCTV system in the place, so we were careful not to show any sign of a gun. The guys we were looking for weren't faces I was familiar with, so Ponny scanned the betting shop floor until he spotted them. Sure enough, there were three of them as expected and as soon as they saw my pal they didn't know where to look.

I brushed past them, making it obvious my companion wasn't alone and, without warning, I pulled back my jacket just enough to show them I was carrying a gun. The atmosphere changed instantly. This trio knew we weren't fooling around. We wanted an address belonging to one of Ponny's main threats and one of these dumplings could provide it. I told them they were in a lot of trouble, that the best thing they could do was to cooperate and we'd be on our way. Again, I gestured to my jacket and minutes later we left William Hill's happy. We had the address we were looking for. It was perfect. No hassle, no stress; it went exactly the way I envisaged it, and this was only the beginning.

As I was now a free man – albeit a fugitive – I decided to track down an old friend of mine. Michael Healy had escaped from Shotts prison and at the time he was the most wanted man in Scotland. He had hidden in the back of a van that had delivered meat to the prison and the van drove him out of the jail to freedom, much to the embarrassment of the prison department.

I managed to trace big Healy through his sister, Janice, who lived in Ruchazie with her boyfriend. I got an address where I could find Michael – a safe house in the heart of the city, with a police station only a stone's throw away. This was typical of Michael's cunning; it didn't freak him out at all.

I went round to see him but only stayed for a couple of hours on my first visit. I explained to him that I was assisting an old friend from way back who was in some difficulties. Michael told me that he was working on a bank job – a big bank job – and he was trying to recruit a few bodies to accompany him on the mission. He explained that the bank was somewhere down in the south of England but wouldn't give too much away. I certainly couldn't do two things at the same time and told him so. Besides, I was committed to helping Ponny fight his corner and I wasn't prepared to deviate from that. I could see Michael wasn't short of firepower: there were two sawn-off, double-barrelled shotguns lying on the sitting-room floor. After a good old catch-up we parted for the night, and I made my way back to my own safe house in Cumbernauld.

Things were hotting up for Ponny in the north of Glasgow. I was in the safe house on my own when the telephone rang. It was Lizzie Scullion, a trusted friend from back when I was 14, and someone who meant a great deal to me. Lizzie was terrified and her voice was shaking as she told me that a group of people had tried to shoot Ponny. He was now in her house covered in blood. He'd had to jump through a double-glazed window to escape.

I armed myself, jumped in the ringer parked outside and drove to Lizzie's house in Braid Street, Woodside, just north of the River Clyde. When I arrived, I found Ponny sitting on the sofa. He was cut from head to toe and had some particularly nasty gashes to his face and forehead. Earlier in the evening Ponny had visited a woman who worked for him stashing drugs. But Ponny's enemies had a contact in the same street where she lived and when he turned up in his car and popped in for a cuppa, he fell into a trap.

Ponny's helper lived in Possilpark. Her house was on the bottom landing of a typical three-storey tenement block on Barmola Street. The house was also very busy, as she was a single mother with five small children. Ponny arrived late at night and parked his car outside. He had hoped that by the time he got there her children would be safely tucked up in bed. It was a quiet night, but it had been a hectic day, and so when he sat down he decided to take some diazepam tablets. Just as the pills started to take effect he was startled by the sound of a car being smashed to bits outside.

Two cars had pulled up outside the house and five or six figures wearing dark clothes, their identities concealed, had jumped out with baseball bats and other weapons, including a loaded shotgun. Ponny's car, a green Ford Escort, was their initial target.

While some of them made sure the car wasn't going anywhere, the remainder headed straight for the house, where he was sitting, unarmed and almost out of it because of the pills. They were soon banging and kicking on the front door. These guys wanted to do serious damage. The children were awake by now and screaming the place down. They were terrified, and the look of fear on their mother's face would have been enough to double their hysterics.

A shotgun went off in the close and the bang would have amplified dramatically in such a confined space. Fearing for his life, Ponny dived through the back bedroom window. Realising that he'd made his escape, his attackers tried to give chase, but luckily for Ponny the back door to the close was locked and this short delay is what probably saved his life. His enemies had missed their chance but had created havoc and terrified the kids in the process.

Ponny took off over the back courts and hid himself under a

Transit van a few streets away. He lay there motionless for half an hour until the big guy who owned the van, Norrie McAlpine, appeared. When he saw Ponny, he immediately offered to drive him anywhere he wanted to go. Ponny got a lift to Lizzie's place.

Lizzie was a special person to me. We went way back as teenagers and had had a relationship when I was only 15. Sadly Lizzie died in her 40s as a result of depression and taking prescription and non-prescription drugs including speed, Ecstasy and the rest. She left behind young children of her own.

As related in various sources, including Alex Shannon's book *The Underworld Captain*, only a couple of hours after the fierce attack on the house where Ponny had been sitting, someone who had heard all about what had happened thought the people responsible had gone too far and shouldn't get away with what they had done. They had crossed the line and broken the unwritten code of never causing trouble if children are present.

Impulsively, he decided to deliver a message right to the heart of the McGoverns' headquarters, the Spring Inn public house on Springburn Road. With no care or thought that his actions could start a full-scale war by hitting the McGoverns' stronghold, he calmly walked into the Spring Inn at the busiest time in the evening. He selected the tallest man in a group at the pool table – who, unbeknownst to the intruder, was one of McGoverns' right-hand men – tapped him on the shoulder and asked him for a quiet word outside. As the two stood just outside the pub door a shooter was produced and pointed in the face of the tall figure.

The gunman then related what had happened at the house in Possilpark, adding that certain people weren't happy about what had gone on, and that this message was to be related back to the McGoverns. The tall figure nodded his head in acknowledgement, and the gunman then ordered him back inside to continue his game of pool.

Like lightning, the guy vanished back into the pub. As the door was closing behind him, the gunman let off a shot as a warning. The bullet went through an ice bucket on top of the bar and then slammed into the gantry.

The McGovern family would now have to consider what had happened in their backyard and to mull over the possibility of further reprisals. Almost straight away the word on the street was that the gunman who had strolled into the Spring Inn that night was similar in appearance to me, and my name was put forward to the McGoverns as the person responsible. Although I was aware of these accusations it wasn't something that bothered me at all because I hadn't even been near the place on the date in question, and the police clearly didn't take it seriously, as I was never even questioned about it. Anyway, that was the least of my worries. As far as I was concerned, they could think what they wanted. Our job now was to find out the names of those involved in the attack on Ponny and figure out out who had frightened the life out of all those poor children when they fired that shotgun in the close. This was first on the agenda, so I came up with an elaborate plan that would enlighten us all as who was responsible.

A guy by the name of Geo Madden lived on Springburn Road, not too far from the Spring Inn. Back in 1991 Madden was an associate of the McGoverns, and he fancied himself as a bit of a lady's man. Ponny, Tam and I singled him out for a visit.

At the time of writing Madden is the business partner of Paul McGovern and together they run the well-established M & M Security (McGovern and Madden) in and around Springburn. Geo had been dubbed 'the Gobfather' and 'Vain George' by the Scottish press at one point after he had a full set of trendy tooth implants fitted at a top Harley Street dental clinic. He reportedly splashed out £90,000 on the titanium implants, a heck of a lot of money, if you ask me, only to fall victim to a serious mouth infection.

It's amazing how sociable people can become when some marijuana and a few tins of beer are produced in exchange for a nice bit of hospitality – and this is exactly how we became acquainted with a young couple who shared a flat just above Geo Madden's place on Springburn Road. They assisted us by allowing us to sit in their flat so that we could watch Madden's movements. This made our task of pinning him down a walkover.

We sat in this couple's house for hours until we were sure Madden was at home. It was first thing on a Saturday morning when we made our move.

The couple informed us that Strathclyde Council had been replacing windows in the area, so I thought I would go to Madden's door disguised as a council inspector. I was very smartly dressed in a grey Dunn & Co. three-quarter length coat. I tucked a folder with some paperwork in it under my arm to give that authentic professional appearance, and to add to my masquerade I stuck on a pair of glasses.

While I knocked and waited at Madden's door my two mates hid themselves just out of sight of the spyhole. He took his time in answering, but then I heard: 'Who is it?' It was Madden, and he took a peek through his spyhole.

'Good morning, sir, I work for the council,' I replied. Before I could say anything else the door opened slightly with the security chain preventing it from opening fully. Madden took a proper look at me.

'Hello there, I'm from the Scottish Special Housing Association and I would like to take some measurements of your windows, if that's OK?' I said. Just as I had anticipated, Madden unhooked the chain and opened the door.

'Just come in,' he said, before walking off along his hallway.

His back was to me and I could see he was wearing a flamboyant silky dressing gown. I grabbed the handgun I had stuck down my waistband and followed him up the hall. Ponny and Tam Shannon came rushing in behind me, with their guns in hand.

Madden was quickly ushered into the sitting room and told to have a seat. I went to have a look in the other rooms to make sure there was no one else present. When I checked the bedroom I came across a nice-looking blonde in her late 20s sitting up in the bed, looking rather nervous and bewildered. She had a quilt cover pulled right up to protect her dignity.

'You OK, hen?' I asked her in a reassuring voice.

'Yeah, I'm fine, thanks,' she replied. I got the impression she thought I was a copper, especially from the way I was dressed.

'Do you smoke?' I asked her.

'Yeah, I do,' she replied, so I took out my Benson and Hedges and offered her one from the packet.

She took the smoke and I lit it for her. She seemed to look

much calmer, but I unplugged the telephone from its socket and told her I had to remove the phone from the room. I wasn't taking any chances. I informed her that we wouldn't be too long, we just wanted a few words with her boyfriend through in the sitting room. She nodded; I left the bedroom and closed the door behind me.

Back in the living room, Madden looked like he'd seen a ghost. My pals were sitting on the sofa, pointing their handguns at him; one of them had a piece of rope in case we had to tie him up. I grabbed a seat just opposite Geo. The plan was that I would do the talking, but Madden had already been subjected to a barrage of abuse from Ponny and his brother, and frankly it all felt a bit amateurish. My pals found it difficult to control their frustrations, so I had to intercede.

Looking puzzled Geo snapped: 'Look, guys, what's all this about? What's the score? What have I done?'

'Nothing Geo . . . Nothing at all, so calm down,' I said, trying my best to reassure him.

Now in control of the situation I continued, 'It's like this, Geo. We want some information from you – information about an incident that took place the other night where five or six guys smashed up a green Ford Escort . . .'

Before I got the chance to say anything else Geo retorted: 'I know exactly what you're talking about. I heard about that carry-on. They were all talking about it in the Spring Inn.'

I could see that Geo was prepared to talk to us so I got straight to the point. 'I'll tell you what, Geo. If you give us the names of all the slags involved, and who gave the orders, then we will leave you in peace to get back to your bed. You've got a nice lassie through there waiting on you.'

'No problem. When I heard about what had happened, I didn't agree with it. They were all idiots firing a shotgun in a close, just no need for it.'

It was obvious Geo just wanted us out of his house as quickly as possible, and who could blame him. He gave us the names and even the telephone numbers of some of the people involved that night, and I was delighted we got the result we came for. But before we left I put my hand into my overcoat pocket and produced a cigarette lighter in the shape of a hand grenade. I had picked this gimmick up in an old Army & Navy store. No one would have known if it was fake or not. It really looked authentic and I could see Geo's face as he gulped at the sight of it in my hand.

'See this here, Geo,' I raised my arm in front of him so that he got a good look at it. 'I want you to pass on a message to the McGovern family for me. I want you to tell them I've been to visit you, and I want you to tell them that if there are any more "liberties" taken like that one the other night, then this grenade will be lobbed through the window of the Spring Inn. You pass that on, OK?'

I stood up, looked at my pals and beckoned them to exit. We didn't hang around for tea and biscuits. That was it, another nice bit of work completed.

The following day we drove past the Spring Inn and to our amusement we could see that every window had been covered with metal roller shutters. I laughed and shook my head. I knew they had taken our message seriously, and I knew that they would want an equaliser.

Tit-for-tat incidents followed, becoming more and more violent. One name in particular kept coming up as the person behind many of them. His name was Duncan McIntyre, a close friend of the McGoverns. It soon became clear that McIntyre had pushed his luck a bit too far. We had to teach him a lesson.

We knew he lived on the ground floor in a block of maisonettes just up behind the Spring Inn, he had had his front door heavily reinforced with an iron grille, so pinning him down there would be difficult. We weren't exactly in the mood for hanging around, though; we were turning up the heat and wanted to make an example of this McIntyre character.

It was around ten o'clock in the morning when we went to McIntyre's door armed with handguns. We had no idea who would be in the house, and we weren't even sure if he would open the door. Our strategy was simple: as soon as McIntyre appeared Ponny and Tam would shoot him once each in the legs, and that was it.

Although I was armed I wouldn't be firing my weapon unless

I really had to. I would keep watch. We were in a rough part of
Springburn and a police motor could drive by at any moment.

All seemed quiet as we approached the front door. No one was
about, so I slipped my hand through the iron gate and knocked
on the door while my two pals stood back from the spyhole. I
tightly gripped the gun in my coat pocket.

'Aye, who's that?' a voice said in a cocky Glaswegian accent.

'I just want a word with you, if that's all right,' I shouted back.
A moment later – I couldn't believe it – MacIntyre opened
the door and stood before us. My pals stepped into view with
their guns at the ready, but something wasn't right. They were
supposed to shoot him, but nothing happened. What was going
on?

I noticed two old women away at the far end of the block of
maisonettes carrying what looked like bags of shopping and I
stood in that doorway with disbelief as a conversation started to
take shape.

McIntyre had opened the door wearing only his trousers. He
looked scruffy, with greasy skin his wavy black hair unkempt.
He looked as though he was heavily pregnant, as his gut flopped
out over the top of his jeans, and it was obvious he had a less
than healthy relationship with chips and beer. For a moment I
thought about shooting him myself. There he was standing right
in front of me, a target a two year old couldn't miss. But no, it
wasn't my call, and I wasn't putting myself forward for this one.
Furthermore, it wasn't what we'd decided. I had seen enough,
but what I found really disappointing was the fact that our plan
hadn't been executed as we'd arranged.

Already I was beginning to regret escaping from Dungavel
nick. I was spotting weaknesses in Ponny's ability to perform
when it mattered: couldn't understand why he didn't shoot
McIntyre when he had the chance. It all seemed a complete
waste of time and effort, and now the other side would be right
on their guard.

Afterwards, all I heard from my pals that day was the excuse
that the old dears might possibly have witnessed the shooting,
but this didn't wash with me. The old women probably couldn't
see two feet in front of them, never mind 30 metres along the

ground-floor landing where we were standing. Their bottle went; it was as simple as that, and if they expected me to do their dirty work that morning then they had another thing coming. I was beginning to think it was time for a change. I had to pursue a different path now, one that would ultimately catapult me into the bigger playing field, the premier division. I was putting in a lot of hard graft in trying to clean up Ponny's mess and I wasn't getting much back in return. I wasn't impressed and I was starting to feel that I was flogging a dead horse. The Shannon cause wasn't going anywhere. They weren't the players I hoped they would be, and they were becoming too slack for my liking.

Chapter Twelve

Embracing a Brother

I decided to spread my wings a bit and so I looked up Paul Ferris, whose number I still had from the time we spent together in HMP Shotts three years earlier. By this time Ferris had well and truly fallen out with Arthur Thompson Senior but was still one of the major players on the Glasgow crime scene.

When I got hold of Ferris on the phone, he told me to come and meet him at the Cottage Bar, Shettleston, in the east end of Glasgow. I got the Shannons together and told them what my intentions were: that I was going to meet up with Ferris. I could see by the look in their faces that they weren't too happy about it. This wasn't what they wanted to hear. It was as if they knew that I was thinking of heading off in search of pastures new, and the mere thought of that must have sent shivers down their spines. They knew how much of a loss I would be to them, especially at such a critical time, when their own little war was on the verge of going full blown. But I wasn't going to give up on them entirely just yet.

I taped a Beretta handgun to my thigh, where it would be secure but accessible, and called a taxi. I didn't know how the evening was going to pan out, so it made sense to take along with me some means of security, just in case I found myself in a position where I had to defend myself. This little compact gun was capable of firing nine .22 calibre bullets, with eight in the magazine and one in the chamber. It was the perfect companion, and lethal if fired accurately.

When I got into the taxi I asked the driver to take me to the Cottage Bar. He seemed to know the pub so we set off from Cumbernauld and headed towards Glasgow. Twenty minutes later we arrived. I paid the cab driver and went inside. The place looked dismal and empty, not what I had expected at all. A few old-timers stood at the bar, chatting over their pints. There were a couple of rough-looking guys playing a game of pool who eyed me up as I entered. But there was no sign of Ferris. I stood at the end of the bar next to the public telephone, expecting a familiar face to appear any second, but still no sign. The few drinkers present were beginning to wonder what I was doing there. I stood out like a sore thumb.

The barman approached me. 'All right, mate? What can I get you?'

'Err . . . give me a fresh orange juice,' I told him, then I asked, 'Is Paul about? I've to meet him here and he's expecting me.'

The barman looked at me befuddled. 'Who is it you're after? 'Paul . . . Paul Ferris . . .'

Now he looked extremely puzzled. 'I've not got a clue who you mean, mate, never heard of him. You sure it's here you're meeting this person?'

Now I was confused.

'This is the Cottage Bar, isn't it?

'Aye, but there's another Cottage Bar in Shettleston . . . you sure you've got the right pub?'

The penny dropped. It never dawned on me that I could be in the wrong boozer. What a start to an old reunion! I felt so embarrassed. I quickly got on the phone and called the right pub to let them know what had happened, and then I called another taxi to take me over there straight away.

When I eventually arrived at the correct Cottage Bar, I noticed the difference immediately. The pub was situated on the corner of Shettleston Road not far from the local cop shop. When I entered, the whole place was full of life. It wasn't the biggest of boozers, but I saw a mixture of old and young drinkers who were all having a good time. I got a good vibe the second I set foot in the door. I could see Ferris sitting away at the back of the pub with various people hanging around him, and as soon as he noticed me he stood up and approached me.

He steered me to the bar and said to the barman, 'Alan, this is my pal, Gibby. Fix him up with what he wants.' ('Gibby' was the nickname I had from years back because of my mother's then boyfriend, Alex Gibb. Some people still used it, and Ferris was one of them.)

I asked for a fresh orange juice. I wasn't a drinker and fresh orange was my preference. I took the glass, thanked the barman and joined Ferris and his company. Two of the main people he introduced me to were Bobby Glover and Joe 'Bananas' Hanlon.

After we got the pleasantries out of the way, Ferris and I then spoke privately for a while and caught up with what we had been doing since we had last seen each other. I explained to him that I was on the run from Dungavel, and I presented myself in such a manner that I left him with no misconceptions as to where I was coming from and what I wanted to do with myself. I got the feeling that everything was going well and I didn't pick up any sort of negativity.

I asked Ferris if he fancied going through to Hamilton for a night out at a place I knew. A good friend of mine was now managing a nightclub there called Gloss. I first met this guy when he ran a different club, the Rococo Club, also in Hamilton, during the days I ran around with Lorny Barclay and Frank Mackintosh. I had been invited through for the opening night of the Rococo Club and we'd hit it off straight away, and I kept in touch with him right until I was sent to prison for armed robbery in 1987. He was aware of my fugitive status, but this made no difference to our friendship. He really respected me and vice versa. He was a big man with tight black curls and a trim Errol Flynn-type moustache. He was the perfect host and knew exactly how to look after people in his club – and he enjoyed rubbing shoulders with the bad boys.

As soon as I explained all about it, Ferris's eyes lit up. 'My girlfriend, Sandra, goes to that club. I've heard all about it, but never been there.'

He wanted to know if my pal would help him to find out what she was up to when she went through there every weekend.

'Listen, Paul, if your bird goes to Gloss every weekend then my big pal will tell you everything you want to know,' I assured him. It all sounded good and we made a decision to head for Hamilton.

Before we set off Ferris explained that he had to stop off to see the other woman in his life, the mother of his young son, Paul Junior. He invited me into the house with him, which was a short drive from the Cottage Bar. As he got himself a change of clothes and a quick wash, I sat in the living room talking to his missus, who was extremely chatty, a very nice lassie. He then shouted me into the kitchen.

'Here, Gibby, cop for that!'

I looked at the small white object he handed me. It was amphetamine inside a cigarette paper – or a speedball, as it's better known.

'I haven't had this stuff in a long time,' I said to him, still looking at the white ball of powder in my hand.

'You'll be all right – look.' He produced a slightly larger ball than the one he had given me and he swallowed it with a glass of water.

'Let's go for it, I may as well,' I replied.

I chucked the tiny ball in my gob and swallowed it. I wasn't thinking straight at all. How did I know what it was he had just given me? What if it wasn't what he claimed it was? Paranoia gripped my mind for a few seconds, and I went back into the living room and sat down. Ferris slung on his Boss designer jacket, we checked our appearances in the hall mirror one last time and we left for Gloss.

When we arrived outside the club, the queue was running the length of the whole street. Hundreds of people were waiting to get in. I spotted my curly-haired pal at the entrance with the bouncers. Ferris had made sure he wasn't alone. He had arranged for some of his own crew to be there, including his girlfriend, Sandra, and one of her pals. With the two blondes in tow, we made our way past the large queue of people and walked right up to the front door. My pal, the manager, saw us as we approached, and like true VIPs, the cordon was pulled back to let us past. From that moment on, we would be shown splendid hospitality. We were escorted into the restaurant area first and then ordered drinks.

I introduced Ferris and the rest of the associates so that everyone was acquainted, and as soon as my pal knew we were content he left us to settle in. It was all looking very promising at this stage and I could tell Ferris was lapping it up. I couldn't have asked for a more impressive and encouraging start to the evening. As we stood chatting away at the bar someone produced some LSD tablets and we necked the acid tabs as we stood there talking. What was I doing? I knew I shouldn't be taking this stuff – it could have been anything – but it was too late. I just got caught up in the moment.

The Gloss nightclub was like a palace. It had three different levels: the bottom part was a huge restaurant and bar; the middle section was the actual nightclub; and right at the top it became a bit more exclusive, designed to appeal to the over-30s. They called the top floor 'Baby Jane's', after the Rod Stewart hit single. It was still being refurbished and therefore hadn't officially opened yet.

After a while, my big pal came back and offered to take us upstairs. We gathered our drinks and made our way up into the middle part of the club, where he showed us to an alcove right next to the dance floor. The place was heaving, the music was thumping, and everyone was having a good time. Ferris's girlfriend and her pal hit the dance floor and my pal took Ferris on a trip upstairs to give him a tour of Baby Jane's. I stayed put as I had been upstairs many times before. After a short while the effects of the LSD started to kick in and suddenly I began hallucinating. My pal brought Ferris back a short time later, and then a worrying thought entered my mind. It dawned on me that I was still carrying a loaded gun. What if Ferris and his pals decided to search me at the end of the night? What if they found the Beretta strapped to my thigh? It was a worrying thought accentuated greatly because of the LSD. I decided to come clean.

I asked Ferris to come with me to the Gents toilet as I wanted a quiet word. The two of us zigzagged our way through the packed nightclub towards the restroom. I selected an empty cubicle and gestured Ferris to come in with me. Once inside I locked the door. There was barely enough room for one person, never mind the two of us. I unzipped my trousers, they slid to my knees, and I freed the Beretta from where I had it taped to my leg.

'Listen, Paul, I carry this gun because some friends of mine have got ongoing trouble with the McGoverns in Springburn. It's just in case I run into any of them.'

He took hold of the handgun, released the magazine to check it had bullets, put it back, and then returned the hammer to its normal position.

'Don't do that with the hammer, Gibby. You'll end up having a nasty accident with it taped to your leg like that.' To be honest I was more worried about it jamming if I had to use it in a hurry.

Ferris paused for a moment and said: 'Gibby . . . can I accept you as a brother?'

Surprised by what he just said, I looked at him: 'Of course you can.'

We shared an emotional hug and in that moment we bonded.

We left the cubicle and I, for one, felt elated and much better than when I had gone in. We made our way back to the alcove and for the next hour or so we stood talking until an extraordinary thing happened. Ferris's girlfriend came up to me and said: 'Get out while you still have the chance.' A strange remark, I thought, and I didn't know what to make of it at the time, so I just carried on talking and drinking.

When we left, I travelled with Ferris, Sandra and her pal back to Glasgow to Sandra's apartment in the Gallowgate. Joe 'Bananas' Hanlon was driving. Dance music was blasting from the car's sound system, deafeningly loud, prolonging the upbeat mood from the nightclub. Halfway along the M74 we could see the blue lights of a police car coming fast behind us. At first we weren't sure if they would speed past. I looked at Ferris, fearing the worst – what if the cops found the gun I had in my possession? Hanlon slowed down and slowed onto the hard shoulder. We were getting pulled over. I sat in the back, waiting for the cops to ask us to step out, but the request never came. Why didn't the cops approach us after they had pulled us over? Perhaps it was because the cars Ferris and his crew drove around in were well known and would have been registered on the police computer as non-approachable. Maybe on this occasion they hadn't checked the registration numbers until it was too late. Who knows, but it made me feel very jittery.

We reached Sandra's flat in the early hours of the morning. Hanlon came up for a while and he and Ferris began communicating in a childish manner as though playing mind games with me. They were attempting to mock me, in a psychological sense, even though they weren't directly having a go at me. I sat there quietly listening to the torrent of abuse, which went in one ear and out the other. It didn't phase me in the slightest. One or two cars drove past the flat, and someone shouted up from the road to find out if everything was OK. I guess Ferris was expecting trouble and wasn't taking chances. It now made sense when I thought back to the remarks Sandra came out with in the Gloss: 'Get out while you can.' Ferris had obviously primed her to say these words, and it was clear that he was paranoid himself and might have thought there was something sinister behind my getting back in touch with him.

I couldn't travel back to Cumbernauld so early in the morning. Also, I had been pushing my luck all night carrying a gun and I didn't fancy getting stopped going home. It made sense for me to get my head down where I was. I handed Ferris the handgun and asked him to put it away for safe keeping. Hanlon left and Ferris retired to the bedroom with Sandra. What a night it had been.

Meanwhile the hostilities between the Shannon brothers and the McGovern clan had reached boiling point. Alex Shannon, the sensible brother who so far had managed to keep in the background while juggling a military career with a more dishonest one, had discharged himself from the army and was now in the forefront of Glasgow's gangland scene – and available for launching a severe assault on his brother's adversaries. I knew that Alex's proficiency and coolness were vital if the Shannons were to have success in the McGovern fight.

Alex, in his semi-autobiographical book *The Underworld Captain* (written with David Leslie), describes how he had played a pivotal role in assisting his brothers by stashing large quantities of drugs, guns and money for their use. Always preferring to keep out of the limelight and in the shadows, Alex's contribution to the Shannon crusade now had changed. He understood the importance of the task, of sorting out his brother's enemies. It was just a matter of time before the McGoverns launched their own deadly assault, and Alex had volunteered to help end this tit-for-tat once and for all.

Alex and his older brother, Tam, had run into some of the main players from the McGovern side whilst taking a shortcut through Springburn. Unarmed and well out of their depth, Alex identified Tony McGovern and Jamie 'the Bull' Stevenson – sentenced to 12 years in 2007 for laundering £1 million of drugs money – amongst their surprise attackers. The McGovern mob produced handguns and quickly gave a half-hearted chase. The Shannons ran for their; they and knew that they faced terrible consequences if caught. They ran in different directions, hoping to confuse their would-be assailants, and Tam, who was fit and could sprint, managed to make good his escape.

Alex hid in a drying room attached to a row of flats. He got lucky. Jamie Stevenson, with his gun still in his hand, had run after Alex and, to Alex's horror and disbelief, had popped his head around the door of the drying room where he was crouched, trembling in the dark. Stevenson gave the place a quick scan, but, seeing nothing, he left. Alex believed Stevenson had actually clocked him but for some reason had decided to keep quiet. There's no doubt in my mind, however, that Stevenson would have blasted Alex without a second thought if he had actually seen him there.

Duncan McIntyre – the McGovern stooge who Ponny and Tam were meant to shoot in the knee but didn't – was in the thick of things in the feud between the Shannons and the McGoverns, and he became the focus of the now frustrated Shannon brothers, who despised him with a passion. Dunky – 'the man no one could kill' – would prove to be an elusive character at this time. He was a lucky individual, fortunate to have survived various attempts on his life. On one occasion, had been the subject of a hit-and-run attack, with witnesses informing the police that they had seen someone run him down and then reverse the vehicle over his body before driving off at speed.

He survived a further attempt on his life when someone ran up behind him and shot him in the back of the head with a sawn-off shotgun. When he was taken to hospital, the surgeons successfully removed countless pellets from his skull. He would become the victim of yet another shooting as he left a barber's shop in Springburn, along with his wife, Linda, who witnessed the whole thing. The gunman shot him in the head with a handgun in broad daylight. A passer-by, who watched the shooting, helped McIntyre to the nearest hospital and this act of benevolence probably saved his life.

I thought it was about time I went back over to see my big pal Michael Healy at his flat in Rutherglen on the other side of the city. I remembered him saying the last time I had seen him that he was still in the process of putting a team together for some big bank job he had lined up somewhere in Devon. On the strength of this, I thought it would be a good idea to take Ponny Shannon along with me, just so that we could both sound out what it was exactly that big Michael had on offer. I had previously told Michael that I was helping out a childhood pal of mine who was at war with a mob from Springburn, and he knew I was committed to seeing that through. That said, it wasn't going to do any harm just listening to what he had to say. And besides, this would also give Michael the opportunity to weigh up Ponny in his own way.

When we arrived at Michael's refuge, we wasted no time in getting down to business, discussing the ins-and-outs and practical details of the bank job he wanted to carry out. Michael explained that he was recruiting several fellow Glaswegian criminals, including his younger brother, James, to carry out the robbery and he emphasised that this was 'the Big One' – the one he had always dreamt of doing. There was never a shortage of candidates for the job. It was just the case of Michael being particularly selective in whom he wanted at his side. This was his baby, the pinnacle of his armed robbery career, and it was evident just how passionate he was about the whole thing.

The bank in question was the National Westminster Bank in Torquay. Michael didn't want to simply stage a hold-up, he literally wanted to empty the whole bank. Michael was after the contents of three massive steel vaults inside. It would be an ambitious job, since the robbers would have to deal with as many as 20 members of staff.

Pressed on how much money he thought might be involved, Michael reckoned it would be in the millions, and I believed him. The three of us sat gabbing for what seemed like hours, and eventually Ponny and I left to head back across the city. In the car on our way home Ponny made it crystal clear that he didn't want anything to do with what he had just heard, thinking it was far too risky.

What put me off was when Michael revealed to me the identity of one of the guys he had recruited as a potential driver. Don't get me wrong: if I had insisted that I didn't want this person to take part, Michael would quickly have got shot of him. His name was Robert 'Plug' Harper, a big gawky fellow with two protruding front teeth and a penchant for car magazines. He was nicknamed Plug after the cartoon character, one of the Bash Street Kids in the *Beano*. I remembered this jumped-up wannabe from Polmont Young Offenders, where he was weak, allowing other young offenders to take his tobacco off him, and the thought of doing such a high-profile piece of work with such a person just gave me the heebie-jeebies. In any case, the outcome of the next couple of meetings with Healy eradicated any vague possibility there might have been of me taking part in this doomed-to-failure job.

Not long after seeing Michael I had arranged an urgent meeting with all the Shannon brothers. I had reached a stage in life where I felt an air of invincibility around everything I did. I suppose we all felt a bit like that; I couldn't care less about those with the big reputations on the opposite side who wouldn't have thought twice about putting a bullet in *my* skull. I remembered what my uncle Robert had drummed into me as a wee boy just before he was shot and killed, that I should never, ever look up to anyone, or the way he put it, never praise false gods. What my uncle said had always stuck in my mind.

I had always respected Alex Shannon, even as far back as when we were just teenagers running about singing verses of a Fat Larry's Band song called 'Zoom'. Out of all of the Shannon brothers I always believed that I had a special and indissoluble

Above left. My grandparents, Nessie and Hector Manson, with me, aged four, outside Peterhead Prison, February 1973, when Robert Manson was on hunger strike there.

Above right. My uncle, Billy Manson (second right), at the top of his game socialising with friends in the early 70s.

Left. My aunt, Patricia Manson, holding one of her brother Billy's model ships.

Below left. Billy Manson (far right) with some of his pals. Notice one of my uncle Robert's oil paintings of Robert Burns overhead.

Below. World champion Vincent Manson at HMP Albany in a warm-up session before he broke the press-ups on fingertips record.

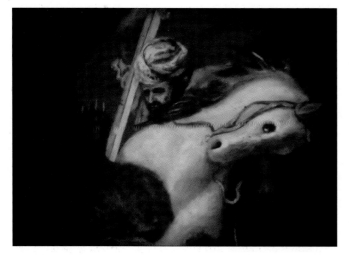

Above left. One of the few surviving oil paintings by Robert Manson.

Above right. The Clown – my personal favourite of Robert's oil paintings.

Right. Robert Manson was like a father figure to me. I still miss him very much.

Below. The New Monaco Bar, which Robert left just before he was shot dead.
(@ oldglasgowpubs)

A mug shot of me as a 19 year old. (Mirrorpix)

My partner in crime, Michael Healy, who was the master-mind of an estimated £6 million aborted bank heist.

Above. Maximum Security Shotts Prison. I served almost a year of my sentence there when I was still only a young offender. (Mirrorpix)

Left. Me (front right) with other prisoners during the annual superstar competition at Maximum Security Perth Prison. The lady on the left handed out trophies.

John 'Ponny' Shannon sitting between my two English Bull Terriers, Bonnie and Rea.

Ponny's brother, Captain Alexander Shannon.

Police SWAT team outside The Ponderosa, the Thompson family home, in Provanmill, Glasgow, in 1991, shortly after the funeral of Arthur Thompson Junior. (Mirrorpix)

Arthur Thompson Junior, the man I was meant to have killed, according to Paul Ferris. His murder remains unsolved. (SMG)

Arthur Thompson attending his eldest son's funeral. (Mirrorpix)

Joe Hanlon (left) and Robert Glover (right), whose murders remain unsolved. (Mirrorpix)

The recovery truck in which Hanlon's Ford Orion was transported to Paisley Police Station. Hanlon's and Glover's bodies were still inside at the time. (Mirrorpix)

Police search for clues while Paul Hamilton's lifeless body sits in his Daimler. (Mirrorpix)

Above left. Paul Hamilton. His murder remains unsolved. (Mirrorpix)

Above right. My mother, Sylvia Lobban, appealing via the *Daily Record* in 1991 for me to hand myself in when I was the most wanted man in the country. (Mirrorpix)

Left. Paul Ferris immediately after his acquittal for the murder of Arthur Thompson Junior. (Mirrorpix)

Below left. Tam McGraw (centre, carrying coffin) at Joe Hanlon's funeral. (Mirrorpix)

Above. The notorious C Hall inside Perth jail, where I held prison officer Terry O'Neil hostage for 13 hours. (Crown Copyright © RCAHMS. Licensor www.rcahms.gov.uk)

Right. This is the exact cell, No. 3 below C Hall, where I started the prison siege. (Crown Copyright © RCAHMS. Licensor www.rcahms.gov.uk)

Below. Maximum Security Full Sutton, where I was caught up in one of the most serious prison riots in prison penal history. (Ross Parry Agency)

bond with him. That bond, however, was shattered in 2011 when Alex published his so-called life story. I had been warned that his book was due for release, and I thought to myself, 'Go on, son. Nice one Alex!' I imagined his book would be well written and about his army achievements; about him having reached the rank of captain and so on.

However, when I picked up a copy of the book I was sickened. Alex had allowed David Leslie, a writer from the *News of the World*, to dictate the gangland theme for his book. I was mentioned no fewer than 169 times by name. It was the same old stuff, the same old characters, all shamelessly sensationalised. Just like others before him, including retired police officers, Alex opted to cash in by jumping on the Glasgow crime book band wagon. It was the ultimate act of betrayal, and I didn't deserve the slagging I got. In one part of the book he claimed that I tried to wipe out his bank account by trying to coax his wife, Angela, into revealing their account details. This is so far from the truth it hurts. It was his wife who moaned about being in financial difficulty and I offered to help out by disclosing a method by which they could con the bank. Alex knows I would never have done that to him, so why did he allow it to be printed? There was also no mention of me buying brand new mobile telephones and other gifts for his three children.

The book also gives an account of what went down during the meetings I had with the Shannons concerning the McGoverns, and he tries to water down the animosity between the two families. He claims that I sounded like an army strategist as I urged that we should go straight for the top and take out the two main players. Indeed, the Shannons and I agreed that this was the best way forward, but not, as Alex claimed, to hit them in front of their families while they sat in their living rooms watching television. This would have been a cowardly way of carrying out a relatively straightforward piece of work, and I for one would certainly have had nothing whatsoever to do with that.

We had agreed in principle that the two main players from the McGovern camp would face execution, and Alex and I had volunteered to carry out the work. We set our sights on a date and time, which, if I remember correctly, would be a Sunday night.

But as the big day approached, for some reason or another, Ponny withdrew and the whole thing went pear-shaped.

I was, by now, beginning to get tired of the Shannons' way of doing things. Ponny was forever sleeping in to all hours in the afternoon, and sometimes I could not get hold of him at all. In addition, although I could not prove it at the time, I was sure Ponny was dabbling in the drugs he was dealing, and I found out some years later that I was spot on.

Then there was Tam Shannon, the brother I got on with least. Alex said in his book that I hated Tam with a passion, but he failed to elaborate on why. I can understand Alex not wanting anyone to know why I disliked Tam so much, but an autobiography should be upfront and truthful. Perhaps he thought it would spoil his book, and I'm quite sure it would have done, if the readers had known the truth. Tam Shannon received an eight-year sentence with some of his pals from Springburn for a heinous crime involving the gang rape of a young girl. Our personalities clashed throughout the time we knew one another, but things got worse after that.

But the thing that got on my wick the most with the Shannons was the fact that I wasn't making any money, despite the hard graft and effort I was putting in on their behalf. I was on the run from a six-year sentence and sooner or later I was either going to get caught or get killed. Worse still, I might have ended up back in jail doing a lifer. My destiny lay elsewhere, and I made a decision to move on and head off in my own direction, and to follow my instincts, which I relied on unreservedly. In my own mind I had done everything I could to help the Shannons. It was now time to sever connections once and for all and let them get on with things themselves. Besides, my sights were set on much bigger things, but it had nothing to do with changing alliances, as was suggested by Alex in his book.

Chapter Thirteen

Promise Me You Won't Shoot Him

The time had come for me to head back over to see Paul Ferris. I told the Shannons exactly what my plans were, that I had decided conclusively to seek out new horizons, and I tried my best not to leave any loose ends behind me. My inclination was to move forward. I was on top of my game and self-confidence was oozing from me.

I knew about Ferris's personal vendetta with the Thompson family. It was common knowledge all over Glasgow's under-world but that didn't bother me in the slightest. I realised that I was putting myself in a dangerous and difficult situation, being in the firing line of his enemies, as it were, but I didn't worry much. Not many villains could saunter into the Ferris camp and be welcomed with open arms, but that's exactly what happened with me.

As soon as we hooked up with each other again, I knew it would be better to use an alias in front of everyone he knew. After all, I was still a fugitive living on the run and the last thing we wanted was the police finding out who I really was. It wouldn't have taken long for word to filter back to the cops through their network of grasses that there was a new face going about in the Ferris camp, so we came up with a snide name. From then on, I would be referred to only as Gary. Of course, the likes of Bobby Glover, Joe Bananas Hanlon and Tam 'the Licensee' McGraw – the main cornerstones of the Ferris clique – knew my real name.

I quickly discovered that the Cottage Bar, where Bobby Glover was the manager, was actually the headquarters of Ferris's deal-ings – a meeting place where the back store was more like an office.

I also had to find somewhere safe to get my head down, so Ferris took me to a contact of his that lived just up the street from where Bobby Glover stayed. The friend was a big guy who was keen on his kickboxing and who had just separated from his partner. It was agreed I could stay at his place until such times as I could move on to more convenient lodgings.

Over the next couple of weeks I would get to know the main players connected to Ferris, and I soon built up a picture of who stood where in the pecking order. Tam McGraw ran his own pub, the Caravel, with his wife Mags ('the Jeweller') and from time to time he would show his face in the Cottage Bar. He was very much a part of what Ferris, Glover and Hanlon were doing. McGraw held the purse strings, he was the man with all the money, and he would call the shots from behind the scenes. Hanlon chose to hang out in the Caravel most nights, looking out for McGraw's interests, but he always made himself available to Ferris. If Ferris had said 'Jump', Hanlon would simply have asked 'How high?' He worshipped the ground Ferris walked on and this foolhardiness would ultimately be his downfall costing him his life. I know Hanlon never had much time for me, but that was down to a clash of personalities back in Longriggend Remand Centre, when we were together there as teenagers.

I was playing the game, trying my best to build a solid reputation within the Ferris camp, and to prove my worth in their eyes I took it upon myself to rob the Pipe Rack public house on Crammond Place, Budhill, in the East End of Glasgow, just up the road from where Bobby Glover lived.

It was a Sunday night, 28 July 1991, and I knew the weekend takings of at least a few thousand pounds would be inside the pub safe. The manager of the Pipe Rack had been winding up fellow publicans on the pub circuit in Shettleston, so I thought I would teach him a lesson and make myself a few grand in the process. I waited until the bar was empty after closing time before I made my move. Wearing a fetching long blonde wig, gloves and glasses as a disguise, I entered the pub via a fire escape door that lay open in a lane at the side of the boozer.

Apart from the manager there were two female bar staff inside, and together they were cleaning up and making sure the pub was in good order before pulling down the shutter for the night and going home. Seeing that the coast was clear, I entered, shouting: 'Here, start making your way to the back office . . . Move it!'

As soon as the three of them saw a figure brandishing a sawn-off shotgun, they froze on the spot.

'Come on, get to the office . . . quickly!' I yelled.

They snapped out of their daze, hurried to the back office as ordered and I was right behind them. The four of us crammed into a tight space no bigger than your average lavatory.

'Right, open the safe, mister,' I commanded. The pub manager stared at me with a look of contempt and cockiness.

'I can't open the safe, the key's broken.'

'What do you mean, the key's broke? Just get it open and hurry up.'

I swung the shotgun around and whacked him across the side of the head, hoping this would make him a bit more cooperative.

'Honestly, mate, I can't open the safe! Look, here's the key . . . try it yourself.'

Shaking and stuttering, he held out a set of keys on a key ring and, sure enough, there amongst the bunch was the stub of a broken key. I looked down at the safe and there, clearly visible and sticking out from the keyhole, was the other part of the key. I cursed under my breath. It was time to go.

'Here, you, take that holdall and put the day's takings in it.'

I chucked a black holdall to one of the barmaids and she did as she'd been told. I left the office, ripped the phone from its socket and locked the office door behind me, with the manager and the two women still inside. They managed to free themselves by removing the facing boards from around the doorframe, some three or four hours later, and then they raised the alarm. I walked away with the day's takings, just under a thousand pounds, and although I missed the bigger prize I still achieved my goal in giving the pub manager the fright of his life. I'm sure he would have known what was going on at the time and why he got turned over.

For weeks, the Shannon brothers had been plotting a bloodbath for their enemies. Their plan was to stroll into the Spring Inn and, without warning, shoot their adversaries dead, once and for all. Alex Shannon, the army officer, found himself heavily embroiled in his brothers' turf war and in his book he compared the planned assault to the St Valentine's Day Massacre.

Ever since I'd left the Shannons to fight their own battles, it was very much on the cards that they would get desperate. Alex was up to speed in what was required, doing all he could to help his brothers out, but he had a monkey on his back. His wife had given him an ultimatum – my way or the highway – and she had announced that she was pregnant. The pressure would have been unbearable in the Shannon camp and, feeling that their backs were against the wall, they decided to come out all guns blazing. It was a madcap plan and one that, if it had gone ahead, would surely have seen them all going to jail for at least 30 years.

Without first thinking things through, Alex, Ponny and Tam decided to drive over to Ferris's stronghold, the Cottage Bar, where they hoped to find me for a quiet word; they were looking for firearms for their planned McGovern massacre. Apart from creating all sorts of paranoia by turning up uninvited, they almost got themselves severely beaten up. If anyone had recognised Tam Shannon and knew about his eight-year sentence for raping a young girl, I am in no doubt what would have happened to him.

When Tam stuck his head in the door of the Cottage Bar to see if I was there, the pub was quiet, so they moved on to Tam McGraw's boozer, which was only a short drive away. This time the three of them went inside, ordered a drink and asked if they could get a word with either William Lobban or Paul Ferris. Naturally, people became suspicious.

Word soon reached Ferris and me that three guys were in the Caravel looking for us. As a precaution, Ferris readied his handgun – Joe Hanlon had already made his way to the Caravel to monitor the three intruders until Ferris and I arrived. According to Alex in his book, Joe Hanlon had a coat on that looked so bulky it was obvious he had a shooter on him.

When I realised it was the Shannon brothers, I told everyone they could relax, that I knew these people, and everything was OK. Ferris asked me what I wanted to do and I suggested that

Ponny come for a drive with us by himself, without Tam and Alex, and that way we could find out what was so important that they felt they had to come all the way over to the East End to see us.

I was driving and Ferris was in the passenger seat. Ponny jumped in the back and then came out with the foolhardy assassination plot, saying he and his brothers were on the hunt for guns. I had already filled Ferris in on the background to the Shannon and McGovern affair, and in the end he chose not to help the Shannons; he wasn't that stupid. Besides he had enough on his own plate.

I managed to nip over and see Michael Healy on a couple of occasions, and during one of my visits I mentioned to him that I was hanging about with Paul Ferris. Michael knew exactly who Ferris was, remembering him from Shotts, when the three of us were in the same hall together in 1988. Michael knew I was friendly with Ferris back then but had never taken to him himself, and he clearly didn't approve of my association with him now. He had something on Ferris and he wanted to warn me about it.

Michael called Ferris a police informer, a grass, someone who I should steer well clear of and not trust in the slightest. As you can imagine, this created a tricky situation between us. I wasn't prepared to accept what Michael was saying about Ferris, but as it was obvious he was sticking to his guns, we just agreed to disagree and left it there. Michael had always been his own man, but never before had I seen him so condemnatory of someone else. I couldn't think of any good reason why he would feel so aggravated. There had always been rumours kicking about that Paul Ferris was a grass, but I had taken the view that until there was solid proof it was simply hearsay.

It later transpired that one of the criminals who Michael had recruited as an additional getaway driver for his Torquay bank job had been bad-mouthing Ferris and calling him an informant. This was based on a duplicated letter on headed paper from the Procurator Fiscal's Office in Glasgow that was in circulation amongst villains in the city and which claimed that Ferris was a police informer. Naturally, tongues were wagging as to the authenticity of the document. Some people were saying Ferris himself put out the letter with the sole purpose of implicating his old rival, Arthur Thompson, by making it look like Thompson had created the document himself. This would all make more sense later. For now it was obvious Michael had been influenced by all this. When I told Ferris about my meetings with Michael Healy, the first thing he said was: 'Did you tell big Mick I was asking for him?'

Well, what could I say to that? I realised that I should have kept my mouth shut. Ferris picked up from my reaction that something wasn't right, and the drama that ensued taught me a serious lesson in when not to open my mouth.

A lot has been said in certain over-dramatised 'true crime' books about the following incident involving Healy, Ferris and myself, and I want to set the record straight about what actually happened. Ferris never at any time primed me with questions to slip to Healy, and I *never* urged Ferris to shoot Healy. Nor did I say anything like 'Put one in his nut, Paul,' as has been claimed in the past. This is absolute garbage. Paul Ferris wrote the most inaccurate account of what happened in his book *Vendetta*. It just goes to show how far some people will go in order to sensationalise their work.

This is what really happened.

Following my awkward reaction to his question, Ferris demanded, 'What's he been saying about me?'

Ferris wasn't daft, he knew big Healy had said something about him and he wanted to hear what it was. The bottom line was that I knew I had to keep things straight with Ferris, no matter what, so I cut to the chase and told him outright.

'Look, Paul, Michael is my pal, you're my pal, and all I'll say is his head's all over the place just now. He's definitely not thinking straight.'

'What do you mean by that? Spit it out, Gibby,' growled Ferris.

'Well, he said you're bad news. I don't know what's up with him, Paul.'

I tried to water things down a bit, but it was no use. Ferris wanted blood.

'So, you know where he's living?' Ferris snapped.

I could see where this was going, but I didn't envisage for a split second that I was about to be thrown into one of the most difficult quandaries I have ever been faced with. Ferris had no regard for my difficult position, and he could at least have handled it in a less confrontational manner.

We got into Ferris's car, and then he was off to get his handgun and silencer – the very same weapon that the police proved through forensics was used to kill Arthur Thompson Junior, and which got Ferris arrested for the killing. I pleaded with Ferris to forget about it, to change his mind and deal with it in a different way, but he was having none of it. He wanted to go over and shoot Michael in the legs as a warning to anyone else who had any ideas about calling him a grass. A can of worms had been opened up and now I was learning what a fundamental error I had made by not keeping my mouth shut.

'Look, if you shoot him, the second you pull that trigger it's curtains for Healy. It's as good as putting him right back inside. Paul, you've got to keep in mind that Michael is Scotland's most wanted man and on the run from Shotts, and if he ends up in hospital with a gunshot wound he's going straight back to the nick.'

When I came out with that one, it seemed to put a different perspective on the matter, and Ferris knew I was right.

'OK, I'll just give him a talking-to. I still want you to take me over there so that I can have words with him.'

That was that, then; there was no way out of this one, and for all I knew Ferris might end up shooting me as well. A surge of paranoia ran through my body and I asked Ferris to pull over.

'Look, Paul, I'm asking you as a pal, will you just leave it out? This is going to create all sorts of problems for me. I know you're angry, and so would I be, but Michael is my good friend and this will destroy everything . . . it could cause murder.'

Ferris looked at me as if to say 'you should have thought about that before you said anything'. He could see I was on edge, but there was no empathy from him whatsoever. If he'd had any respect for me at all, he would have listened to me, but he wasn't interested in anyone else's feelings. Looking back, it was as though he wanted to drive a wedge between big Healy and me, although in fairness I'd done quite a good job of that myself.

'Gibby, I'm going to speak to him. I can't have people going about saying these things about me. Just relax. You're worried that I'm going to shoot him, aren't you?'

'Well, promise me you won't shoot him. In fact, swear on your kid's life that you won't shoot him, because remember you'd be putting him back in the jail.'

Ferris did as I asked, and this did alleviate the tension slightly. All I could do now was clench my teeth and hope things didn't get too messy.

We arrived in Rutherglen and parked the car about 50 yards from Michael's bolthole. We agreed that I would go up to the flat on my own, knock on the door, get inside and make sure no one else was in the house. Then I would come back and open the door for Ferris as soon as I felt it was safe to do so – a very different sequence of events to the one Ferris relates in his book, in which he claims I had a key to the flat and that I let him in myself. That's just rubbish. Michael opened the door to me and let me in on my own. Ferris stayed out of sight up a flight of stairs in the tenement close. I went inside, and I will never forget the tune that was playing on Michael's ghetto blaster – 'I Want to Give You Devotion' by British dance outfit Nomad – not Bob Marley and the Wailers as Ferris claimed.

For a moment, I sat listening to the song. My heart started pounding in my chest at the thought of what was about to happen. 'I need to go to the toilet,' I said to Michael. There was no drink by his side and certainly no long fat joint in his hand, as Ferris has suggested. I knew beforehand that Michael had two shotguns that he kept in a suitcase in the flat, and I saw the case lying on the living-room floor, but for all I knew Michael could have had another gun somewhere that I didn't know about.

From the living room, a small hallway led to the toilet, which was right by the front door. I walked down the hallway, and unhooked the security chain on the front door, turned the Yale lock and Ferris came rushing in shouting at Mick to sit where he was and to put his hands on his head.

Ferris fired a warning shot from the handgun, and the bullet went straight into the little ghetto blaster, putting a swift and unanticipated end to the song that Michael had been enjoying seconds before. Ferris was now in charge of the whole situation.

There was a three-piece suite in the living room. Michael sat on one chair, I sat on another opposite him, and Ferris sat on the couch by himself. For the next ten minutes or so, Ferris quizzed Michael about this, that and the next thing during which time big Healy was ordered to sit with his hands clasped on top of his head. There was no sign of Michael's fingers gripping the arms of the chair or his knuckles going white, as Ferris has claimed. I have to hand it to Healy, he kept his calm despite having a maniac pointing a shooter at him, and he gave as good as he got, even having a go at me on one occasion! That's when I reminded Michael that *he* was the one who had a gun pointed at him and that he should listen to what was being said.

I've no doubt that Michael would have blown my head off if he had been able to at the time. But if he thought hard about what had just taken place he would come to terms with the fact that I was simply the messenger relaying the rumours that had landed us both in trouble. Before we left, Ferris asked me to look for the spent casing from the bullet he had discharged. He also asked me to grab hold of the suitcase containing the two shotguns, otherwise Michael would have come chasing after us for sure. We were leaving big Mick without any firepower and I knew this would hurt him the most. He had a major robbery looming and the loss of his shotguns would be a drastic setback for him. In the end one of the shotguns did get returned, but the other one mysteriously disappeared.

That was it. With my integrity in tatters, we left the flat and drove back to the Cottage Bar. Ferris had made his point, and I had to fight with my own conscience because of what had happened. If Ferris's version of these events are anything to go by in his book, then what does it say about the rest of what he says?

The next time I saw Michael would be in a courtroom at the Old Bailey when he called me as a defence witness at his trial for bank robbery. His younger brother James and another five fellow Glaswegians would receive 16 years apiece for the Torquay bank job. Michael got 19 years for being the ringleader. On reflection, I sometimes wish I had taken part in that job. If I had known what cards Old Mother Fate was going to deal me, I would gladly have accepted a 19-year prison sentence. I chose my path, though, and this decision would inadvertently propel me forward into a predicament so abysmal and unforgiving that today I look back and wonder how I coped.

Around this time I always endeavoured to nip over to Possilpark to see if my mother was OK. Even though she was a chronic alcoholic with severe mental problems, I still made an effort to visit her whenever I could. She had a man living with her at the time by the name of Charles Halpin and, like my mother, he was an alcoholic with problems of his own. The two of them were well suited, but I always got the impression he looked after her. The way I saw it, at least there was someone there to keep an eye on her, and that, for me, was the main thing. In addition to the fleeting visits, I would ring her most nights, even if it was just to say hello. When I looked at her, I could see that she was slowly deteriorating with the effects of the drink, smoking and general neglect to her health, and it was hard seeing her in that state. I did try to help her, but it was all in vain. She simply didn't want to know: it was obvious she had lost her resolve and will to live.

Anway, visiting her would soon become difficult, as Ferris offered me a place to live in Finsbury Park, north London, and he assured me that a nice Glaswegian family based there would welcome me with open arms. I jumped at the chance, as I felt I was beginning to draw a bit too much attention to myself in Glasgow's East End. The last thing I wanted was to end up back in jail. I had to be more phlegmatic, find the time to unwind and quieten down a bit, and so within days of his offer I travelled to London with Ferris, taking only a holdall with a few belongings.

The Glaswegian family who would shelter me in London were a middle-aged couple with two grown-up sons. I could tell immediately that they were not the criminal kind, though it later transpired that they would provide Ferris with an alibi in the Arthur Thompson Junior murder trial.

One of their sons thought he was a bit of a Jack the lad, and within a week or so of knowing him he thought he could trust me enough to show me a handgun Ferris had asked him to stash away. Of course, the first thing I did was to get straight back to Ferris and tell him what this fool had done. I wasn't sure if I was being put to the test, so I had no choice really. By Ferris's reaction I got the impression that this time I wasn't being tested. The son took an immediate disliking to me after that.

The apartment was part of several in a new-build block right in the heart of multicultural Finsbury Park. It was luxurious, and two flagposts – complete with flags fluttering – stood imposingly at the entrance. At the back of the apartments there was a private car park with security gates. There were three Irish occupants in the adjoining flat, two men and a woman, and I got on well with this lot, so well that they got me a job working as an apprentice in an Irish firm called Pro Flooring. I must have made a good impression because the Irishman who ran the firm, a smooth character who drove a top-of-the-range black Mercedes S Class, took me on no problem, even though I didn't have any qualifications or skills in that particular trade.

First thing every morning I would meet the boss and a select group of fellow workers for a fry-up in a café in Muswell Hill. He would then hand out the worksheets for the day. The work could involve heading off to a well-appointed hotel to lay carpets in 50 bedrooms, or it might be off to a top-class Indian restaurant to fit a marble surface in the foyer. Anything involving flooring, Pro Flooring specialised in it. The business had three big Mercedes vans and there were two workers to each van. After only a few days, the boss allowed me to take one of the Mercedes vans home with me. This was perfect because it gave me a chance to blend in to the London scene. All the while I was still using the alias Gary.

At this time, Ferris and I often went out socially, frequenting trendy wine bars and nightclubs, where we would dance the night away. I was never one for boogieing, and judging by Ferris's moves I don't think he was either. It was the early 90s and the rave scene was in full swing. We would swallow an Ecstasy tablet, and as soon as the drug started taking effect we would hit the dance floor and go wild like everyone else. It wasn't about being a good dancer; it was more about letting yourself go and being a part of the immense energy generated under the same roof.

One night we hooked up with a couple of female friends of Ferris's who were also from Glasgow and were now living in London. I started seeing one of them, a nice young girl with a strong Glaswegian accent who specialised in dancing, sex, taking E and smoking hash, but not necessarily in that order. She was a bit loopy but such a lovely bird.

One of the effects of this mind-bending drug is a feeling that you're emotionally connected to people. One night we all ended up back at one of the girl's flats. I was absolutely flying because of the effects of the Ecstasy; we all were. I felt I was on a different plane, on a higher level, and when Ferris and I lay back on the sofas and closed our eyes it felt as though we were united, communicating telepathically, if you like, on a subliminal level. It was a very powerful indeed. As daft as this may sound, that's exactly how it seemed. I felt it, and so did Ferris.

As the weeks went by, Ferris would bounce back and forward from Glasgow to London whilst I continued working away for Pro Flooring and living it up. Then, right out of the blue, Ferris phoned, asking me for a favour. He said someone by the name of Dick would be dropping by the apartment in a bit so I had better make sure to stay in. He went on to say Dick would be giving me something that I had to bring back to Glasgow for him. It wasn't rocket science to realise what was going on, but I was in a bit of a catch-22 situation. I felt I had to go along with the plan.

Ferris told me that a ticket had been booked for me at Heathrow under an alias. I was to take the flight back to Glasgow and then make my way to the Cottage Bar. I waited for the mysterious Dick to appear and, sure enough, he did, complete with a package the size of a bag of sugar. Dick just dropped off the package and left without saying a word.

I got myself smartly dressed and stuck on a tie – Ferris had even told me what to wear – ordered a taxi and made my way to the airport. I never flinched, but I can't say I was happy about what I was doing. I was starting to realise exactly why I had been offered a nice apartment in London.

As I paid the taxi driver and stepped out onto the walkway leading into airport terminal, I remember thinking to myself 'Here goes.' I prayed that I'd be all right. I walked up to the check-in desk and got my boarding pass. It was my first time flying and I was feeling rather excited about this part of the jaunt, like some big kid taking in the scenery and lapping it all up.

As I went through security I could see three or four customs officers. I walked past them – they never as much as blinked an eyelid. I had the package squeezed down the front of my waistband, supported only by the belt around my trousers, and my jacket was all that hid the package from view. An hour later I touched down in Glasgow, home and dry. Again, I walked out of the terminal without any problems, hailed a taxi, and told the driver to take me to the Cottage Bar in Shettleston. Job done!

When I arrived, Ferris and a couple of unfamiliar faces were waiting there to greet me. Whoever the guests were, they were obviously waiting to collect whatever it was I was dropping off. I was ushered into the back store of the pub and asked to hand over the package. One of the guys picked it up, stuck it up his jumper, and left the pub. I could swear blind that one of the strange faces belonged to Paul Hamilton, a member of the Thompson outfit. This belief is based on photographs I've seen since, as I hadn't met Hamilton at this point. Ferris handed me £250 and told me I would get a further £250 within a few days. What a joke. I probably risked at least ten years in jail for what I later found out to be hundreds of thousands of pounds' worth of acid tablets for a paltry 250 quid. A few days later Ferris drove us back down to London in a red Porsche. I never saw the other £250. Instead, he treated me to some designer clothes in a trendy menswear store. Perhaps he had taken into account the fact I wasn't paying any rent in Finsbury Park.

At the time I hooked up with Ferris and subsequently became criminally active with him, in April/May 91, I had been on the run from Dungavel for three months. In *Vendetta*, Ferris mentions that I lived with his friend Bobby Glover and his wife Eileen for *nine* months. But how could I, when I had only been involved with him and his associates for approximately four months tops? Most of the time I was involved with Ferris I spent living down south in London, and the record speaks for itself. I don't deny having lived at Bobby Glover's house in the East End of Glasgow on three or possibly four different occasions, because I did. What I have never accepted is the way that Ferris and others such as Alex Shannon – one of my so-called childhood friends – have spread lies about me in their books with the sole purpose of blackening my character to bolster their own.

Chapter Fourteen

The Killing of Arthur Thompson Junior

On Friday evening, 17 August 1991, approximately four months after bolting from Dungavel, I was in Bobby Glover's house along with Paul Ferris, Joe Hanlon, Bobby himself and his young son Robert, who was perhaps three or four years old at the time and in his bed fast asleep. It seemed like any other normal weekend until Ferris, Glover and Hanlon disappeared upstairs to put the finishing touches to the murder plot they had waited so long to execute. At this stage I knew nothing about what was happening, or what was about to happen, although I did suspect something very serious was looming that night.

As I sat downstairs on my own, I could hear their voices as they laughed and joked up in the bedroom. The time had arrived when they were going to shoot and kill Arthur Thompson Junior, the eldest son of the Glasgow crime boss Arthur Thompson Senior, right outside his home on his first weekend leave from Noranside Open Prison. Arthur Junior had been convicted back in 1985 for possession and supply of heroin, and many believed he had been set up by none other than Ferris himself. Young Arthur had waited a long time for this weekend home leave, and so had his enemies. The execution Ferris and his two pals were about to commit would go down in Glaswegian underworld history as igniting a murderously gruesome chain of events that subsequently claimed the lives of many other criminals. This was a do-or-die mission where everything was at stake, and Ferris and Tam McGraw, the masterminds behind the murder plot, knew that if they botched this hit then there would be swift revenge. They would be as good as dead themselves. Although Hanlon and Glover were heavily involved in the murder they were about to commit, they were merely the footsoldiers for Ferris and McGraw in this ruthlessly executed and well-planned hit. When Ferris, Hanlon and Glover came downstairs, I noticed that Hanlon was wearing a fake black moustache and was carrying a duplicated set of square taxicab licence plates. Ferris then frivolously chucked what I believe was a fake handgun at me, saying, 'Feel the weight of that thing.'

I had no choice but to catch the weapon in mid-flight, but I remember thinking to myself, 'What's he doing this for? My dabs are on that now.'

I got the impression that he wanted my prints on that gun, imitation or not, and he didn't give me time to check to see if it was the real thing. It might have been a fake that Glover wanted out of the house before they left. Annoyed, I made sure I wiped it clean before I handed it back. I was still very much in the dark as to what the three of them were up to, or where they were going, but there was no doubt in my mind they were up to no good. Ferris looked relaxed, or it might have been a show of contrived composure under the severe pressure of what it was they were about to do. Hanlon was just delighted to be at Ferris's side, whereas Bobby Glover appeared disconcerted and looked very much out of sorts. He certainly wasn't as comfortable as his mates.

'I've got a wig in my holdall if you want a shot of it, Paul,' I said to Ferris. I had used the same wig in the raid on the Pipe Rack pub, so I thought I would offer it as a disguise.

'A wig? Let me see it, then,' Ferris said. I took the wig from my holdall and handed it to him and he tried it on.

'What do you think?' Ferris asked the three of us standing there, as he persevered with its positioning until it sat properly on his head.

We all sniggered and passed light-hearted observations at the weird sight before us, but I could tell immediately that he liked his new disguise.

'That actually looks the part, Paul,' I told him as he soaked up the approval. 'Look, keep hold of it, because I don't need it for anything and you can just bin it when you're done,' I added.

'I think I *will* keep hold of it. Right, come on, you two: are we ready to hit the road?' Ferris said. I could see he was itching to get a move on. He put the wig inside a bag and beckoned the others to follow him.

'You'll be all right watching the wee man until I get back, won't you?' said Glover, referring to his son upstairs in his bed sleeping. 'I shouldn't be too long.'

'No problems . . . see you when you get back, and best of luck with whatever it is you're doing,' I replied.

The three of them then left through the side door of the house and drove off into the night.

Tam McGraw, of course, knew exactly what was going to happen to young Arthur Thompson that night, and he knew that he had to find a cast-iron alibi. He chose to go out with some friends to a fancy Chinese restaurant in the centre of Glasgow. Young Arthur had also been out at a restaurant with some friends that night, but with his feisty reputation and contempt for the likes of Ferris and McGraw, he had rejected sound fatherly advice to wear a bulletproof vest. Thompson Senior knew only too well what dangers lurked beyond his doorstep, what menaces could strike from the shadows at any second. Young Arthur knew this as well, but his was an egotistic personality. He seriously underestimated his rivals and treated them as if they didn't exist. In the end, this would prove to be his downfall.

Bobby Glover drove Ferris and Joe Hanlon to collect a stolen Nissan Bluebird car they intended to use as the getaway vehicle. Much has been said about this stolen car, where it came from, and I'll elaborate on this later. The important thing here is that they quickly altered its appearance so that it would pass off as a private taxi. This was a significant part of the murder plan. Tam McGraw was in the private taxi business at that time, so there was no one better to provide false plates.

Hanlon, who was still incognito, wearing his fake moustache, got himself into the driving seat of the stolen Nissan. Ferris got in the back seat, and that's when I suspect he would have put on the long blonde wig I had given him back at Glover's house. They drove to Provanmill Road, site of the enormous Thompson family home, where they knew Young Arthur would appear at the end of his night out. Details of Young Arthur's movements came from a spy inside the Thompson camp. I believe this person was Paul Hamilton, a defence witness for Ferris in the subsequent murder trial and someone who paid the ultimate price when he was shot dead at the wheel of his Daimler in November 1993. There's certainly no way Ferris and Hanlon would have taken the chance of sitting in a stolen car with a loaded gun without being certain that Young Arthur would eventually appear.

Glover's job was to wait for Ferris and Hanlon at a prearranged spot immediately after the hit, and that was the only part Glover played in the murder of young Arthur Thompson. Ferris and Hanlon waited in the bogus taxi on Provanmill Road across from the Thompson house, knowing that Young Arthur would show up at any time.

It was dark, just after 11 p.m., and this provided great cover, but in reality no one would have paid much attention to what looked like a woman sitting in the back of a private taxi. Ferris was sitting in the back seat clutching his .22 calibre handgun with silencer, ready to pounce at the first glimpse of his enemy. Ferris knew he would only get one chance and knew he wasn't going to miss. He had built himself up for this moment for months, rehearsing the scene over and over in his mind's eye until he visualised it as clear as day.

Ferris was about to shoot and kill his childhood friend – a person whose family had taken him under their wing and cared for him. This wasn't just some random shooting, it was all about a power struggle, and most of all it was about eradicating the competition. How did it get so bad that it had come to this? It didn't matter now – suddenly Young Arthur came into view and the wait was over.

Ferris, still in disguise, got out from the back of the stolen car and rushed towards Thompson Junior, who was now making his way to his front door, unaware that an assailant was right behind him. Ferris pulled the trigger, and three of the .22 bullets went crashing into the front wall of the house. Three additional bullets found their target, hitting Young Arthur in the head and body. While Thompson Junior staggered towards the door for help, his strength becoming weaker by the second, his younger brother Billy came to his aid. Within seconds, the wounded man was drifting in and out of consciousness, gasping for breath.

Ferris was gone by this time, having jumped into the back of the bogus taxi, which then sped off into the night. Ferris and Hanlon met up with Bobby Glover, who was waiting for them and quickly took them to safety, ditching the stolen car in the process. It's at this point that the three of them went their own separate ways, but not before Ferris had given Glover a detailed account of what had just happened. Glover came straight back to his house, as he said he would, and told me everything about what had just happened, including the fact that Ferris, still in possession of the handgun he had used to shoot Young Arthur, and fearing some sort of reprisal, had hastily begun making his way to London.

News of the hit would have been music to Tam McGraw's ears, and he wasn't worried in the slightest about being implicated in the ensuing police inquiry, since he had a clear alibi. Loads of witnesses would testify that at the time of the murder he was in a Chinese restaurant with friends.

After the shooting, the whole of the Glasgow underworld was placed under heavy scrutiny. This wasn't just some run-of-the-mill, random shooting; it marked the start of one of the bloodiest, most ruthless, gangland upheavals Glasgow ever had the misfortune of witnessing. It would also change for good the way the underworld in the city operated. From this point on, my life would never be quite the same, and neither would that of anyone else who was ill-fated enough to have been caught up in the case.

All night Glover and I waited for news, any sort of news that would alert us to what was happening at the hospital where Young Arthur had been taken. Was Thompson alive? Was he dead? All we knew was that Ferris had definitely shot him in the back at least three times. It wasn't until early in the morning, just after 6 am, that Bobby came rushing into the bedroom where I was resting and said, 'Arthur Thompson has croaked it. I've just heard it on the radio . . . You'd better think about what you're going to do.'

I could see by his expression that he wasn't too happy.

'I don't really want to be hanging around here if there's a murder inquiry on the go now,' I told him. 'The last thing I need is to be pulled in by the police. They'd just love to know who I am, and as soon as they find out they'll know I'm an escapee from prison.'

'So what do you want to do, then?' Glover asked.

'I think I'm best off heading down to London for a while because it's going to get red hot around here shortly.'

Glover agreed that it was unwise for me to hang around when the police were more than likely to come knocking on his door at any time. The police knew Glover as one of Ferris's main associates, so they would want to know what his movements were over the last 24 hours. I got some things together, put them in my holdall and got myself down to the station as quickly as possible, jumping on the first train to London.

Although I didn't realise it at the time, Ferris must have already been visualising a special defence of incrimination, in which he would name me as the killer, should he be questioned and charged by the police over the murder. I had no idea how expendable I was to him. I believed he was my pal, someone I had known as a 15-year-old schoolboy in Longriggend; a true mate who had accepted me as a brother. For now, I was on my way to London, and the first thing I would do when I got there would be to visit him, since I knew exactly where he was.

On the journey down I started to look at things in a different perspective. The game was about to become clearer for the first time. Bobby Glover would have managed to get a message to Ferris saying that I was on my way to see him. Ferris had plenty of time to think about his fall-back plan should things not have gone his way, and little did I know that I would be used as a scapegoat.

Ferris has given a different account of what actually happened when I travelled to London to see him, even swearing under oath in the High Court in Glasgow. In his version of events he claims it was me who shot Arthur Thompson Junior, and after the shooting I travelled to London, taking the murder weapon with me. He went on to say he took the gun off me for safe-keeping when I arrived, and this gave him a feasible explanation as to why he had the murder weapon in the first place.

But this is what *really* happened when I arrived in London to see him.

I knocked on the front door of his flat and waited for a response, but there was no answer. I chapped the door again, this time a bit harder, but still nothing. What's up here? Is Ferris even in there? I asked myself.

Just as I was about to forget it and walk away, the door opened and there he was, standing in the doorway half-smiling and looking very smug indeed.

'Sorry about that. I was on the phone; quite an important call ... Anyway come in ... and what are you doing here?' Ferris asked.

'I thought, since Thompson is dead, I ought to get as far away from Glasgow as possible. There's no way I was hanging about up the road with the place crawling with police. I thought I'd head down to London and stay with you,' I told him.

What a clanger that was. If looks could kill, I would have dropped down dead immediately. Ferris was having none of it. The negative vibe between us was clear to see. Ferris wanted to play the big boss now – it was ripping out of him. The telephone was ringing constantly, and I remember Ferris gloating, smirking, just revelling in the knowledge that he had shot and killed his old friend without as much as a second thought. While he sat there, giving it large, the gun that he used to kill Young Arthur lay on the floor between his feet. If he left the room to go to the toilet, he took the gun with him. It never left his sight.

Over the course of the evening, Ferris said that I could stay the night, but he wanted me to leave first thing in the morning, pointing out I would have to find somewhere else to go. Then he had the cheek to say, depending on how things panned out over the Thompson shooting, we could perhaps hook up after the dust had settled. He was putting me out in the cold, washing his hands of me. It felt as if I were talking to a complete stranger.

Why was he doing this? In retrospect, there is only one answer: his plan to incriminate me in the murder would have failed if I had been anywhere near him during an arrest. It was therefore in Ferris's best interests to distance himself from me as quickly as possible. He couldn't make his plan too obvious in case I twigged, and that's why he allowed me to stay that one night. I must admit he was streets ahead of me when it came to his devious ploy, but in my defence I was just far too trusting to see it.

That night he gave me a couple of blankets and told me I could sleep on the floor at the foot of a luxurious, king-size, pull-down sofa divan in the lounge while he lay in complete comfort and warmth. In the morning there was a steady continuation of phone calls and more gloating. When I finally got my act together and got ready to leave, we shook hands and said our farewells. I grabbed my bag and got out of there. I looked up at the flat as I was walking along a concrete footpath and there was Ferris leaning out of the window.

He shouted down to me: 'Plan it well!'

That was the last time I ever saw him.

Back in Glasgow, the Thompson family were grieving the loss of their own flesh and blood. It was a sad end to what should have been a weekend full of laughter and celebration. Young Arthur Thompson had spent eight years locked up in various prisons throughout Scotland; eight long years he had waited for his first bit of freedom, only for him to end up in a refrigerated unit at the hospital morgue after less than 24 hours of home leave.

On the night of the shooting, old Arthur came rushing from the house, saw what was happening, and quickly put his dying son into the back of his car and drove him at speed to the Glasgow Royal Infirmary. Racing through red traffic lights, he pushed the vehicle to its limits, praying it would somehow make a difference. It was no good. Surgeons battled in vain to save his son's life, but one of the bullets had pierced his heart. At exactly 18 minutes past midnight, the doctors pronounced Thompson dead, and in doing so hammered a nail in the coffin of the Thompson criminal empire.

This wasn't the first time the Thompson family had had to deal with heartache and despair at the loss of a loved one. In 1966, old Arthur's mother-in-law, Margaret Johnston, had died when someone placed a bomb under his MG sports car. Mrs Johnston was getting a lift from Arthur and was sitting in the passenger seat when the bomb went off. In 1989, one of old Arthur's daughters, Margaret, died of a heroin overdose. In May

1990, old Arthur was almost killed himself himself just yards from his own home when a white Ford Escort XR3 mounted the pavement, smashed into him at speed and sent him flying against a fence. Witnesses said the white car then twice reversed over his body before shooting off along Provanmill Road at high speed. Bobby Glover told me that the occupants of the XR3 were Paul Ferris and Joe Hanlon. Glover also told me that a man by the name of Thomas Bagan was the person responsible for shooting old Arthur outside the Provanmill Inn that day. When old Arthur turned up at a hospital with a gunshot wound to the groin, he told medics that he had been carrying out some home improvements when the drill bit he was using shattered, sending a piece flying into his body. This was a likely story for an old-school gangster who would never have reported the incident to the police.

The police now had the arduous task of piecing together the little evidence they had on Young Arthur's murder to try and pinpoint exactly who his killer was. On top of that, they knew that old Arthur would want to exact his revenge for the callous murder of his favourite, eldest son. The press were having a field day and reported that at least 30 detectives were in the team set up in an incident room at Baird Street Police Station, and that they had called upon the services of HOLMES (Home Office Large Major Enquiry System) police computer technology to deal with the complex investigation.

Because of the long-running feud between the Thompsons and Ferris and McGraw, the focus of attention was steered towards Ferris and McGraw. The wheels were set in motion to get a conviction, and the police began pulling in people for questioning.

One of the first on their list was a man by the name of William Gillen, a harmless crook with links to Ferris. Gillen claimed that sometime in May 1991 Ferris and Bobby Glover had taken him for a run in Glover's black Volkswagen Golf GTi, and as soon as they were on the A77 near Kilmarnock, they pulled over into a lay-by. Gillen gave a statement to the murder inquiry team that Ferris then told him to get out of the car. Once he did so, Ferris shot him in the leg.

Initially Gillen refused to name Ferris as the man who had shot him, and it wasn't until the police assured him that Ferris would be going away for life for the murder of Young Arthur Thompson anyway that he agreed to cooperate and give evidence in a court of law.

Next to be hauled in for questioning was a fellow by the name of David Logue, a self-confessed car thief with a thick scar running down the side of his face. Logue had given a statement to the murder inquiry team saying Ferris had ordered him to steal a car for a job he had planned. He went on to say Ferris later asked him to set the same car on fire. The car in question was the Nissan Bluebird used as the getaway vehicle in Young Arthur's killing. Fearing he would be charged with acting as an accessory to murder, Logue caved in and cooperated fully with the murder inquiry team. The police thought that they now had enough evidence against Ferris to ask the Procurator Fiscal for an arrest warrant, and that's exactly what they did. Their next move was to apprehend Ferris, who was due to appear at Hamilton Sheriff Court for some minor road traffic offences.

Ferris travelled up from London to answer to these charges, and that's when he was nabbed and charged with shooting Gillen in the lay-by. Because Gillen had mentioned Bobby Glover as being present in the car when Ferris had shot him, the police also pulled Glover in and charged him, too. Ferris and Glover then appeared in court and were both remanded in custody.

Meantime, I had made my own way back to Glasgow to stay with some friends, being careful to keep my head down amid the heavy police presence. I'd been back and forward to London that many times over the months it was now ridiculous. I managed to get my head down at a pal's vacant apartment in Abercromby Street in the Calton area. The flat had bare floorboards throughout and no furniture apart from a double bed. There was electricity; there were some cups and saucers and an electric kettle for making tea, and that was all. My pal handed me the keys and generously assured me I could use the place whenever I wanted. All he asked of me was that I post the keys onto him as soon as I moved on, and so he left me a forwarding address.

With Ferris and Glover banged up on remand in Barlinnie, my main contact during the time I lived in the flat on Abercromby Street was Tam McGraw. I got to know McGraw far better in the short time I lived in that empty flat than I had done the whole time I'd known him before Young Arthur was killed. I had only spent a short time in McGraw's company before – whenever he popped into the Cottage Bar in Shettleston, or when I sometimes went into his own pub, the Caravel. There was one occasion when McGraw invited me to the modest council house he shared with his wife, when they lived in Barlanark. I always found McGraw to be a bit of an overwrought type of character, who never seemed able to settle in my company.

We sat in his parked car the first couple of meets before he plucked up the courage to come upstairs with me – it took a lot of persuasion to get him to leave his BMW. I remember saying to him, 'Just come up for a cup of tea, Tam. We shouldn't be sitting here in the car.'

As he locked his car and followed me up three flights of stairs to the top of the close, I teased him by saying, 'Don't worry, there's no one going to jump out on you!'

With him being jittery at the best of times, I think those comments just made him worse.

The only place to sit in the flat was on the double bed, and I asked him to have a seat while I put on the kettle. He was having none of that sitting-by-himself lark, preferring instead to follow me closely as I moved about the apartment. He never let me out of his sight, and he never accepted a cuppa from me either.

This was the only time that McGraw actually came into the flat, and his visit lasted about 20 minutes. It was on that occasion that he handed me a wad of cash and planted a seed in my head about some friend he had over in Ireland, assuring me that if ever I had to get out of the country in a rush he could arrange it through this contact and I'd have somewhere to stay. Although this didn't make much sense at the time, it wouldn't take long before it did.

Bobby Glover had made a successful bail application at the Sheriff Court in Glasgow over the shooting of William Gillen.

But Ferris, Glover's co-accused and, according to Gillen himself, the person who was responsible for shooting him in the leg, wasn't as lucky and was kept banged up in Barlinnie jail. The police also went on to charge Ferris with the murder of Arthur Thompson Junior, along with a mass of other crimes involving firearms and attempted murder. Ferris would stand trial for the Gillen offence within the 110-day time limit set down in Scottish law. With Ferris safely locked up on remand, the police had time to work on the case as a whole, and at that point they would, I believe, have been quite optimistic about securing convictions against those they thought were responsible for these crimes.

Perhaps the police thought that putting Glover back on the streets would prove more beneficial than keeping him banged up in jail beside Ferris. Maybe Glover would slip up and provide them with some sort of a lead that would blow Young Arthur's case wide open. After all, if the police had wanted to keep Bobby Glover off the streets, there's absolutely no chance he would've got bail – it's as simple as that.

Some months later, it would be widely acknowledged by Strathclyde Police that they *did* put Glover under 24-hour surveillance when they sanctioned his bail and let him walk free. At the time the coppers would not have known that by letting Glover out they were actually sealing his fate, and that he would soon be permanently removed from the marathon murder investigation.

Meanwhile, Ferris would most definitely have been feeling the pressure, wondering whether or not he'd go down for killing young Arthur Thompson. The weight of that on his mind would've been far heavier than anything he'd been used to dealing with in the past. As he lay stewing in the segregation cells in tough Barlinnie jail, he must have been haunted by visions of spending the rest of his days behind bars. How could he get out of this one?

Tam McGraw was in close contact with Ferris by way of third parties, and it's true he visited him himself. He was able to keep Ferris up to speed with the gossip on the street, as well as keeping him posted with the info that he'd been seeing me on a regular basis. Ferris would've been told about my return to Glasgow, and that I was now shacked up in some flat in the Calton area of the city. McGraw would've got word to him that I was on my own and that I might be useful to him. In other words, I was on standby. Ferris sincerely thought he could move me about like a pawn in a game of chess. He had already proved to me that I meant absolutely nothing to him by treating me the way he did in the flat back in London, but his complacency was such that he genuinely believed he could manipulate me however he wanted.

The next time I saw McGraw we sat talking in his dark-coloured BMW, parked downstairs from my flat.

'I've got a message from Paul,' McGraw said. 'He wants you to shoot old Arthur Thompson for him.'

During this intense conversation, we sat in the car watching each other, each weighing up every inch of the other's body language. After a moment of silence – and just enough time for me to fully register what he'd just put to me – I asked, surprised, 'What? He wants *me* to shoot old Thompson?'

'Yes. That's the word coming straight from Paul himself, and he wants it done as soon as possible.'

McGraw went on to tell me that the handgun he intended to give me was ready and waiting, but it was up to me as to how I pulled the trigger. He offered me no help whatsoever in planning the hit; he didn't want any part of that, and he made this crystal clear. He did remind me of the contact in Ireland and that getting me there wouldn't be a problem. We ended the conversation over at McGraw's house in Barlanark, and I remember his wife being there. Margaret would've known all about this incident, and that Ferris wanted me to shoot Thompson. She knew that her husband would be the one who would supply me with the gun as soon as I wanted it.

Ferris thought he could rely on me to shoot old Arthur Thompson, but what was the ulterior motive behind this? In his mind, and possibly that of Tam McGraw too, Ferris wanted a fall guy, someone who would fit the bill of a cold-blooded killer – and someone who ultimately Ferris could blame for the killing of Arthur Thompson Junior. Ferris knew that if he could get me to shoot Arthur Senior and face prosecution for that crime, he could lodge a special defence of incrimination and it would clearly look as though *I* was responsible for killing both father and son. The fact that during his eventual trial he told the jury I was the one who killed Thompson Junior makes this look very likely

And why would Ferris have wanted old Arthur killed when that would simply worsen his own predicament? It would've been absolute lunacy for him to go down the road of thinking, 'I'm in jail, I'm finished, so I may as well get old Arthur killed as well.' But where there's a will there's a way, and Ferris wasn't going to throw in the towel that easily. He saw what he thought was a viable escape route and, come what may, he was going to take it. For his plan to bear fruit, though, he first had to make sure I was definitely going to shoot old Arthur. He relied on McGraw to deliver the message and to give me the gun as soon as I was ready.

The meetings I had with McGraw began to reveal what was *really* happening; just like a jigsaw puzzle, the pieces were there, I just couldn't put them in their proper places quickly enough. I was still a young man – 23 years old – and I was still learning the game. The bundles of cash McGraw gave me on at least two occasions were not acts of generosity. The money was to sugar-coat his interceding and were given on the orders of Ferris. The talk of me going to Ireland to stay with a friend of his was also part of the planned exploitation. If I'd made it that far, I doubt very much if I'd have come back.

Chapter Fifteen

More Murder on the Streets

On 18 September 1991, the day after Bobby Glover walked free from court because of the insubstantial evidence in the William Gillen case – and on the very same day as Arthur Thompson Junior's funeral – Glover's body, along with that of his friend Joe Hanlon, were found lifeless in Hanlon's metallic blue Ford Orion.

They had both been shot in the head and the chest before being driven to a spot in Darleith Street, just a few feet away from the Cottage Bar in Shettleston. Leaving their bodies outside Ferris's HQ was an added insult. The press reported it as if it were a hit right out of a Mafia movie.

As related in *Gangsters, Killers and Me,* the memoirs of retired detective Gerard Gallacher, both Hanlon and Glover had apparently been responsible for a catalogue of armed robberies on banks and building societies all over Glasgow, and the police had been keeping close tabs on them for some considerable time. Hanlon and Glover were key players in the Ferris and McGraw camp and, all together, the four of them were the cornerstones of an alliance hell-bent on taking over from the Thompson criminal empire and, subsequently, the entire Glasgow criminal underworld.

There's no doubt that Hanlon and Glover were removed from the game because of their involvement in the murder of Arthur Thompson Junior, although it has also been suggested that perhaps they were killed because they knew too much and had become a potential liability to Ferris and McGraw. Since prosecutions have never been forthcoming in all three gangland killings of Thompson Junior, Hanlon and Glover, people can speculate all day long. The bottom line is that 22 years later the

167

case remains as much of a mystery today as it was all those years ago. Ferris has been blaming me for years, saying that I was behind not just Hanlon and Glover's demise, but all three killings, but he does have a tendency to change his tune. Let's not forget, during his 54-day trial at the High Court in Glasgow back in 1992, he accused me of being the person who shot and killed Arthur Thompson Junior, only for him to change his story and then accuse someone he refers to as 'the Apprentice' instead. The *two others,* according to Ferris, with whom I'm supposed to have shot Hanlon and Glover – my own uncle Billy and Paul Hamilton, the man I believe passed on information to Ferris and McGraw about Young Arthur's movements so they could plan his murder – are now dead and gone and cannot now defend themselves. Where does Ferris gets this information? He never discloses his sources. He only ever points the finger.

Then there's the press. Never has there been such a journalistic frenzy. Year after year the media remains obsessed with reporting what happened to Thompson Junior, as well as to Hanlon and Glover. If neither Hanlon nor Glover had been removed from the picture, the police would probably have charged them both with shooting young Arthur Thompson. Along with Ferris, the three of them would have stood trial for that crime in the High Court in Glasgow.

But this is where the plot thickens, because on the same night Hanlon and Glover were killed, I had actually arranged to meet Glover at a prearranged spot on Abercromby Street, just beneath the flat I was living in, the exact same spot where I'd meet McGraw.

According to at least two retired police officers who worked on the triple murder inquiry and who wrote about its aftermath in their autobiographies, I became the prime suspect in the double slaying because I was the last person on record to have seen them both alive. My name had been fired into the frame by Bobby Glover's partner, Eileen, who had told the murder squad that I'd made a phone call to their house and spoken to Bobby the night he was killed. There was nothing sinister in this – Bobby and I would often talk on the phone. On the strength of what Eileen said to the police I subsequently became the most wanted man in the country.

It didn't help matters when the cops realised I'd been using the alias 'Gary' (Eileen knew me only by that name), as it probably looked as though I had something to hide. The Strathclyde murder squad now had the enormous task of integrating the double murder of Hanlon and Glover with that of young Arthur Thompson, while simultaneously treating them as two separate inquiries.

To give an insight into the sheer size of the police operation during these investigations, detectives involved in the case reported that they moved from Baird Street Police Station, where they set up base to begin with, and took over the entire top floor of the gigantic London Road Police Office building. Each half of the top floor of the building was used to conduct separate investigations, and by the time they'd reached the point of a trial the 'productions' (the exhibits used in court) alone totalled more than 800. This was a major and highly interconnected operation, in which dozens of experienced detectives would embark upon the biggest inquiry of their careers. It was a mammoth assignment.

With Darleith Street in Shettleston taped off from the public, scene-of-crime officers positioned their sophisticated equipment and began taking photos and videos of Joe Hanlon's car from all different angles. Experts from the forensic science laboratory attended too. Their job was to search for any chemical or biological evidence. It was reported that ballistics officers showed face as well, but only to familiarise themselves with the scene for the job that lay ahead. Their work wouldn't begin until they had full access to the inside of the vehicle.

At the scene, newspaper journalists mingled with members of the public and scores of uniformed police. From behind the cordon, their notepads and cameras were ready to capture the mood of the people who stood mesmerised by the unfolding events. After preliminary investigations, Hanlon's Ford Orion, complete with the bodies still inside, was picked up meticulously using a harness and, like a toy car, placed onto the back of a lorry. It was then taken under special escort for 20 minutes or so along the M8 until it reached Paisley Police Office. Once there, the forensic experts could begin their work, as the police office in Paisley had a specially constructed area to carry out forensic examinations of this kind.

Glasgow has always been known for its many brutal gangland murders and its criminal networks, but the events of August and September 1991 took things to a whole new level. The press coverage was also stratospheric. One particular article, in which I was pictured wearing a pair of shorts, made the front page of the *Daily Record* and must have had people all over Scotland choking on their cornflakes as they read the fictitious account. The headline was 'Tootsie on the Run' and it's a story I found very amusing indeed. Based on malicious lies, hearsay, and without a single shred of factual evidence to back it up, the story began: 'Scotland's most wanted man is dressing up as a woman and is wearing a fetching blonde wig, tight mini-skirt and high heels to avoid being captured by the police.'

The *Daily Record*'s 'insider' – it's always an 'insider' – who provided this fanciful information went on to say that I'd tottered into the Cottage Bar in drag and, as I stumbled in the heels and almost fell over, everybody in the pub burst out laughing when they realised it was me. Yes, it's a comical story. Yes, it makes an interesting read. Was it true? Most certainly not!

It wasn't long before the triple murder inquiry took a dramatic turn.

Only a couple of days after the burial of Arthur Thompson Junior, blue-bereted SWAT teams armed with machine guns and police dogs were preparing to storm the Thompson family home, nicknamed 'The Ponderosa' (this being the name of the ranch owned by the Cartwright family in the popular TV Western series *Bonanza*). Consisting of what were once two separate houses knocked into one, it was the strangest of homes, considering old Arthur could've afforded to live almost anywhere.

As police vans sealed off both ends of the street, armed cops wearing bulletproof vests positioned themselves behind police cars, aiming their guns at the windows and doors of the giant property. A police helicopter hovered menacingly in the early morning sky above. Inside Riddrie Cemetery, which is at the rear of the Thompson home, and where Young Arthur was laid to rest only days before, more armed police crouched behind gravestones ready to pounce on anybody who tried to exit the house from the back. With all angles covered, their next move was to shout via a loudspeaker, 'Come out slowly and put your hands on your head!' A short time later old Arthur Thompson, his wife Rita and daughter Tracy came out and were immediately placed in the back of police vans. Young Billy Thompson, the only surviving son, remained in his dead brother's part of the house while detectives using sledgehammers and crowbars caved in the front door.

After methodically turning all parts of the property upside down, a police spokesperson reported 'Nothing of any significance has been found so far.' There were also police with shovels digging in the gardens; they really did go to work on this place. They were searching for guns or anything that might connect old Arthur to the double murder of Hanlon and Glover. His family solicitor and leading Glasgow lawyer of the time Joseph Beltrami told reporters that his client was a businessman and had nothing to fear from the police. Thompson went on to sue a Scottish newspaper for £10,000 damages after the paper claimed he was involved in crime. He gave the money to charity, presenting the cheque to Tiger Tim, the popular Radio Clyde DJ.

Because my status had overnight gone from being that of an absconder from a semi-open nick to that of the most wanted man in Britain, I was left with very few delusions as to the gravity of the situation I faced.

I didn't fancy going back to jail just yet and Glasgow was the last place on earth I needed to hang about, so I set out on a journey back to London. In the autobiography of a retired police officer working on the murder investigation, it was stated that I cycled back to London on a mountain bike. This is true. I did get to London using a mountain bike. I was super-fit, I enjoyed cycling and I had a lovely black, hand-built 21-speed pro-bike called 'The Ghost'. Before departing, I had kitted myself out with all the cycling gear I'd need, from windproof cycling gloves and sports helmet to a high visibility reflective bib-vest I'd wear at night. But the secret was to travel light, and so, apart from a London A–Z and an ultra-light set of waterproofs inside a bumbag clipped around my waist, it was just me, the Ghost and lots of fresh air for the whole journey.

After I reached London I would regularly shift from place to place, booking myself into different cheap lodgings or tourist hostels across the city. But before long I had half the Metropolitan Police Force pursuing me and I knew it was only a matter of time before they caught up with me; my spell on the run in London came to an end.

One day at the beginning of January 1992, I was on my way for a sauna not too far from New Scotland Yard, when all of a sudden I found myself being chased along what was a very busy Victoria Street by a swarm of armed coppers, screaming, 'Stop or we'll shoot!' At that moment, everything around me looked like it had gone into slow motion. I saw people running for cover. For me, there was nowhere else to run. At both ends of the street police vans blocked my escape, and everywhere there were plain-clothes coppers holding guns. Trapped amongst central London shoppers, unarmed and with no escape route, there was not a lot I could do. Fearing that one of the armed police would shoot me, I crouched behind a couple of people inside a shop doorway and asked them to shield me from the men who were chasing me, brandishing guns. These folk must've got the fright of their lives, but when it comes down to survival you're not thinking straight and you'll do whatever you have to. For a split second, I thought some trigger-happy copper might've done the naughty and taken a pop at me, but in reality there were far too many pedestrians about and I probably over-reacted a tad. However, it isn't fun when you're being chased along the street by scores of coppers with guns, I can assure you.

Everything happened so fast, and before I knew what was happening I was overpowered, handcuffed and hustled into the back of a police van like a rag doll. A plastic carrier bag I had with me, which contained a small mirror, shaving gear and toiletries, fell from my grasp during the struggle and the mirror smashed into a thousand pieces. Was this a sign of what was to come?

From the day my name went into the papers as the most wanted man in the country to the day I was actually caught,

I'd been at large and living in London for over 13 weeks. There had been much speculation as to my whereabouts, and it was even rumoured that I'd been shot and killed, and so until I surfaced it would have been a very frustrating time for everyone concerned. This included my mother, who appeared on television as well as the front page of the *Daily Record* pleading for me to give myself up before I was shot by the police. A dozen armed detectives stood in her house and terrorised her to the point that one of them pulled back his jacket to reveal his .38 special saying, 'You'd better tell your son to give himself up as we're not messing about.'

I know that the Glasgow murder squad would've been thoroughly delighted that such a lengthy investigation into my whereabouts had finally paid off. In the back of the police van, the English coppers knocked me about a bit before taking me to Paddington Green Police Station, where suspected terrorists go to await trial, and which is the most secure police station in the UK. Situated beneath ground level, it has 16 cells complete with its own custody suite, and the minute I arrived there the coppers stripped me naked and, in front of a doctor, they cautiously examined me for a gun or any other concealed weapon.

I remember the police saying they were looking for a gun in particular – they obviously thought I might be armed. After putting me through this humiliating process, and with no trace of a firearm in sight, the police handed me a white paper-like set of overalls and told me to put them on. I was then off to a windowless strip cell to be alone with my intensifying thoughts, as I wondered what would happen when the Scottish police took me back to Glasgow. I had no choice but to face the music, and I can't say I was enjoying the prospect very much.

The following day, Detective Superintendent Jimmy Johnston of Strathclyde Police and one of his sidekicks waltzed into my cell, quickly introduced themselves and said, 'You know you're in a lot of trouble, Willie, and if I were you I'd start thinking about what you're going to say to us.' Johnston was the main man in charge of the investigation into the double murder of Hanlon and Glover, and I knew exactly what he was trying to do. I'd seen it all before, albeit not on this level. He'd waited months for this day, as all his colleagues had, and the excitement of being able to interview the person who'd eluded them for so long would've felt really uplifting for him. My name was heavily in the frame for the Hanlon and Glover deaths, and although I knew there was nothing to worry about, my worst fear was that the police might try to set me up somehow.

'We'll be taking you back to Glasgow shortly,' said Johnston. 'Tell me, Willie, do you have any preference as to the way we take you back? Are you OK to travel by plane?'

It was obviously more convenient for the police to put me on an aircraft and fly me back to Glasgow in just over an hour as opposed to using a vehicle, which would've taken all sort of security measures and most of the day to get there.

'Flying back is fine with me. I'm not fussy,' I told him.

They then left the cell to go and book tickets for the flight. A short time later, I recall the custody sergeant telling me whilst I was being handed over that I had better not try anything stupid on the way back to Scotland, as I would be making a big mistake. He then leaned under his counter at the uniform bar and picked up a Smith & Wesson .38 Special, looked at me and said while gesturing with the gun: 'That's what your escorts are carrying, so if I were you I'd behave myself.'

I didn't even bother replying. Jimmy Johnston and co. appeared again, cuffed me and then we were all off to Heathrow Airport accompanied by the English division as extra back-up. I'd never witnessed this much security before in all my dealings with the police. At the airport, the four detectives walked me through a specially designated area in order to get to the plane, but there was a problem. The men in suits carrying the .38 Specials thought they could just waltz right through the detector apparatus without declaring their guns. I watched as the security staff had a quick word, and then the police took their guns from their holsters and placed them into a suitcase. I could tell by the look on their faces that they weren't too happy, but what did they expect? They should have known better.

Then there was more drama on the plane itself when Johnston refused to remove my handcuffs. To be honest, I wasn't aware of the rules and regulations regarding prisoners in flight, but apparently no one should be shackled during take-off or for the duration of the journey. The captain of the plane wanted the cuffs removed, otherwise the aircraft wasn't going anywhere. The pretty flight attendant had to ask my captors twice to remove the restraints from my wrists; they were very reluctant to do so.

We did eventually get airborne, and midway through the flight one of the coppers sitting next to me thought he'd play the card he had up his sleeve. I was in the middle seat of the three, sandwiched and reading a magazine when the cop nearest the window thought he could lighten the mood by trying to get into my head. Without warning, he leaned over and whispered in my left ear: 'Willie, I just want you to know that if you wish to talk to someone off the record, you know, and in total confidence . . . then I'm your man.'

Well, I had to give him full points for trying, and I suppose someone had to plant the seed, but there's no way I was playing along. I told him politely that I'd cooperate fully with police inquiries, but only when my lawyer was present. When the plane touched down at Glasgow Airport later on that afternoon, there to greet us on the tarmac, in full view of everyone, was a procession of police vehicles that looked as though it were there to escort royalty. I couldn't believe my eyes. I was back on home soil, Strathclyde Police territory, and there was no doubt about who was now in charge. In a massive show of force, leading the way were two police motorcyclists followed by a Transit van with eight coppers inside. The unmarked car I travelled in came next, and right behind us there was another Transit with another eight police inside. With blue lights flashing, the police convoy drove all the way from the airport to London Road Police Station, right on through red traffic lights, and never stopped once. During the 20-minute drive, the police helicopter tailed us overhead. I could actually hear the rotor blades, it was that close above us.

In the police station I was allocated a cell and informed that I'd be interviewed about all three gangland murders in due course. With my solicitor present, I was quizzed over the deaths of Bobby Glover and Joe Hanlon but only in an interview that lasted no more than ten minutes. I cooperated with the murder squad as much as I could until they began bullying me with questions like 'Did you shoot those men?' and 'Come on, tell us, was it you, Willie?' Up until that point the interview had been flowing without any difficulty and I was answering every question the cops put to me, but then Kinloch advised me not to answer any more questions. Strangely, I was never questioned over the shooting of Arthur Thompson Junior.

The same police who had escorted me from London to Glasgow drove me back to Barlinnie jail. I received a six-month sentence at Hamilton Sheriff Court for absconding from Dungavel, which is standard in these sort of situations, but I could see the distinct possibility of more sentences looming ahead. After spending a few days in the Wendy House segregation cells inside Barlinnie I was taken to Perth Prison under heavy escort.

Back in London, a team of handpicked Glaswegian detectives received orders from their commanding officer to stay there and try their best to find out where I had been living prior to my arrest. Because I was the last person to see Glover and Hanlon alive, I was now the number one suspect. Then of course, and let's not forget this, I had Ferris blaming me for the killing of Arthur Thompson Junior, so it's perfectly understandable why the police were so keen to trace my London refuge.

The retired officers from Glasgow who worked on both murder inquiries and later wrote about them in their memoirs spoke at length about the vast assignment of resources used in trying to find my flat in London. When they commented on this particular mission, they both said conclusively that the police had hoped they might find a gun or maybe blood-stained clothing. The only clues to help them find my base was a single Yale key and a return ticket for the tube from Earls Court. These were the only two items I had in my possession that could provide them with some sort of lead. Strangely, they never once asked me about where I lived.

After some good old-fashioned police work, as well as bursting a gut or three, these two small clues would eventually take the cops straight to my basement apartment, deep within the heart of Earls Court bedsitter-land – but only after a stroke of pure luck. After weeks of disappointment they'd almost given up the search. Earls Court is a multicultural district in Kensington and Chelsea, and a magnet for students from all over the world searching for cheap accommodation. At the other end of the scale, there are many multimillion-pound apartments and houses in plush garden squares and residential streets. Now, the police had to find out where it was I was staying. They had the Yale key, but how could they find the door it fitted? This would have been like looking for a needle in a haystack. Their first move was to take the key to a professional locksmith to find out what information he could give them, but he told them that there were hundreds of thousands of that same lock in the area. No luck there, so there was nothing for it but to coordinate a gargantuan lock-testing operation. The first thing they did was to tack a street map of Earls Court to the wall of an incident room in Kensington Police Station. The idea was to split the map into small, practicable sections and then cross-reference them as they went along. Forty identical keys were cut from the one they found on me, and these were dished out to every available police officer they could summon into helping them with the operation.

Teams of police officers from all different ranks hit the streets and industriously began trying the key in every lock they could find. After each punishing shift, the disconsolate coppers made their way back to Kensington Police Station to cross out the streets they'd covered. This uneventful procedure went on for *two weeks* non-stop, and still they hadn't found the door the key fitted. Frustrated and homesick, the team of Glaswegian detectives felt their mission wasn't going to produce the desired result and were on the verge of throwing in the towel.

Then, from out of nowhere, they had an extraordinary piece of luck. By complete accident one of the officers and a female detective bumped into each other right outside the business premises of the landlord I had rented a small flat from just weeks before. This small, dingy, inconspicuous letting agency had advertisements in the window for bedsits and flats. Curious, the two murder squad detectives wandered in and asked the owner if he'd rented a property to anyone matching my description. He just laughed in their faces and told them he sub-let thousands of flats and bedsits to people so he couldn't possibly remember one person.

The police then produced a photograph of me and showed it to him. He told them that I'd not only rented a flat from him, but also become quite pally with him. Well, that cancelled out our friendship right there and then. The police couldn't believe it. After trying literally thousands of doors in and around Earls Court and getting absolutely nowhere, all it took was sheer chance to unlock the mystery of the Yale key. The landlord took them straight to my flat and the police sealed off both ends of the street, as if it were now a murder scene. A team of forensic experts entered the property and searched every inch of it. My personal property, including the mountain bike I'd cycled to London on and a rowing machine, was photographed, finger-printed and then sent back to Glasgow for further examination. But nothing in the flat linked me to any crime committed back home, so it would seem the laborious workload put in by the police was a complete waste of time.

Chapter Sixteen

Back to Perth Prison

On leaving the reception area after my arrival at Perth Prison, two prison guards escorted me towards D-Hall. It was a cold morning and I gazed up at the cell windows as we passed by. Suddenly, I heard a voice; it was loud and it shouted a moniker I'd become familiar with from the unfounded *Daily Record* story. Someone in one of the cells could clearly see me being escorted along the forecourt, but I couldn't see them. There were dozens of cell windows to choose from, and I could only listen as the voice screamed down: 'Tooooooootsie!'

The screws looked at each other and smiled; I was not happy at all. In fact, I shouted back:

'Why don't you identify yourself, loudmouth? Come on, big man, who are you?' But they weren't so keen to say another word. It was the perfect welcome back to HMP Perth.

This was it; there would be no room for let-ups or stupid mistakes. I knew what I had to do and I was ready to deal with any situation. It had been almost two years since I was last in D-Hall so I knew the changes would be great, and that prisoners I'd known when I was last serving time would not necessarily be there now. That aside, I was also deemed a high-security risk, what's known as a Strict Escapee, so all eyes would be watching.

The last time I had been in Perth I had managed without too much difficulty to keep a low profile. Blending into the background wasn't an issue because it allowed me not to get involved with the hardcore elements running the show who were forever in the forefront of things. Things were different now; the spotlight was very much upon me, so I was prepared and up for whatever lay ahead.

I entered D-Hall and the atmosphere was tense. It felt strange being back in my old hall, and I had a feeling that everyone in sight was watching me, this quiet young man from Glasgow accused of all those killings. It makes no difference what prison you go to, existing inmates will always be well informed and a step ahead of any newcomers. They know exactly when a high-profile case has landed in the hall and who is due in from the courts. It's the way of the jail and that's how it works. I quickly scanned the surroundings, looking for familiar faces, but I couldn't see anyone I knew. Surely some old faces would appear, I told myself.

The Principal Officer, a man by the name of John Glen, called me into his office for the usual pep-talk.

'Hello, Willie. So, you're back with us.'

He greeted me like an old buddy and informed me what cell I was to go to. It so happened that the cell was on the second flat, just above the screws' office. It was obvious the guards intended to keep their eye on me. With my kit in hand, I made my way up the stair.

One of the first prisoners I came across was Colin Murdoch, from Wishaw. I wasn't quite sure how to take him at first, or how the meeting would go between us, as he had had some sort of trouble back in Shotts with my co-accused, Michael Healy. In fact, Murdoch had been responsible for starting the 1988 Shotts prison riot. He was a fearsome character in appearance, with piercing dark eyes. He had thighs like tree trunks and this affected his walking pace. A fanatical Glasgow Rangers fan, he would also sit in front of the telly glued to *Coronation Street*. For the rest of the day, he would sit in his cell listening to Pink Floyd songs on repeat. He was a definite weirdo and highly unpredictable – a perilous combination. He had stabbed someone in Barlinnie and received an additional eight years to run consecutively with the five-year stretch he'd started with. He wasn't the sort of person you could share the same hall with if he was your enemy, that's for sure.

I remembered that in Shotts he had strapped a kitchen knife to each of his wrists and walked out of his workplace in the cooks, past the prison guards, then made his way towards the Halls. Unchallenged, he calmly strolled right into the same hall as me and shouted to Gerry Rae, a nutter of a prisoner I've already mentioned, to come out and face him. Guards managed to peacefully defuse that particular incident. However, it wasn't long before he found himself locked up in solitary for a couple of years for his role as the instigator of the riot.

Another prisoner in D-Hall was a man called Kenneth Kelly. Kenny was in his 50s and was from the Anderston area, one of the old-school brigade. Nicknamed 'Kansas' Kelly, he was a good friend to the respected Glasgow hardman Colin Beattie. Kenny was of stocky build and had a receding hairline. An armed robber, he had an old boxer's face which you could tell had done the rounds. He would have all the other cons transfixed with tales from Glasgow back in the 60s and 70s. He lived on the ground floor due to ongoing health problems – he'd been diagnosed with angina. His mind still functioned sound enough though, and that's what mattered.

A prisoner by the name of Thomas Bagan – the same Thomas Bagan who, according to Bobby Glover, shot Arthur Thompson Senior in the groin – had stabbed Kansas Kelly in Barlinnie while they were doing time there together. Old Kenny said it was a botched stabbing, as the homemade knife Bagan used didn't penetrate him properly. During a fierce struggle old Kansas managed to grab the knife and chased Bagan until he caught him and stabbed him back. Kenny Kelly would become a good, trustworthy pal and someone on whom I could rely.

It didn't take me long to find my feet in D-Hall. I'd managed to work out a happy equilibrium where buoyancy and high spirits presided over any misgivings I had about coming back into the prison system as a high-profile convict. No one posed any realistic threat towards me, and I was content with my surroundings and everyone else around me. The only real issue playing on my mind was knowing that the big trial at the High Court in Glasgow had started, and I knew Paul Ferris was planning to blame me for the killing of Arthur Thompson Junior by lodging a special defence of incrimination.

Ferris had the cheek to send his legal team to speak to me at Perth. I gave his team the courtesy of seeing them on an 'agent's visit', and there was no doubt in my mind that the purpose of this unsolicited appointment was to get a feel for where I was coming from and what I might say if I were called to give evidence. They asked me what I would say in court if I were called to give evidence. Instead of giving them the answer they had perhaps hoped for, I informed them that I was not interested in anything they had to say and could not assist them in any way. I told them to take that message back to their client. They didn't waste any more time, took the hint and left. Whatever Ferris thought might be achieved by sending his legal team to see me I've no idea. This didn't stop my name being bandied about the High Court in Glasgow in such dramatic fashion.

I know that old Arthur Thompson never saw Ferris as a major threat, because if he had he would have dealt with him straight away. My uncle Billy told me old Thompson wasn't interested in Ferris, and that he was more concerned about Tam Bagan, because he was the one who shot him in the groin outside the Provanmill Inn. Bagan was a lucky man because Billy had been watching him for some time and he had him firmly in his sights. Bagan was the one who was to be dealt with, not Ferris. Thompson had therefore made a fundamental error by over-looking Ferris's intentions, and as a result his son lost his life.

As for McGraw, he wasn't considered a big-enough threat either by Thompson, but that didn't stop Ferris keeping him as a pal, albeit an arms-length one, and Ferris thought McGraw was inferior to himself. There's no doubt that Ferris received a proper education from old Thompson, and by the time he left the Thompson camp for good he had secured a diploma in how to work subterfuge at the highest level.

The Ferris trial at the High Court in Glasgow took a dramatic twist when the Procurator Fiscal introduced his star witness: kidnapper, sex offender, sadist and supergrass Dennis 'the Menace' Wilkinson, or 'Woodman' as he'd become known.

Woodman had been a key prosecution witness in no less than eight major criminal trials in England, alleging in every one that the person on trial was a fellow inmate who had confided in him crucial details of the crimes they'd allegedly committed and for which they were being tried. He helped secure convictions against 20 men who were jailed for a total of 90 years between them. The duplicitous reprobate had become an invaluable asset to the police, the Crown Prosecution Service and the whole English judicial system.

A *World in Action* documentary produced by Steve Bolton was aired on television after Woodman gave evidence at Ferris's trial. The programme focused on Woodman's activities as a registered police informer in England, and the question on everyone's lips was how he ended up in Scotland giving evidence against Ferris in such a high-profile case.

Steve Bolton said: 'When we heard of Wilkinson/Woodman's use as a prosecution witness in the Ferris case, we were astonished because we already knew a lot about his background.'

Ferris was being held in the Barlinnie segregation unit for the duration of his trial and Woodman was also being kept there on charges including the kidnapping and torturing of a Dumfries farmer. There's nothing particularly suspect about Ferris and Woodman being banged up together, although Ferris would later claim that the authorities moved Woodman there as part of a conspiracy to set him up in court.

Another prisoner in the segregation unit at the time was an arsonist by the name of Mark Leech, who was finishing off a five-year sentence, and he, along with Ferris and Woodman played chess by shouting out moves to each other from behind their cell doors. Leech was a very clever man who would go on to pen his autobiography, *A Product of the System*, amongst other titles relating to prison establishments and penal reform. Ferris claims in *Vendetta* that Mark Leech knew Woodman from the English prison system, knew all about his activities as a paid police informer and duly warned him to stay on his guard. I find this strange since Leech himself was no angel and has also been labelled a police informer.

What Ferris didn't mention in his book is that his brother Billy also knew Woodman from the English prison system, and they were very good pals. The governor of Barlinnie received a report that Woodman wanted to speak to him. Woodman told the governor that Ferris had confided in him about the shooting of Arthur Thompson Junior while they were playing chess together and out in the exercise yard, where it was possible to whisper to other inmates. This was, of course, Woodman up to his old tricks again, or so you would think; but this time Woodman had offered his services to Ferris, as opposed to being called upon by the police. Woodman, at this stage, felt bitterness and resentment towards the police, whom he'd helped so many times in the past, because they never kept to their promise of giving him a new identity and a fresh start in Canada. This was revealed in the *World in Action* documentary. Woodman knew exactly what he was doing, as he'd played the courts umpteen times. He knew how to address juries and sway their opinion, and the link between him, Paul Ferris and the Procurator Fiscal would ultimately spoil the prosecution's chances of securing a guilty verdict in the Ferris case. Woodman was called as a prosecution witness to testify to what he claimed Ferris said to him in the segregation block at Barlinnie.

For five days he stood in the witness box being grilled over what was and was not said, even at one stage offering Donald Findlay QC a fist fight – not exactly the behaviour of a man supposed to be working for the Crown, is it? Clearly Woodman wanted to look bad in front of the jury, and his act was just part of a clever strategy designed to make the jury dismiss him as a credible witness. The Procurator Fiscal must've been trembling at the knees at the sight of his star witness making a complete and utter fool of himself in the witness box.

What sealed the deal was Woodman swearing in open court on the lives of his dead children that he was telling the truth, the whole truth and nothing but the truth. Who could fail to be moved by this and grant Woodman 'a vote of sympathy', as Ferris put it in his book? Unfortunately, the effect of this was somewhat spoiled when, overnight, Ferris's defence team did some digging and the next day Woodman's ex-wife appeared in court to reassure the jury that their kids were in fact alive and well! A clever move, wouldn't you agree?

In the short time I had been back in D-Hall everything had seemed nice and quiet, then out of the blue I heard an awful racket coming from outside my cell.

As I went out to investigate I saw a prisoner chasing another con around the gallery. The taller of the two, the one who was giving chase, had some sort of knife in his hand. Just another couple of cons sorting out their differences, I thought to myself. This type of incident was common in Perth. Round and round the gallery these two ran until fatigue kicked in. Then, just opposite my cell, I saw the one with the blade stab the other guy three or four times.

The stabber was from Edinburgh and was serving a three-year sentence for a minor offence. I'd seen him wandering about the hall but hadn't given him a second thought. His name was David Rafferty. The guy who Rafferty was chasing was also from Edinburgh. His name was Pete Marshall, and he was an amateur boxer. The two of them had been at loggerheads on the outside and the bad blood between them had followed them to Perth, where it had led to blows. The guards eventually intervened and dragged them both away. Rafferty went to the segregation block over in C-Hall and Marshall went to the surgery for treatment. These incidents were commonplace and nothing out of the ordinary, but Rafferty had come to my attention and I decided to keep tabs on him, as I thought he might be useful. As a big guy he looked the part and might provide some useful muscle. Little did I know that, far from being useful, he would be the catalyst that led to one of the most miserable episodes of all my years in prison.

One day, quite unexpectedly, one of the guards downstairs called out my name: 'Lobban! The PO wants to see you.'

I knew the Principal Officer wasn't about to tell me I'd got my C-Category back. On entering his office I saw that the number one governor, Ron Kite, was also sitting there. It was obvious something was going on, and what I heard next didn't surprise me in the slightest. The governor said: 'Just to inform you, Mr Lobban, that Billy Ferris [Paul's brother] will be coming to this jail tomorrow. Do you have a problem with that?'

He went on to say that he had to put these questions to me in order to assess whether or not there would be trouble when Billy arrived. I remember thinking, 'You cheeky bastard! You know what the answer to that is!' I mean, even if I had said 'yes' there would be trouble, what difference would it have made? I am certain of one thing: the prison authorities are masters of divide and rule, and they knew that transferring Ferris's brother to Perth would most certainly provoke trouble to some degree.

Those in high places had carefully planned and orchestrated this move because there were other jails more suitable that they could have sent him to. So, you have to ask yourself: why send him to Perth to be next to me? Before leaving the office, Ron Kite said: 'It's OK, Mr Lobban. Although we are bringing him to Perth he will be housed in a different hall from you.' I turned to the governor and just laughed.

Now, if news of that mug coming to the jail wasn't bad enough, there was something much worse about to hit me like a ton of bricks. I thought I'd seen the last of the murder squad back in London Road Police Station, but I was wrong.

To my complete dismay the same group of police who'd dealt with me over the Hanlon and Glover affair suddenly appeared at Perth and took me under heavy escort back to London Road in Glasgow for questioning over the armed robbery at the Pipe Rack in Shettleston in July 1991. I had, of course, carried out this robbery and I knew I had my work cut out if I was going to convince the police I was innocent.

The person who put my name forward for this crime may well have been Bobby's partner and mother to his son. She probably believed, as many others did, that I was responsible for her man's death. As I've written earlier, the basis for this belief would have been my phoning to arrange to meet Bobby on the night he was shot and killed. Since the police failed to prosecute me over Bobby's death, it's easy to understand why she might have grassed me for robbing the boozer just up the road from where she lived. The coppers would have been ecstatic with this development, thinking that perhaps they could use the robbery at the pub as some sort of bargaining tool; that I would open up and tell them something that would assist them in their ongoing murder inquiries. This wasn't to be, and instead I would take it on the chin but deny all knowledge of any involvement. I stayed tight-lipped and said nothing, refusing to answer any questions. I had to stand in an identification parade and the police asked me to wear a long blonde wig and a pair of glasses, exactly what I had been wearing on the night of the hold-up, and the same wig I gave to Ferris the night he shot young Arthur Thompson. Everyone standing in the ID parade wore similar blonde wigs and glasses, but this didn't throw the witnesses on the other side of the two-way glass. The two barmaids and male manager picked me out as the person who had robbed them that night, which wouldn't have been difficult since my picture was plastered on the front page of every newspaper in Scotland. A clear-cut case, the police must have thought, and when they drove me back to Perth they must have seen the embitterment etched in my face.

Meanwhile David Rafferty was back in D-Hall, which didn't make much sense considering what he'd done to the boxer Marshall, but this was typical of the pressure the prison authorities are constantly under. Some prisoners shouldn't be allowed to roam freely amongst other cons because of medical conditions and so forth, but in reality that's exactly what goes on.

The prison governor had moved Marshall to Saughton Prison in Edinburgh and decided to put Rafferty back into the same hall as before, as if nothing had happened. I approached him and congratulated him on his return back to the nut house. Gradually, I built up a sort of rapport with him to the extent that I managed to get him a cell right next door to mine. The way I saw it was that he obviously had bottle; he looked the part and he was prepared to listen. It was good to cultivate guys like this inside. Rafferty could be useful, or so I thought.

Meanwhile, Billy Ferris landed in the prison, just as the governor said he would. I heard that he had been placed over in A-Hall, and I thought I'd send him a message and play with his head a little bit. I didn't know much about Billy Ferris. He had spent most of his time down in the English system, where I believe he was initially arrested for murdering some bloke who was sleeping with his girlfriend. The fact he was Paul Ferris's brother was enough for me to keep a watchful eye on him and my spies in A-Hall would keep me posted on what he did with himself during recreation periods.

Every inmate in Perth was required to work, so I found myself a job in the tailors' workshop, always regarded as a cushy number. The tailors employed something like 30 prisoners. During my spell there, we were making yellow waterproof jackets and trousers, similar to those you might find fishermen wearing on the boats.

I had made a corner of the workshop my own personal space and I was very particular as to whom I allowed to sit with me. For the short time I was there, I didn't make a single waterproof; it was a bit of a joke me being there at all. But no one bothered me and it was an easy part of the day. As it was the tailoring workshop, there were a couple of pairs of industrial scissors available to prisoners on request. A prisoner usually signed these out and it was their responsibility to return them. I wanted a pair – they might come in useful for other things than making waterproof jackets – but how could I get them past the strict security measures and metal detectors? I knew that the scissors going missing would send shockwaves right across the prison and that the governor would not be happy, but what did I care? It was obvious that the mind games had started with the transfer of Billy Ferris, so I was upping the ante. Why not create a bit of paranoia throughout the prison, I thought, while I sit back and have a chuckle to myself.

On D-Hall bottom landing I knew a prisoner called Cat (after the 70s TV character Catweazle), an old-timer with long hair and straggly beard who worked outside in the garden party. This meant he was able to walk around the prison grounds unescorted by the guards, picking up litter and other less desirable objects inmates had chucked out of their cell windows at night – I'm talking about the days long before inside sanitation was introduced. My plan went into action immediately. I would throw the scissors out of the tailoring workshop window and Cat would then pick them up and stash them for me in a safe place. Cat was old-school and didn't ask any questions, so it was straight forward enough coaching him with details of what he had to do. We arranged a time when the scissors would be ready for pick-up and he assured me that he would bury them somewhere in the grounds as soon as he had them in his possession. Perfect.

As everyone working in the tailoring workshop cleared up to go back to the halls that day, the guards realised that a pair of scissors was missing. This sort of thing had happened many times before but usually they turned up after a thorough search – this time they didn't. Next, every inmate was subjected to a vigorous strip-search, but the scissors remained elusive. The whole jail went into lock down for 24 hours after that, during which time a huge search-and-locate operation swung into action, as this was a serious breach of prison security. But they never did find the scissors.

As soon as things had settled down, over the coming days a sort of normality crept back into the jail. You could bet your bottom dollar Billy Ferris was feeling the pinch, though. It had come to my attention that Rafferty had been seen going in and out of Colin Murdoch's cell, which was located on the top floor landing above me. There was nothing wrong with this in itself, but what stank is the fact Rafferty didn't say anything to me about him meeting Murdoch. It's impossible to keep something like this quiet in such an enclosed environment without being detected. This was worrying. I couldn't have Rafferty coming into my cell and overhearing conversations only for him then to go into Murdoch's cell and possibly repeat what he had just heard. I had to put a stop to this, but I decided to wait until I had concrete evidence that Rafferty was up to no good.

Kenny Kelly had sent someone to tell me that I was to go and see him straight away. When I went down to Kenny's cell, he had the company of three or four other prisoners, including Tommy Gordon from Dundee. (Tommy Gordon was the young guy who had stabbed and killed 18-year-old Mark Mulheron in Greenock back in 1988 and was in D-Hall serving out the lifer he had received for that crime.)

'Wait until you hear this,' Kenny told me. 'I've got some very important news you'll want to hear.'

The guy from Dundee had overheard a couple of prisoners from his neck of the woods talking about stabbing someone in the hall. Instead of keeping their mouths shut and carrying out their mission, it would appear they were going about the hall bragging about it.

'Two halfwits have taken on a hit to stab you. Billy Ferris has given them a lump of hash and a blade.'

It was all beginning to make sense. In a desperate bid to have me nipped, Billy Ferris had recruited two of the biggest dunderheads in the prison to stab me. On a good day such a plan might have worked, but on this occasion it ended in complete farce.

I selected the taller of the two, who we'll call Dumb, and entered his cell just before bang-up. As I went in I closed the cell door over to prevent anyone else from looking in. When Dumb turned and caught a glimpse of me standing there, I could see the blood drain from his face; he went as white as a sheet. He blurted out that it wasn't him, that he was sorry and didn't want to have anything to do with it in the first place, all in the same sentence. Pointing to his bed, Dumb said: 'It's under the mattress, it's under the mattress.'

I lifted his mattress and found a lump of marijuana. I placed that in my pocket and told him to think himself lucky that he wasn't going to be seriously harmed. I produced a little blade I had on me and punctured his left cheek just below the eye. I told him: 'Every time you look in the mirror, always remember how foolish you were to get involved in something you shouldn't have messed with.' On leaving his cell I could see his pal, Dumber, across the gallery go expeditiously behind his cell door and bang it shut. He'd obviously sensed what had happened to Dumb and didn't fancy being next.

That night, I broke a piece of the marijuana off and gave the rest to old Kansas Kelly to do whatever he wanted with it. Smoking that stuff sent me scatty but on this occasion it felt appropriate to treat myself to a big fat joint.

Sitting back in my cell I penned Ferris's brother a note, or 'stiffy', as we called it, to be sent over to him in A-Hall first thing the following morning. Because of what had transpired I suggested that we meet up in the gymnasium to sort out any differences between us. It was now a case of waiting to find out which way the wind would blow, but my guess was that he wouldn't appear.

As suspected, my reservations about Rafferty turned out to be well founded. More stories were beginning to filter back to me that suggested not only was he visiting Colin Murdoch in his cell, but he was also saying to certain people that he believed he could batter me in a square-go. Yeah right! I got together with old Kenny to discuss what my next move would be. The heat was building in the hall; you could feel it. My senses were always very accurate and they warned me of some sort of danger, so I was glad I still had access to the scissors I'd taken from the tailors. I talked with Kenny about how I should tackle Rafferty. I never saw Rafferty as a threat, and when it came right down to it I knew he was a coward. He was just a big pest who needed taking down a few pegs.

While all the focus was on Rafferty, Murdoch remained in the background, probably instigating the whole thing, and it made sense to call Murdoch down to Kenny's cell to find out what he had to say for himself. While we were waiting for Murdoch to come down, I happened to clock Rafferty hanging about on the bottom landing. I told Kenny I was going to have words with him right there and then.

'Don't be mad,' Kenny said to me. 'You're not even tooled up and that big parasite will be carrying something.'

A couple of weeks previously it was rumoured that Rafferty had stolen a couple of massive screwdrivers from the tool bag belonging to a worker who was fixing some cell lights in the hall. I didn't care if Rafferty had a screwdriver on him or not; feelings were running high and there he was in front of me, so I said, 'Hey, Davie, can I have a word with you in the dormitory?'

Just opposite old Kenny's cell on the bottom flat there were a couple of dormitories that were used solely for the kitchen workers. Kenny suggested I get tooled up before I went in there, but the only tool I needed was the psychological type. I could read the game perfectly, and I was about to call his bluff. I had committed myself to a confrontation by asking Rafferty for a word, but in any event I felt I was in total control of what I was doing and regarded him as a pushover.

I entered the dormitory and told a kitchen worker who happened to be sitting in there to give me a moment, as I had a bit of business to attend to in private. The con took the hint and got out quickly, and then Rafferty came in and stood just inside the door. At this stage I was right inside the dormitory, unarmed, and I had positioned myself facing my opponent.

I was sure that Rafferty had the screwdriver on him. He could have pulled it out, and I would have been in severe trouble, no doubt. He had every advantage under the sun: he was both taller and heavier than me; he was almost definitely armed, and he blocked my exit. The odds were clearly stacked against me. I quickly put it to Rafferty that I knew all about the things he had been saying about me, regarding beating me in a square-go, and that now was the time to sort it all out. 'Come on then, let's see what you can do. Now's your chance, so come ahead,' I said.

Well, just as I had anticipated, he didn't want to fight and just weaseled his way out. That was the end of that, and I walked out of the dormitory victorious, at least in a psychological sense, proving my point that Rafferty was simply a big coward with a loose tongue. From the dormitory I walked right over to Kenny's cell and guess who was sitting there? Murdoch.

'Hello, Colin. I've just put Rafferty in his place,' I told him. On hearing this he looked surprised; perhaps he was expecting or hoping for a different outcome. I told Murdoch: 'Go and take the screwdriver from Rafferty. Slap him on the face and tell him that silly boys shouldn't be carrying weapons. Oh, and if you do that, then we can forget all about everything else that's been said.'

He accepted this and seemed relieved that the matter would finish there. Rafferty was now sitting at the end of the hall, by the window on the first landing. I watched as Murdoch approached him, and I even saw him slap Rafferty on the face just the way I'd asked him to. Kenny and I burst into a fit of laughter. When Murdoch came back to Kenny's cell, he handed me a screwdriver. It was ten inches long and there's no doubt this thing would have inflicted serious damage if it had been used against me earlier. Rafferty's sense of self-worth had taken a beating, and psychologically he would've been down in the dumps, knowing everyone was now laughing at him, and this was something that would have an almost instant repercussion.

The next morning I made my way over to the gym to see if Billy Ferris would turn up. To my frustration and anger – though not to my surprise – he didn't. He obviously didn't fancy seeing me that day and I don't blame him. He knew I would have destroyed him with my bare hands. Billy Ferris was prepared to use the weaker element to do his dirty work but couldn't do it himself. That was the measure of the man; he was a coward just like Rafferty.

When I arrived back in the hall from the gym, it was late in the afternoon and the food was being served. I was still in my gym kit, wearing only a pair of shorts and a vest, when I went to collect my meal. Just before mealtimes everyone would normally be locked up for a number check, then the guards would open up one landing at a time to prevent a large number of prisoners queuing for their meal at the same time. Prisoners would collect their food from the pantry area on the bottom landing and take it back to their cells to eat it. There was no dining hall. By the time I'd come back from the gym the whole of the bottom landing, where Kenny's cell was located, had been served their meal and were locked up in their cells.

I remember seeing Rafferty standing outside his cell and hanging over the railings. Since my cell was right next door to his it was difficult to give him a wide berth. With the psychological wounds still fresh in his mind from the day before, he couldn't have felt good about himself at all. As I left my cell to head downstairs for my meal I noticed he was still standing holding onto the railings, as if he were waiting for something. I pressed on along the landing and made my way downstairs towards the pantry area. I collected my meal, which came in a tough, mustard-coloured plastic tray with a lid on top to keep it warm. After the usual banter with the pantry lads who served the meals, all seemed fine. I picked up my tray and started to make my way back up the stairs.

There is a saying that you should never trust the person who you meet on the stairs, and suddenly this thought flashed through my mind. As I started to walk up the steps I looked up and could see Rafferty storming down – he was coming down fast and he had his hands behind his back. In that moment I knew exactly what was going to happen and my reflexes sprung into action. I threw my meal tray at him and tried to swing round in order to get into some sort of position where I would be able to defend myself, but it was too late.

Thump! He was on top of me, and I remember seeing this enormous flash. There I was, receiving a thumping from a big wimp who hadn't had the bottle to deal with things in the dormitory when no one else was around. He had obviously decided to commit a cowardly act of revenge in an attempt to save face in front of the prison guards, knowing full well he would be dragged away immediately afterwards before I had the chance to strike back. The weapon he used on me was a six-pound cobbler's last – in effect, an iron shoe. How he managed to sneak it past the security – past rubdowns as well as the once-over with a hand-held metal detector – is way beyond me and is anybody's guess.

To give credit to the prison guards, they intervened quickly and pulled Rafferty off me before he did more damage. I was completely dazed; the barrage of blows I received had blurred my vision. It's the only time in my life when I felt completely out of it and incapable of defending myself. I was helped to the nearest sink on the bottom landing and one of the guards gave me a towel to stem the flow of blood which by this time was streaming down my face and neck. For a moment I thought I was in serious trouble.

Rafferty was taken to the separate cells in segregation over in C-Hall. I was taken to the surgery block to find out how serious my head wounds actually were, and I received 18 stitches in two separate lacerations. Immediately after the stitches were inserted I was escorted to C-Hall and chucked in a cell – right next door to Rafferty! I couldn't believe this; it just didn't make any sense other than it was designed to wind me up. Was the governor making sure he got the last laugh? Ultimately the decision rested with him. If anything, I should have been taken to hospital, where my head could have been properly examined and possibly X-rayed for potential fractures. It wasn't right that I was being sent straight to a cold and filthy cell below ground level. It felt like I was the one being punished.

The segregation unit was located beneath C-Hall and

comprised six individual cells, which were used for prisoners who were either disruptive or violent. The security consisted of three prison guards. With blood still seeping from my head wounds, I began pacing the cell. I was raging.

Typically, the cell in which I found myself was filthy; there was a wafer-thin durable mattress with a matching blanket, and not surprisingly there was no pillow. How could Ron Kite possibly justify the treatment I was receiving? As much as I protested that it was wrong I had been put there, it made no difference and fell on deaf ears.

Just when I thought matters couldn't get much worse, I felt the wall nearest me begin to shudder. It was Rafferty banging on the wall and shouting: 'How's your head, Lobban?' This went on for some time, and it was obvious he was getting a kick from all the abuse he was shouting. To say he was rubbing salt into the wounds would be an understatement. It really was doing my head right in. All night I had to endure Rafferty's rants.

The following morning I was in a right mood and all I thought about was how I could get my hands on him. The prison nurse came to see me and she noticed I didn't have a pillow. On enquiring as to why this was the case, the screw informed her that it was because I hadn't asked for one they had assumed I must have had one already. I remember the nurse making a note of this and expressing her deep indignation about the conditions in which I was being kept. She actually appeared to be on my side and she told me she would be going straight to see the governor to raise her concerns.

But what was about to happen next turned out be far more a cause for concern, and would change the way security was handled within the segregation block.

Chapter Seventeen

Prison Siege

I made a request to have all my paperwork brought down from D-Hall to my cell, as reading it would give me something to do and keep me occupied during my time in the segregation unit. I asked for my whole portfolio, every piece of paperwork about me on file, and then I sat back and waited to find out what exactly they would deliver. That same afternoon my cell door swung open and the guards handed me an assortment of paperwork. This was a box full of official documents which had been accumulated since my arrest in London. There was all sorts inside what I called 'the magic box'.

I came across a folder that felt hard to the touch at the bottom. On closer inspection I couldn't believe my eyes. There, in between the paperwork, was my steel Parker pen. In that split second a burst of energy swept through my body, and I felt hot and sweaty. This was it; I knew what I had to do. I had to get to the coward next door who had been winding me up all night. As soon as the guards went for their break I quickly got down on my hands and knees and like a maniac I started to sharpen the steel nib of the pen. The stone floor was perfect for this and in no time I had the pen looking like a lethal weapon.

Three of the segregation cells in C-Hall were occupied during this time: I was in cell 3, Rafferty was in the next cell to me, number 4, and there was some unknown prisoner in cell 6, the end cell. For security reasons prisoners did not associate with each other and this meant the screws only opened one cell at a time. Under no circumstances did this rule ever change. Inmates could expect one hour of exercise every day and were locked up in their cell for the other 23. The only other times the guards opened the cell door were at mealtimes and for a quick slop-out afterwards. Outside the cells, the area where the guards patrolled and sat drinking tea was cramped and poorly lit. There was a desk and a kettle and that was about it. Before the guards went home at the end of the day my cell was scheduled for one last slop-out. Of the three guards who would open the door that night, one wouldn't make it home.

It was around 9 p.m. on Wednesday, 22 June 1992 when the guards finally opened up my cell door to offer me the last slop-out of the evening. When the door swung open, there were the usual three guards. At first glance they looked alarmed, not to mention apprehensive, at the sight standing in front of them. My aim was to get precisely this reaction, and it was clear I had achieved it. I must have had the look of a complete lunatic.

I was bare-chested, with a piece of torn cloth from my vest wrapped around my forehead, and was sweating profusely from the non-stop exercising I'd done to psyche myself up. Holding my plastic piss-pot in one hand, I had a towel draped around my forearm concealing the sharpened pen in the other. The atmosphere was very tense indeed and I could sense the fear coming from all three of them. As I passed the guards I got myself into position just in front of them. Then, placing the piss-pot down on the floor I pulled the towel away to reveal the sharpened parker pen compressed tightly in my grasp.

'Move away from the riot bell,' I ordered them quietly. 'Just do as I say and no one will get hurt.'

Gesturing with a nod and pointing towards the cell next door to me, I assured them that Rafferty was the one I wanted to get my hands on. He had pushed me over the edge and all I wanted to do was exactly what I should've done back in the D-Hall dormitory when I had had the chance. Above the silence that gripped the tiny holding area, all you could hear was the petrified screaming of Rafferty, who by this time had cottoned on to what was going down. 'Heeeeeelp! . . . Heeeeelp!' he shouted at the top of his voice.

The first thing I demanded was the pocket knives I knew most screws carried on their key-chain. These were little red-handled penknives and they were issued to all prison guards on qualifying for the job. The purpose of the knives, at least in theory, was to give them a better chance of quickly cutting a prisoner down should they find someone hanging in their cell. Of the three screws I now had hostage, two of them had their penknives.

By handing over these deadly weapons the guards had reinforced my position, and in doing so blew any chance they might've had in regaining control of the situation. In fairness, two of the screws were young and not that long in the job, so they simply froze on the spot, while the more senior guard, a man by the name of Terry O'Neil, showed his experience and courage in what happened next.

Immediately after the two screws handed me their penknives, my next move was to send one of the guards upstairs to C-Hall and inform the governor that there was now a full-blown hostage situation in progress. I ordered Terry to stay behind, since he was the man with the cell door key, which was obviously vital for gaining access to Rafferty's cell.

Then I asked Terry to select one of the other two guards to go upstairs to pass on the message to his colleagues. 'I want you to bring me back a set of handcuffs,' I told the young screw in a stern voice. My plan was to handcuff myself to Terry as soon as I was finished with Rafferty. Terry signalled to one of his mates, telling him: 'Do what William wants. Go upstairs and tell the management that he has us hostage and bring back a set of handcuffs while you're at it.'

With his orders, the guard vanished from sight. Little did I know that this was the last time I would see him. I turned to Terry and asked him to hand over the cell-door key. 'I don't have it,' he said.

'What do you mean, you don't have it? I saw you open my cell door, so don't give me that nonsense,' I told him.

'Yes, but for security reasons we always change keys.' Terry had unlocked the cell door, but then given the key to one of the other guards, on this occasion the young officer I had just sent off upstairs.

I was seething when he told me this. What was I going to do now? I shouted to the young screw, but he was now out of

earshot. I had made a fundamental slip-up by not taking possession of that cell-door key straight away, and this turn of events
totally changed the game. The other young screw still had what's
called a single key, but this only opened grille gates and suchlike,
so was useless for my purposes. It now looked as if Rafferty
would live to see another day.

Full credit to Terry O'Neil, though, for having the guts to send
his colleague upstairs with the cell-door key. I think that Terry
was very courageous in doing that. Given the situation we were
all in, and how dangerous I was supposed to be, he couldn't have
been sure how I might react? Terry probably saved Rafferty's
life that night, and me from a certain life sentence.

Suddenly, I heard a door open upstairs, followed by footsteps,
then the Principal Officer's voice called out: 'Willy Lobban, it's
John Glen. Can I speak with you for a minute? Come on, now,
Willy. You can stop this and we won't take matters any further.'

There's no way I was surrendering now, so I politely told him
to go back the way he had come. He listened to me and hastily
withdrew back up the stairs.

Ten minutes or so had gone by at this point and it was obvious
that the young screw I sent off to fetch the handcuffs wasn't
coming back. There was a walkie-talkie radio attached to Terry's
belt but it was dead. He explained that all communications via
radio would be terminated in these situations. The only move
I had left was to make my way upstairs, and perhaps I could
demand a cell-door key in exchange for a screw. It was the only
thing left to do.

The gloves were off and I was determined to get Rafferty's
door open. He was still screaming to such a degree and volume
that the whole prison must have heard him. 'Heeeeeelp! ...
Heeeeelp!' That's all you could hear. I went over to his cell, lifted
the spy-hole cover and he was sitting down with his back against
the cell door and his feet up against the concrete plinth for the
mattress. Being wedged between the two must have given him
some feeling of defence.

'I'll be back for you in just a bit, so you'd better prepare
yourself for when I come through your door,' I shouted to him.
He continued to scream the place down. Holding Terry by his

trouser-belt I whispered in his ear that no harm would come to
him.

'Terry, I've got to make it look as if I mean business; it's the
only way I'll get a cell-door key.'

I asked him to acknowledge me and he nodded his head to
say he understood. I couldn't afford any further mishaps at this
stage. With my right hand, I pressed the penknife against the
leather of his belt to ensure the point of the knife wouldn't cut
him in any way. I ordered the other screw, who by this time
looked as though he'd seen a ghost, to stay close to us but press
ahead and move slowly up the steps towards the door which led
out onto the bottom flat of C-Hall.

Slowly we all made our way up the stairs, the young guard
leading the way. There were only two small flights of stairs, each
containing about ten steps. As we reached the landing the three
of us stood cramped together. I told the young screw to go on
up and open the door leading to the hall. Terry and I looked on
as he moved slowly up towards the door. When he reached the
top, he turned to look at us as if waiting for further instructions.

With Terry still pulled close to me, I told the young screw to
open the door with the single key he had in his hand. He gave
a half-smile then proceeded to open the door. As he turned the
key I looked on with eagerness, but what happened next caught
me with complete shock: the young screw had no sooner turned
the key in the lock when suddenly he was carried away like a
log of wood. There must've been at least six pairs of hands that
grabbed him. Like some sort of snatch squad the dark figures
in blue overalls and helmets pulled him off out of sight. The riot
squad had clearly arrived in force. What we had just seen didn't
put me off from moving on up; I simply waited a few minutes
until I managed to compose myself. There was a moment of
eerie silence before Rafferty's screaming started again.

I was holding Terry very close now, and again I tried to reassure him that everything would be fine. But looking back I
understand that it must've been absolutely terrifying for him
regardless of this. Holding Terry in front I nudged him forward
as we moved slowly up, one step at a time. I shouted up ahead
that I wouldn't hesitate in hurting their colleague should there

be any more surprises. Again I whispered to Terry that I was just bluffing and would not hurt him in any way.

We now stood at the top of the stairs and I could see out into C-Hall bottom landing. The place was deserted. As we poked our heads out to have a better look around, the only activity I saw was away down at the other end of the hall near the screws' office. There were three or four guards rushing in and out of the room, clutching what appeared to be folders and paperwork. This was probably case-sensitive material they didn't fancy me getting my hands on, and far more important than the documents they'd brought to me shortly before in the segregation unit. Not that I was even remotely interested in that stuff.

As soon as the guards saw Terry and me standing at the door entrance to the segregation block they didn't hang around for long. They bolted the office door shut, ran to the grille-gate and locked it up behind them. That was it; I was now alone with Terry and we had C-Hall all to ourselves. What could I do now? Where could I go? What would my next move be? It was all a bit confusing and mentally draining. My plan had gone terribly wrong, and the chances of me finding assistance to batter down Rafferty's cell door were zero. What a mess!

My thinking became a bit more rational but I still realised there was no way back. I wasn't about to throw in the towel just yet, though, so I decided to play the scenario out. That way the rest would take care of itself. My first thought was to get myself off the bottom landing of C-Hall. It was pointless going back down to the segregation block. My instincts told me to go up. Through the wire mesh that's used to prevent prisoners from jumping off the balconies I selected a spot midway along the first gallery that I felt offered me the best possible position to defend myself.

I asked Terry to turn to his side. With me standing behind him, we took sideways movements along the middle of the bottom landing, so that I didn't have to worry about being rushed from behind. I wasn't taking any chances. Eventually we reached the staircase which led up onto the first landing. We then progressed up the stairs and onto the first landing itself.

From there I positioned us both outside a cell door midway along the gallery. This is where we stayed until the siege ended 13 hours later.

I didn't know the name of the prisoner in that cell; all I know is he was a local lad from Dundee. Actually, the music coming from inside was what drew my attention to it in the first place. When I approached the cell initially, I opened up his spy-hole and kicked the door. He must have thought it was a screw asking him to turn his music down. I stood back, and with the peephole opened and still holding Terry, I said to the guy: 'Look, pal, I've got a screw here and I'm holding him hostage,' then asked him for a cigarette. Seconds later, he pushed three roll-ups under the cell door followed by a match. I offered Terry a fag, but he didn't smoke. I sat on the cold stone floor with my back pressed up against the cell door. Terry sat in between my legs and we chatted away quite the thing for ages. I asked the prisoner in the cell to play his music but not too loud, sort of background music to help ease the tension. The song that stands out in my memory from that night was a Bob Marley number called 'Could You Be Loved?'. Whenever I hear that song it immediately takes me back to that time and place.

The main gate opened downstairs and I heard footsteps approaching. Terry and I got to our feet. I could immediately see a couple of people staring up at us. One of them was Eric Duff, the senior physical training officer and the head of staff training in the use of control and restraint. He was unquestionably a hard man. I knew Eric very well from the days he had helped me train for my world record for dips on the parallel bar when I'd been at Perth back in 1989. He'd come along to make me an outrageous offer. He wanted me to exchange Terry for himself. As if I would do that!

He knew I had two penknives but, even so, he would still have fancied his chances disarming me. I thanked him for trying and wished him all the best.

Shortly after Eric left some people arrived and introduced themselves as members of the Incident Command Team. These guys were trained negotiators from the Scottish Prison System who deal exclusively with hostage situations in the early stages until the so-called professionals arrive. I told them to go away and sat back down with Terry for another marathon conversation.

I think that over the course of the night I must've given Terry my whole life story. It's strange, but you know what it's like when you have a heart-to-heart with someone and you feel totally elated and happy afterwards? Well, it was a bit like that when I spoke with Terry O'Neil that night. For a few hours we were simply two human beings getting to know each other without the barriers that normally separated us.

Over the course of the siege I spoke to three different negotiating squads. A woman headed the last of the three and she persevered with the negotiations right up until I let Terry go. My main demand was for a cell-door key to the segregation block. I never did get one. The coward Rafferty was taken to safety sometime during the night, so even if I had managed to get a key it would've made no difference. I had also asked for two jerseys so that Terry and I could keep warm. The offers of cups of tea I rejected because they would certainly have been made with more than just Tetley teabags. Throughout the night the hall was reasonably quiet.

The prisoners on C-Hall weren't aware of the hostage situation until the following morning when their cells weren't opened at breakfast time. That's when everyone started banging on their cell doors. C-Hall was mainly for remand prisoners, and I know that not all the prisoners who were due in court that day got the chance to appear. I permitted prisoners to receive their medication and I gave instructions for inmates to receive their breakfast, albeit a late one.

Just after 10 a.m. on 23 July I brought the whole matter to a peaceful conclusion. Terry, the prison guard who showed remarkable courage throughout his terrifying ordeal, started to break down in front of me. He said to me: 'Look, William, I can't take any more of this. I miss my wife and kids and I feel if you don't let me go now it might affect me mentally.'

This was a brave man. He had tears in his eyes and I've no shame in saying I did too. There's no way I was prepared to hold him any longer after he'd said that to me.

'You're free to go, Terry,' I told him.

He looked at me as if I were kidding.

'Can I really go? Are you sure?' he asked and, still slightly hesitant, he began walking away from me. He must have been 20 feet away from me, with the negotiators downstairs shouting at him to run, when he did something no one expected.

He could've taken off downstairs to safety, but instead Terry actually turned around and came back towards me. As he came within reach, he held out his arm.

'Can I shake your hand, William?'

I couldn't believe it! Here was a prison guard, who I'd kept hostage for over 13 hours, and he wanted to shake my hand! I raised my arm for a handshake and Terry said, 'I think you're a gentleman,' before walking away again.

'Thank you!' I shouted. Twenty minutes after letting Terry go I finally gave myself up.

I made my final demand in the Perth siege situation to the female negotiator who was standing patiently on the bottom landing. I wanted my grievances broadcast on local radio news, and I made a point of asking to see my lawyer. I was told that he was on his way to the prison. I was promised a nice warm shower, a change of clothes and something to eat. All that sounded good to me.

Terry had long gone. I saw him disappear into the swarm of riot-squad officers who were waiting for him as he went downstairs. Now it was my turn to go downstairs, but this was something I found difficult to do. The riot squad could have come bursting up the stairs at any moment. I was asked to throw down the two penknives and the Parker pen. After I did this the negotiator gave me one last warning, saying, 'If you don't come down now, the riot team will have to come up and get you.'

Anyway, I began walking along the first flat landing until I reached the stairs. All I could see below me was a line of riot-squad officers that stretched from the bottom of the stairs right along to the main entrance of the hall. There must have been 30 of them; it was like a scene from a *Star Wars* film, a really big show of authoritarian strength. As I walked slowly down the stairs it sounded as if every prisoner in the hall was banging and simultaneously kicking their cell doors. The noise was deafening.

Prisoners were shouting, screaming and howling in chorus and, amazingly, when I reached the riot-squad officers not one of them manhandled me in any way.

I expected at least to be frog-marched to wherever it was they were going to take me, but that didn't happen either. Instead I was told to follow the line of mufti along to the end. I tried to look at some of their faces as I walked past them, but their visors were pulled down and I couldn't see a thing. A couple of their colleagues followed closely behind me. As I passed the sea of blue overalls I noticed a couple of prison governors along with the doctor and a male nurse standing outside a cell just up ahead. My guess was that this cell was for me, and I was right. Nothing was mentioned about this before I gave myself up, and so I was now beginning to feel slightly uneasy.

I had no sooner gone inside the cell than a nurse in a long white coat came right in at my back. Then the two riot-squad officers who had followed me along the bottom landing came in too. I was told to remove the clothes I was wearing. A Polaroid camera was produced and I was asked to lift up my arms so that a picture could be taken both front and back. I was actually pleased about this because when the pictures were taken I had no marks or bruises on my body. If anyone had any plans to show me any kind of brutality, then they would have to think twice.

Immediately after my picture had been taken I was escorted over to the reception area in bare feet and with only a prison-issue towel to hide my modesty. Where was my nice warm shower and change of clothes? Where was the hot meal I had been promised? And, more importantly, where was my solicitor? I had been led right up the garden path, conned, and taken for a ride – quite literally in fact, as within ten minutes of my surrender I had been photographed, escorted barefoot to the reception, then placed in a waiting van which took me straight to Peterhead Prison. I had left Perth for good.

As for some of the others that were in Perth nick at this time, Colin Murdoch was murdered in Wishaw, his home town, on his release from prison. Old 'Kansas' Kelly hanged himself in his flat in Anderston five or six years after his release. David Rafferty was transferred to Glenochil prison in Clackmannashire, where he was severely scalded on the face when a fellow inmate threw a kettle of boiling water at him. The brave prison officer Terry O'Neil went back to work. After his release Billy Ferris proved to be the beast I always thought he was when he was subsequently sentenced for life, with the recommendation that he serve at least 22 years, for stabbing to death a 15-year-old schoolboy. He knifed the boy 15 times as he lay sleeping in his bed and then set fire to the kid's body. Prison officers throughout the Scottish Prison System were stripped of the red-handled penknives because of what went down on the night of 22/23 July 1992.

Chapter Eighteen

Banged Up in the Napper

The journey north to Peterhead was not a particularly lengthy one – with a distance of about 100 miles to cover it took about two hours. I shall never forget it, though – and not because of the beautiful countryside. I had my face squashed into the floor of the prison van while two screws sat on top of me. They had waited until we had driven right out of Perth and then pinned me down to the floor of the van. There was absolutely no need for it. I realise feelings were running high, but still, they didn't have to behave like animals. In total there were six prison officers escorting me to Peterhead that day.

Peterhead Prison was built in 1888 and designed to hold just over 200 prisoners. Additional buildings were erected in 1909, 1960 and then in 1962. Right up until the early 1990s it housed the most dangerous criminals in the Scottish Prison System. A high-security prison – just 32 miles north of Aberdeen, it is staffed by guards who are mostly big, tough-skinned Highlanders with a profound dislike for prisoners from Glasgow. By the time I arrived in 1992, the whole prison, with the exception of one small hall, was solely for sex offenders. What a place!

The guards weren't prepared to let go of my arms as they took me into the prison reception. What were they afraid of? That I was going to swing for them perhaps? The ride up north had been uncomfortable enough; all I wanted now was to get to a cell so that I could lie down and rest. I hadn't slept for over 48 hours and I was knackered. Waiting to greet me were six prison guards wearing full riot gear. What was all this about? I was soon to discover that this would be normality, and the sooner I got used to the idea of seeing prison guards in full riot gear the better.

I was being placed in G-Hall, where I would see the riot-squad 24-7. This place was the end of the road, a dumping ground for inmates the prison system considered extremely dangerous. 'The National Lockdown Facility' was its official name. I knew G-Hall existed, I had heard some menacing stories about the place, and here I was about to experience it first-hand. My first impression was that it was very small; there was not much to it. I was taken up a flight of stairs and onto a landing where I could clearly see a cell door lying open. It had all been prepared for me. Still naked and in handcuffs, I was led inside.

The cuffs were removed and I was informed that the prison governor would be coming to see me shortly. The guards left and banged the cell door shut. Inside the room there was a cardboard table and chair. A steel bed was bolted to the floor and the mattress was wafer-thin. On top of the table there were some prison-issue clothes. I stuck on the jail pants to restore my dignity and, exhausted, I fell on top of the bed. All sorts of thoughts ran through my head, but one thing was for sure: I knew I would be locked up in G-Hall for quite some time – and indeed I was, for 18 months.

The governor did eventually come round to see me. The cell-door peephole opened and a screw's voice said: 'Right, Lobban, stand at the back wall and face the window.' As soon as I had done so, the door opened. Quickly, three prison guards entered in full riot gear and stood right in front of me, followed by the prison governor, Alex Spencer, who had been Governor at Dungavel when I was there.

'OK, Mr Lobban, you're in Peterhead now and you will be staying with us for the foreseeable future. Have you any questions you want to ask?'

I knew it was a worthless exercise asking about anything and just kept my mouth shut.

'OK then, if you need anything you can always ask my staff, thank you.'

And that was it. I was now officially part of the G-Hall regime.

I will try my best to describe what it was like living in 23-hours-a-day lockdown conditions with six prison guards in riot gear on the other side of the cell door. I mean, you wouldn't keep an animal cooped up for 23 hours a day in a space only 6×8 feet, would you? To be locked up in solitary, in a tiny, often cold and filthy cell with only a cardboard table and chair is one of the most negative experiences anyone could have. It's a time to wallow in a mire of total meaninglessness, a complete waste of life. The night-time lock-up is bad enough, but you can at least get a sleep. It's during those daylight hours when the sun shines through the bars of your window that it's at its worst. That is one of the most debilitating and spirit-breaking feelings you can experience. It's utterly cruel.

The layout of the place was very simple. There were 16 cells in G-Hall, eight on the top landing and eight on the bottom. The eight cells on the top landing were divided into two sets of four by an archway. The bottom landing was the same as the top but with the difference that the shower was situated downstairs. The archway in the middle was where we could wash and have a shave.

In the morning before breakfast, the prison guards in riot gear came to your cell door, opened the spy-hole and shouted to you, asking if you wanted a slop-out or a wash. This was your chance to leave your cell, empty the plastic piss-pot and have a quick wash, if you were fast enough. You only had ten minutes to do all of these things, and I mean ten minutes, not a second over. During the last two minutes you were given a verbal tirade by one of the guards, warning you that time was almost up. If you were not back in your cell in time, and if, for whatever reason, you didn't take heed of this warning, you would be manhandled back to your cell with no questions asked. It was that strict.

At breakfast time the guards would come to the cell door and you were told to stand at the back wall. When the door was opened, a screw would stand at the cell entrance with a tray in his hands and you were asked to come forward and collect your meal. Breakfast was normally a bowl of porridge, which was more like thick, lumpy wallpaper paste, and tea. The tea was never hot, warm at best. As soon as you picked the items that you wanted from the tray, the guard would take two steps back and another two steps to the side. When he was clear of the doorway, one of his colleagues would step forward and lock the door with his key. Everything the guards did, they did with precision; every step, every movement. It was a bit robotic, but that's how they operated, and it worked. When I arrived in this place, this operating system had already been going for a very long time, so they knew exactly what they were doing.

Around mid-morning you were offered 30 minutes' exercise, and the same procedures would apply. The peep-hole would open and you had to acknowledge the guard if you wanted to go outside. When the cell door opened, a screw would stand there with a hand-held metal detector. After giving you the once-over with it, you were escorted downstairs by six guards and taken outside to the exercise enclosure. There were three individual exercise pens separated by a solid wall. The roof of each pen was lined with steel-wire mesh, so it was impossible to escape. Three prisoners would be outside at any one time, each in their own pen, and this was when most of the prisoners communicated with each other. Just above the exercise enclosures there was a walkway where a guard would continuously pace up and down. We called this the 'catwalk'. During exercise was the only time that the guards would remove their riot helmets, and they did this so that they could listen to what prisoners were saying. It was impossible to have a conversation with another prisoner without someone hearing what you were talking about. It was that sort of environment. The screw on the catwalk would listen to everything that was being said, as well as observing every move you made. When the 30 minutes were up, you would receive another going-over with the metal detector and you were taken back to your cell. Then there was nothing until the next meal came round.

In the afternoon you would be offered another 30 minutes' exercise and you would go through the same procedure as before. The reason the exercise was split into two sessions, as opposed to the one full hour, was because of security and time. G-Hall had sixteen cells, but would only hold twelve prisoners at any one time. Any more than twelve would have made it impossible to run the place properly. The guards had to take meal breaks and would knock off home at a set time, and the prisoners on lockdown therefore suffered.

If you wanted to make a telephone call or have a shower, you would have to request it first thing in the morning. The reality was you were lucky if you managed two showers a week. Twenty minutes was permitted for a shower, with another verbal two-minute warning being shouted as your time was ending. You were allowed a five-minute telephone call every couple of days. If you ever left G-Hall for any reason – going on a visit perhaps – you would be handcuffed there and back. In fact, any movement around the prison would involve you being cuffed.

And that was my daily routine, day in day out.

As the months passed in G-Hall it became clear to me that I was there for the long haul. Every time I requested a move I was met with the same answer: I was a danger to prison officers and therefore would be kept in lockdown until further notice.

But perversely the longer I was kept in solitary confinement the easier it became. Don't get me wrong – there were times when the impact of being locked up really got to me and sometimes it felt like mental torture. But these negative feelings were mainly experienced in the early days. I have a tough spirit and I decided that the prison system wasn't going to break it. My attitude was that you can deprive my body but not my mind. In the end I sailed through the 18 months I spent confined to a tiny cell. Some others weren't so fortunate and during my time there I must have witnessed at least five or six prisoners being dragged off to Carstairs. Some prisoners just couldn't handle the lock-up and suffered dreadful consequences. For example, a prisoner by the name of Joseph 'Psycho' Boyle came into G-Hall a few months after I got there. He was a good friend of mine, as we'd met during a spell at Polmont Young Offenders Institution in the 80s. The last time I had seen Joe was when he came into Perth serving a five-year sentence for assault and robbery.

Back in October 1986 Joe, along with his pal William 'Baba' Kilpatrick, robbed a sewage works in Dumbarton of £80,000. Splitting the cash between them, they went their own ways until the heat died down. However, a couple of days later the door of the house where Joe had been lying low got booted in. A gang had received information that Joe was holed up in the house with plenty of money. A shotgun was fired in warning at a television and Joe was robbed of the takings from the robbery. He also received multiple stab wounds and nearly died. His liver had been penetrated, and his stomach and a spinal nerve were damaged, which almost crippled him.

It took months before he could walk again, and when we were in Perth together that's all he seemed to talk about. Joe was obsessed with the people who had done this to him and often threatened to kill them. When he landed in G-Hall, his head was all over the place. Within days he had started an argument with another prisoner, a real clown whose name I can't now remember. The show had well and truly started.

Joe would place his mattress against the wall of his cell so that he could use it like a punch bag. All day and night he would punch it constantly, the sound amplified and echoing all about the place. That's fine during the day, but when it goes on throughout the night it becomes more than just a distraction. Joe actually got released from G-Hall without having any form of treatment or counselling. I fail to understand how the prison authorities could justify releasing him back into the community with all the mental problems he had.

On 29 May 1993, six days into his freedom, he was in his mother's house in Govan when he saw one of the men who had attacked him walking past the window. He grabbed a kitchen knife and ran from the house. In broad daylight and in front of horrified onlookers, including children, he caught up with his quarry and plunged a knife right through his heart. The blow was so severe that it sliced through the sixth and seventh ribs, and the victim died at the scene within a couple of minutes. Joe had got his revenge, but it cost him a life sentence. He was sent to the state mental hospital at Carstairs, where he remained for years.

The worst thing about the lock-up was that there was just no human contact apart from with the six prison guards in full riot gear. It got to a stage with me that I would pace up and down the cell all day long just to pass the time. When I wasn't pacing the cell, I would take my mattress off the bed and do step-ups on the steel frame. I would sometimes go on and on until I literally fell down exhausted. Instead of walking in the exercise pen for

30 minutes I preferred to jog. In a space no bigger than one half of a tennis court I would run round in circles, one way in the morning and the other way in the afternoon. By the time I left the place there was an ingrained track where I had been jogging. You could say that I left my mark!

I also went through a phase of heavy reading. I got a book sent in to me called *A History of Western Philosophy* by Bertrand Russell. I must have read this book three times from cover to cover – and it was two inches thick! Because of my poor background and inadequate schooling I was hopeless at reading and writing. In particular, my spelling was useless. My prolonged confinement, banged up in G-Hall, certainly played a part in me becoming interested in reading and writing. I taught myself how to use words properly. I remember studying a Collins Dictionary and underlining the words that I found appealing. Then I would go back to the beginning and go over those words again until I understood exactly what they meant. It was definitely a huge learning curve and it improved my vocabulary dramatically.

One of the most memorable experiences of my time at Peterhead happened downstairs one day. Having had a shower, while I was drying off I noticed some people in suits who looked very official. I couldn't help being inquisitive, so I walked up to the gate for a better view. It was the governor, Alex Spencer, along with various other members of the prison department. Amongst them was Jimmy Boyle, the man they once called 'the most dangerous prisoner in Scotland'. I hadn't met Boyle before, but I recognised him from pictures that I had seen. Boyle had spent many years banged up exactly where I was, in G-Hall. He also went on to write his autobiography, *A Sense of Freedom*.

The governor had read an article written by Boyle about Peterhead and was so impressed by it he had invited him back to show him how much things had changed. This upset many prison guards, who still bore grudges towards him, and the occasion was marred when most of them boycotted the special event. As I stood next to the gate Boyle came over to me and stuck his hand through the steel bars to shake my hand. It was a pleasurable experience, considering he knew exactly what I was going through, having been there himself.

By the time a year had gone by I was as content and focused as I possibly could be under the severe pressures of solitary confinement. Then, in July 1993, just over a year after being locked up, my cell door opened and I was informed that a solicitor from London wanted to see me. This sudden and incongruous request left me baffled. I didn't like it one bit. The information I was given was imprecise at best, but my curiosity was aroused, and the only way to find out what he wanted was to meet with him.

After a quick scan using the hand-held metal detector one of the guards escorted me, handcuffed of course, to the main part of the prison, where the meeting would take place. I could see two men in pinstripe suits through the large window of the agents' visiting room. When I entered the room, I must say I was slightly taken aback by the appearance of this pair. In addition to the flashy pinstripes and serious Cockney accents, I noticed one of them had a scar on the side of his forehead and wore a small earring. They were a right dodgy-looking duo, that's for sure.

We got the pleasantries out of the way before the more senior of the two said, 'I represent Michael Healy, who's on trial at the Old Bailey for robbing the National Westminster Bank in Torquay. He would like to know if you would come down to the Old Bailey as a defence witness?' Well, this was just great. I had barely seen any daylight for a year and right out of the blue I was being asked if I would go to London as a defence witness for Michael Healy. I was speechless!

As I was sitting there mulling it over, the lawyer continued: 'If you do agree to come down to London as a witness for Michael, then I'll see to it that you're on the first flight tomorrow morning.'

I wasn't getting any time to think about any of this; it was either a yes or a no – simple as that! I felt it was my duty as a criminal, if nothing else, to help a fellow crook win his case in a court of law, especially when he'd asked for my help. I told the lawyers to let Healy know he could rely on me, and win or lose, I'd be there. It turned out that big Healy was actually handling his own case and was representing himself in court – quite a daunting task for anyone.

This was the third attempt at Crown Court proceedings

against Michael and his gang. Two previous trials in Devon had collapsed because of a serious breach in security. The police had received reliable information that a woman was preparing to sneak a handgun into the court building and as a precaution the authorities shifted the case to London. The Old Bailey is the highest court in the land, and Michael would surely have known that his chances of an acquittal were extremely poor.

The robbery itself, which was described as 'terrifying and highly professional', was what Michael regarded as 'the big one' – the kind of job he had dreamed of carrying out for years. When the bank was closed, Healy and his gang, with the exception of the getaway driver, who had no part in the actual hold-up, gained entry using a set of keys he had managed to get hold of and copy.

When they got inside the premises, they cut a hole in a partition wall just under a staircase, and this is where they stayed hidden until the following morning. As soon as the bank staff began arriving for work, they were ambushed, threatened and told to lie on the floor face down. In this way Healy and his gang took each one of them by surprise as they arrived.

There were three massive steel vaults in the building which had already sprung open under a time-locking device, but big Healy hadn't banked on being faced with the one obstacle that would prevent him from getting his hands on millions of pounds – a simple grille gate in front of the vaults which had to be unlocked with a special key. The bank manager was dragged towards the grille gate and told to open it, but he refused, saying he had no means to do so. Michael then fired his sawn-off shotgun into the ceiling. This caused a bit of masonry to fall from the roof onto a young female employee, cutting her head and scaring the life out of her and everyone else.

The bank manager – who it turned out actually had the key in his possession all along – insisted that one of his assistants, who was late that day, had the key. By this time telephones were ringing all over the place, with business colleagues and clients trying to get through. Terrified bank staff lay face down all over the floor, moaning and crying, fearing the worst. It was the ultimate nightmare scenario, a total shambles.

All the robbers had to do was to take the bunch of keys from the bank manager and try them in the keyhole, but they never did. All their planning and work had been pointless, and the attempted robbery ended in disaster when they aborted the raid and fled empty-handed. Although they did manage to get away from the bank itself, the serious crime squad caught up with them soon afterwards.

When I instructed the London lawyers to go back and tell Mick not to worry, that he could count on me as his star witness at the Old Bailey, the ball was set in motion. I would be flying down to London handcuffed to two senior prison officers the following day. Brixton Prison was my destination that's where I'd be held until I finished giving my evidence.

Healy's case was my first time inside the Old Bailey. It was a scene like nothing I'd ever experienced before: it felt as though a small piece of Glasgow had taken over a section of the notorious London court of law.

The courtroom resembled a miniature coliseum. Michael and his five co-defendants sat positioned on a specially constructed raised podium for the purposes of security. Dozens of uniformed police officers in hats and white shirts stood directly behind them with long batons in hand. Below the defendants sat a sea of black gowns and grey wigs, which made up the defence teams, Queen's Council, as well as all the legal eagles for the prosecution side. It really was a remarkable sight. Up in what looked like a huge balcony at a night out at the theatre, people in the public gallery sat glued to every detail of the trial, which went on for five weeks.

Just before I was called to give evidence the jury were asked to leave the courtroom so that the prospect of anonymity could be discussed in front of the trial judge, Lord Verney, a move orchestrated solely by Michael and his lawyers – not me! It also made sense for me not to have my name printed in the Scottish newspapers, so I felt comfortable going along with the proceedings.

Anything I could do to help Michael and his co-defendants wasn't a problem for me. After some legal arguments, which seemed more of a formality – and, bear in mind, big Healy was conducting his own defence – the trial judge ordered that after the jury were called back I would be referred to only as 'Mr A'. The 12 jury members were then asked to return.

The night before I was due to appear I remember the minister from Brixton Prison coming into my cell and leaving me a New Jerusalem Bible. Back then it was normal for men of the cloth to visit new inmates. I don't know what possessed me but I took the Bible with me the next day and walked right into the Old Bailey courtroom clutching it in my hand. I had prepared a section to read out in open court which related to friendship but as soon as I started to read Lord Verney stopped me right in my tracks. I must have been in the witness box for a whole afternoon session.

I did all I could to help in Healy's trial and, in the process, I had put myself through a lot of unnecessary aggravation and stress. I know at least big Healy and Micky Carroll appreciated it. In the end, it made no difference how many defence witnesses Michael called because the weight of evidence against him and his band of merry men was such that the jury found them all guilty. They received sentences totalling almost a hundred years.

I'll never forget walking past a line of Glaswegian detectives who had all been called to give evidence in the case. Ranging from serious crime squad, murder squad, you name it, they all stood staring at me as I swaggered on past them in my suit, shirt and silk tie with Bible in hand. They looked at me in disparagement; they probably thought I'd committed the ultimate act of blasphemy. I overheard one of them calling me an evil man as I walked past. I wondered if they would have done the same if they'd been in my shoes.

After spending another few days in Brixton prison I was then placed on the national draft heading back to the Scottish jail system. I arrived back in Peterhead lockdown unit about three weeks later and I was straight back to where I left off. At least I had been on a short jaunt and out of solitary for a few weeks.

There was to be more travelling ahead of me, this time on my own account. The Perth Prison hostage trial was approaching and so was the trial for the Pipe Rack pub raid in Shettleston. In the end I would receive an additional 18 months for the siege at

Perth, a great result considering the severity of what I'd done. The formidable Donald Findlay represented me in that case and I believe he helped me get a reduced sentence. He managed to get me a deal I couldn't refuse, namely, if I pled guilty I would receive just 18 months. At the last minute I had changed my mind from pleading not guilty using a special defence of temporary insanity, as I was determined to take the case to trial.

Before someone can use such a defence they first have to produce a written report from a psychologist/psychiatrist who will testify to that end. I spoke with a senior lecturer in psychology from Stirling University for well over six hours, and although he identified ten very important factors he felt contributed to my state of mind in the hours leading up to the hostage incident, it didn't amount to me being temporarily insane. Terry O'Neil, the prison guard I held captive, told the truth and never at all twisted his evidence to put me in a bad light. This helped in terms of the leniency of the sentence, there's no doubt about it. There was also all the evidence relating to the circumstances before, during and after the siege. I was the one who had been seriously assaulted, locked up next door to my attacker and left without a pillow. Then there was consideration of the way in which the governor had handled the matter. All these things went in my favour.

On 3 September 1993 at the High Court in Glasgow, Lord Kirkwood sentenced me to a further six years for the Pipe Rack robbery, to run consecutively with the original sentence of six years for my part in the Group 4 security hold-up in Rutherglen. That took my total sentence to 14 years, with the 18 months for the Perth hostage incident and the six months I received for escaping from Dungavel.

This was a hard pill to swallow, but the way I saw it, my best years were still ahead of me, so I wasn't going to let these extra sentences get me down. My release date was a long way off, so all I could do now was concentrate on my present incarceration in Peterhead's lockdown facility. Eighteen months later I got the break I'd been waiting for, but long before then I had a devastating piece of family news.

Chapter Nineteen

Vincent Manson

My uncle Billy showed up right out of the blue. Billy hadn't been to see me since my arrival at Peterhead, and suddenly there he was.

I accepted only two visits during the 18 months I spent in the lockdown unit; that was my choice. One was from the Shannon brothers; the other was from my uncle Billy. I never had a strong appetite for visits, as they invariably messed with my mind and, frankly, I just couldn't handle it. I seemed to get through my time much easier without them. So on this rare occasion, the guards in their full riot gear escorted me, handcuffed, across to the visiting area. Apart from half a dozen cameras, Billy and I had the visiting room to ourselves for a whole 45 minutes. After greeting each other with an affectionate hug, I could tell that all was not as it should be.

'Sit down, son, I've got some really bad news to tell you,' Billy said to me.

'It's Vinnie, son . . . he's been shot through the neck trying to rob a jeweller down in Hertfordshire somewhere, and it's very serious.'

I just looked at him. I'm sure he could see the pain in my eyes just as I could see the pain in his. I couldn't believe what he was telling me about my uncle, the man who had inspired me to try and break his own world record for parallel bar dips when I had been in Perth Prison.

'I've already been down to see Vinnie, and he can't speak or move. He can't do anything. He's just lying there in a coma and he's on a life-support machine . . . We're debating whether or not to turn it off. When I got to the hospital, there were armed police with machine guns outside his room and outside the hospital. The doctors have said that his neck injury is so severe that it will definitely leave him brain-dead, like a cabbage . . . He's finished, son.'

'Are the Mansons never going to have any luck?' It was all I could think of saying. I couldn't help but feel anger, revulsion even, towards whoever had shot Vinnie, but that was just a gut reaction. I now take a completely different view, having established what actually transpired that night, and how the victim of the robbery turned the tables during an attempted tie-up and shot not only my uncle Vincent but also Vincent's fellow robber.

On Sunday evening, 25 May 1992, Vincent, along with two of his pals, drove some 50 miles along the M1 from Northampton in a stolen Ford Escort XR3i. Their mission that night was to carry out a prearranged tie-up and robbery at a luxury home in the Hertfordshire countryside. The target was a well-known jeweller and expert in firearms called Malcolm Hammond, who was 44 years old at that time and who lived with his wife, Elisabeth, in a secluded house in Rushden, near Baldock.

At the time Vincent had recently been released after serving a 25-year prison sentence for armed robbery. He had become pally with a con by the name of Fredrick Usher. During a stint in Albany prison they planned the raid in Hertfordshire after a fellow con provided them with details of Hammond's house safe, which contained cash, diamonds and other precious stones. Usher had finished his sentence a couple of months before Vincent, so the onus was on him to make sure the job was all ready when Vincent got out.

Like the hardened, old-school villain Vincent was, he was straight back into the thick of criminal activities as soon as his sentence was finished. He'd been out of the nick for just six weeks. He would have seen this bit of work as an opportunity to get himself back on his feet, and Vincent was putting all his trust in this Usher. There would have been no doubt in his mind that this was a relatively straightforward in-and-out job. The third accomplice, Douglas Bacon, sat parked in the stolen XR3i well away from the huge property and waited for Vincent and Usher to come back with their expected haul of cash and jewels.

With everyone in place, Vincent and Usher waited for the right moment to strike. Hammond had been out at a restaurant with his wife and some friends earlier in the evening and they didn't arrive back home until about 10 p.m. It was a hot summer's evening, so the Hammonds decided to open up their conservatory doors to let the cool breeze run through the house. Some 15 minutes later, Vincent and Usher, in dark clothes and balaclavas, walked in through the conservatory doors and confronted the Hammonds, who were both standing in the kitchen area at this point.

Wielding a single-barrelled sawn-off shotgun and a claw hammer, Vincent and his pal ordered Hammond and his wife upstairs and threatened to shoot their two pet dogs should they refuse to cooperate. They tied Mrs Hammond's hands and feet, made her lie down on top of her own bed and put a pillowcase over her head. What they didn't realise at the time was that Elisabeth Hammond was actually four months pregnant. While Mrs Hammond lay on the bed terrified out of her wits, Vincent and his pal forced her husband to reveal the combination to their safe. They then quickly emptied the contents of the safe into a bag before tying up Hammond and leaving him trussed up next to his missus.

At this point, Vincent and Usher made a fatal error. Instead of leaving the property and disappearing with the prize they now had in the bag, they continued rummaging through the Hammond household to make sure they hadn't overlooked anything else of value.

Most people subjected to this level of violence would have been too terrified to budge an inch just in case the robbers came back, but not Malcolm Hammond. While Vincent and his pal were roaming through the house, they had no idea that Hammond had somehow managed to wriggle free and that he was now about to turn the tables on them. The jeweller reached under his mattress and grabbed his powerful handgun, a .38 Smith & Wesson revolver he had concealed there as a safety precaution.

Having expertise in firing weapons, Hammond felt he now

had the upper hand and with no reservations whatsoever he went flat out to exercise his right in defending his wife and property. Just as Vincent and his pal were getting ready to leave the house, the incensed jeweller emerged from his bedroom, took aim and began firing. Two shots ripped into Vincent's neck and hand, disarming him instantly and forcing him to the floor.

While Vincent choked and gasped for breath, the jeweller took aim and fired off another volley of shots in the direction of Frederick Usher. One of the bullets found its target, hitting Usher in the back of the shoulder. The jeweller now proceeded to handcuff Usher with a set of cuffs he kept in the house. He had beaten the odds to turn the tables on two violent criminals who had come to rob him. Now he would be hailed a hero, or would he? With both Vincent and Usher immobilised, Mr Hammond went into the bedroom and untied his wife, and only then were the police called and an ambulance summoned to the scene.

By the time the medics arrived at the Hammond household my uncle Vinnie was in a poor state, unconscious and fighting for his life. The ambulance rushed him to the nearest hospital, but no oxygen or blood had reached his brain for six minutes. Paralysis was inevitable and in the end this would render most of his brain inoperative. Although Vincent may have understood some things, by and large he would remain almost completely brain dead until he died as a result of his terrible injuries eight years later on 18 March 2000, in Harrington Lodge nursing home in Kettering, Northamptonshire.

It is very sad to think what Vincent might have done had he gone straight. There's no question he was a super-talented man when it came to physical endurance, sports and weightlifting, in particular. In addition to his world records for the most parallel bar dips and press-ups on his fingertips, he also held the current world record for bench pressing his own body weight a staggering 940 times over a one-hour period. Vincent was only 56 years old when he died.

Frederick Usher recovered from his gunshot wounds but received ten years in jail for attempting to rob the Hammonds. The third man, Douglas Bacon, who waited in the stolen XR3i close by, received seven years for his part in the plot.

Malcolm Hammond always maintained that he wrestled the powerful handgun from Usher and then shot both robbers. However, Frederick Usher had a different story to tell, namely that when he and Vinnie had put their weapons away and were ready to leave, Hammond produced the .38 from under his mattress and shot them. During a separate hearing at Luton Crown Court, which started in February 1993, Mr Hammond stood trial charged with having a firearm with intent to commit an indictable offence and having a firearm when prohibited.

Mr Allan Maindes, prosecuting, told the jury that Hammond, who pleaded not guilty, had a firearms certificate which enabled him to possess several other guns, but he never had a certificate for the Smith & Wesson.

After a four-day trial the jury found Hammond guilty of all charges, disregarding his version of events in favour of Frederick Usher's account. Hammond was fined £2,100 and ordered to pay costs of £1,050. Just six months previously, Judge Rodwell had awarded Hammond £300 from public funds, saying: 'He showed great gallantry in tackling these dangerous men and protected his pregnant wife from further harm.'

Outside of court Mr Hammond is quoted as saying: 'I did what I had to do; it was a question of survival.'

Chapter Twenty

The 10-Man Unit

Life in the lockdown facility went on interminably until one day, completely unexpectedly, the guards came to my cell and asked me if I fancied going over to the new ten-man unit that had opened up within Peterhead Prison.

There was a whole bunch of guards standing right outside my cell door, which was lying wide open at this point, and they wanted an answer, fast. As they stood talking amongst themselves, giving me a minute or two to make up my mind, I thought to myself that anything would be better than staying locked up 23 hours a day in G-Hall, so I jumped at the chance of getting a break from the horrible place.

There had been no warning about this move, no assessment of any kind; it was a total surprise. At the time, it didn't make much sense, but nothing did in that soul-destroying environment. In due course, it would become clear why the prison authorities had kept the new unit a closely guarded secret for as long as possible. For now, I grabbed the few belongings I had, put them into my pillowcase, and went along to the arch to empty my plastic piss-pot.

A strange sight caught my attention as I stood rinsing out the piss-pot. I remember looking at my reflection in the wall mirror, where normally I had a quick shave. I could see how the lockdown had tired me out. I looked dishevelled and my complexion was an ugly grey colour due to the lack of natural light. Being restricted to a tiny cell for the biggest part of two years had definitely taken its toll on my appearance. This was the first time I had properly looked at myself without the feeling of having six sets of eyes peering at me through a large metal grille.

I couldn't help but notice that the guards now appeared helpful, as opposed to their usual impassive and aloof selves. Normally there was a barrier between us and very little communication, if any at all. That's just the way it was in that pitch, day in, day out. The guards then opened up Wullie 'Cad' Cadder's cell and asked him if he wanted to go as well to the new unit. Like me he jumped at the chance; like me he looked awful, but the opportunity of moving clearly raised his spirits no end.

Despite having both been in the same unit for so long, this was actually the first time that Cad and I had come face to face, and I remember the two of us standing in the archway emptying our piss-pots and looking at each other with disorientation written across our faces. It was quite an adrenaline-charged moment, as if our captors were finally releasing us. I can imagine how the likes of Terry Waite felt when his abductors released him after years in solitary confinement. When we were ready to go, a senior officer and a basic grade escorted the two of us to the reception area without handcuffs, but not before I said a last farewell to the cell I had been confined to for the past 18 months.

I went back and stood in the tiny space one last time, as if to try to disengage my spirit and energy from the cocoon that had housed it for so long. I stood shaking my head slowly from side to side, staring at the walls, at the cardboard table and chair, and I remember thinking to myself what a waste; it isn't right locking someone up in those conditions for that length of time. Then I thought about the next prisoner who would be moving into the cell and what mental battles he would have to go through to maintain any level of sanity. Then I heard the sound of the screw's voice: 'Hurry up, Willie, we have to go.'

Cad and I were now standing in the reception area and I couldn't help but think I was getting shanghai-ed to a different jail. This was usually the case when you found yourself being whisked off to reception unexpectedly. But my mind was put at ease as soon as all of my property was handed to me, including my mountain bike and my rowing machine. These two items were part of the property seized from my flat in Earls Court, so they followed me about everywhere I went. Although I couldn't use them – well, not yet anyway – I was told I could take a pair of jeans, a few pairs of socks, this, that and the next thing from the pile of clobber sitting on top of the desk. It was an unbelievable feeling, a relatively small piece of compassion that cost nothing, but to me made all the difference. The screws even offered Cad and me a cup of tea or coffee while we waited!

After this pleasant interlude in reception the same two guards escorted Cad and me over to the purpose-built ten-man unit that was aimed at providing a stepping stone out of the lock-down unit in G-Hall. It was a sort of halfway house, where you had to spend at least six weeks before you were eligible for a move on to a different part of the prison system. Where I might go from here largely depended on which prison governor in the Scottish Prison System was prepared to accept me. I was now seen as a hostage-taker, someone who was unpredictable, and I knew there weren't many governors who would fancy me going to their prison.

The guards asked us if we wanted to watch a bit of telly. 'Do what you want, guys. Chill out and relax,' they told us.

This was going to take a bit of getting used to. I mean, it was like going from one extreme to another, and I was already noticing that I was sweating a bit more than usual and was feeling rather agitated. I put this down to being out in wide-open spaces again after being kept in such a closed environment for so long. I knew I would have to readapt to normality, and that wasn't going to happen overnight. The prison system had taken its pound of flesh. It had made its point; now it was time for it to repair the damage. For the time being, no more prisoners would be joining us in the unit. The guards weren't prepared to take any chances, so it was just big Cad and me for now – and this was just as much a psychological challenge for the guards as it was for us. To be fair, the screws must have felt bare without their protective riot gear, and the trust between us wasn't exactly flowing in abundance. I had my full privileges back as an inmate in the ten-man unit and it felt great. It was as if time had stood still for the duration of the lockdown, but now I was up and running and totally switched on again.

Over the next couple of weeks, the guards and us two

prisoners would become guinea pigs for the system. There was a small television room with some plastic chairs. There was a shower and a bath. That was about it, really. The place looked very basic, and that tang of fresh paint was lingering in the air.

The reason why the prison management had kept the opening of the new unit so low-key was that they had tried opening up the same unit in the past, long before my time, but on each occasion it had been a complete and utter failure. Prisoners, especially violent and aggressive ones serving long-term sentences, always have a tendency to spoil things for themselves. I've seen it umpteen times throughout my time in jail. Cad told me a story about how some prisoners from the lockdown in G-Hall had beaten up the screws with barbells and other weightlifting equipment and smashed up the unit on a previous attempt at opening up the place. It started with a disturbance over poor living conditions, but there would also have been an element of bitterness and built-up aggression because of years of lockdown. That part I could relate to, and it would have been hard not to get involved if I had been there.

With that level of violence, it's understandable why the Peterhead management would feel extremely cautious about opening the unit up again. But pressure from the Home Office meant the management had to at least *appear* to be doing something constructive with the prisoners held on 23-hour lockdown. Despite my record, I posed fewer problems than some of the other inmates, as did Cad, and this was the reason why we had been selected for the unit's re-opening. I wanted away from Peterhead as soon as possible, so I was keeping my nose clean.

The six weeks I spent in the ten-man unit flew past. After a lot of discussion, compromise and meetings with prison governors and suchlike, everyone concerned with my case felt the only feasible move forward for me was a transfer to the Special Unit (SSU) in Shotts Prison in Lanarkshire, and the SSU management travelled all the way up to Peterhead to interviewed me, with the prospect of going there. The prisoners who currently lived in the Special Unit at Shotts would also first have to agree to it, and if, for some reason, there were objections, that would prevent me from going: no ifs or buts, that would be the way it was.

There was only one prisoner in SSU I didn't get on with, a crackpot by the name of Jim McLeod from the Yoker area of Glasgow, but I kept my mouth shut when the governor read me a list of names and asked me if I had any problems with any of the prisoners already in the unit. McLeod and I had never seen eye to eye, and this was purely down to a clash of personalities, which had been intensified under lockdown conditions in Peterhead. McLeod was a prolific stabber. He was serving a life sentence for stabbing his friend to death over a fur coat that went missing from a turn they had done together. This earned him the nickname 'Jimmy Fur Coat'. The story went that he and his pal had turned over a place for loads of expensive fur coats and when he discovered they were one short he immediately suspected his pal had taken it for his girlfriend. When McLeod went to his pal's house to challenge him about this, his pal pulled out a shotgun from a holdall and tried to shoot him. Luckily for Jimmy the gun jammed. His friend wasn't so fortunate, as McLeod pulled out a knife and in a frenzied attack stabbed his mate to death.

Then, during his life sentence in Perth Prison, McLeod stabbed a fellow prisoner – a quiet and harmless man – in a similarly frenzied attack in front of the whole hall. This was why the prison authorities deemed McLeod a danger to other inmates, and why he was in the SSU.

I finally received the news that I had been waiting for. The SSU had accepted me and had given me a place within their community. I was delighted because options weren't exactly coming at me in droves, and besides, the Special Unit's ethos and policy stated that new admissions would be encouraged to start a project of their choice. And the best bit was that the prison department would pay for it!

Shotts Prison sits in the countryside south of the M8 motorway near the town of the same name. It was built in 1978 with a capacity to house approximately 528 inmates. The Special Unit there was created in 1990 because of the success of the Barlinnie Special Unit whose first admissions had arrived back in the 70s.

By the time I arrived at Shotts the unit had been going strong for almost four years and during that time it had shown a lot of success.

The unit was unlike any other mainstream part of the prison system in the sense that you could have private visits from family and friends inside your cell. You could also keep potentially offensive weapons in your cell such as tools, scissors and knives.

It was more like a miniature sports complex with workshops than a prison establishment. It boasted a full-size tennis court, and there was a five-a-side Astroturf football pitch with mobile floodlights for the darker nights. There was also a multi-gym, punch bag and weightlifting equipment. I even had access to my bike and rowing machine, not that I used them much. The doors stayed open all the time, which meant you could wander about the unit's grounds whenever it took your fancy. Just before the guards and unit management went off home for the night you were expected to go back into your cell, and that was the only time you were locked up, with the exception of the duration of the weekly staff management meeting.

A lot of thought had gone into the grounds. Beautiful flowers, nice grass verges, sheds and walkways were a common sight outside. Indoors was just as impressive. Everything hugged the 'concourse' inside the unit. The concourse itself was an open-plan living space that was hugely spacious, with ten cells spread right across the far end wall. Ten cells was the maximum capacity, but I don't think they had ever been that full, certainly not during my stay. On the concourse, there was a full-length snooker table, table-tennis table, and a room where you could play chess and other board games. In addition, there were about a dozen comfy chairs positioned in a circle and they were used mainly for group meetings that anyone in the unit could call at any time.

Once a week everyone in the unit was obligated to sit down and discuss their progress, their projects, and anything else that living in the unit might throw up. This was a constructive way of venting your feelings, as opposed to keeping things bottled up. It was all about being able to express yourself in a positive manner, although not everyone was actually capable of playing the game according to the rules. A prison psychologist would always sit in on these weekly meetings, taking notes as we went along. If someone had a grievance about something, it didn't matter if it was a prison guard, prisoner or even someone from the management side, we all had the same right to call what was called a 'special meeting'. If someone called a special meeting, then everyone in the unit had to stop what they were doing and head straight to the concourse. Sometimes it was embarrassing having to sit through one of these meetings that had been called for the most trivial of matters, but you had to attend no matter what.

Once a week a couple of women would come into the unit just to make everyone, guards and governors included, a lovely home-cooked meal – it was always a proper three-course extravaganza. We also had visits from other people from outside the prison, known as 'unit friends', including some members of the Salvation Army, who would come in to chat freely with us about anything and everything. I got speaking to one of them, a man called Jimmy McIver, after I discovered how he had helped a prisoner in Saughton jail in Edinburgh trace a long-lost relative. I had always been curious about what had become of my father, David Lobban, so Jimmy offered to find out what he could. I was really thrilled about the possibility of finding out more about my dad and perhaps even meeting him one day.

The visiting area was huge. Instead of sitting at tables and chairs, you sat with your visitors in what looked more like the alcoves you would find in a pub lounge. These bay areas offered adequate privacy, and there was no time limit on how long your visitors could stay. Despite the rules stating that you could show your visitors the inside of your cell on their first visit, I lost count of the times I sat with my visitors in my cell with the door closed. No one seemed to mind, or perhaps the guards just turned a blind eye.

On arrival in the unit, you got an allowance for wallpaper, paint and a choice of wood so that you could make your own built-in furniture. The cell would be an empty shell to begin with, and the idea was that you could decorate to your own standard and taste. Personally, I didn't bother with the wallpaper but I chose a black ash wood for my furniture and it was delivered to the unit in two full-length sheets the following day, just as if it were your home address. An inmate in the unit by the name of Christopher 'Crazy Chris' Howarth was a joiner by trade, so the unit employed him to make furniture for every new arrival. He was serving a 25-year sentence for being involved when the UK's largest seizure of pure Colombian cocaine – half a ton, to be exact – was made. When he sorted my cell, I ended up with a complete set of wall cabinets, sideboards, a desk and even a base for my single mattress.

As for a personal project, that was entirely up to the individual. For instance, one prisoner had a stained-glass project that involved him having his own workshop and plenty of materials to make whatever he wanted. He was Danny Graham and some of the stuff he made was very attractive indeed. If your project meant that you might be able to find an outlet to sell your products, then the unit would support that, split the profits with you, and the cost of the materials would be deducted from whatever yield you made. This served not only as a financial incentive, it also gave you the opportunity to explore your business skills and to build up a network of contacts in a particular field.

When the unit management asked me what sort of project I wanted to do, I told them that I had always fancied breeding tropical fish but had never had the chance to do it. No problem, they said, and I received an allowance to order fish tanks, equipment and tropical fish for breeding. It took me a few weeks to get the project properly up and running, but when I did I had no fewer than six four-foot tanks and a couple of six-footers as well. I had a storeroom converted into a multiple aquarium, which really looked the part when you went in for some peace and quiet with the lights out. I even had a six-foot fish tank in my cell built into the black ash wood furniture, and I put another large tank in the visiting area to brighten up the place.

When I was in the unit, I had a burning desire to study astrology – not the typical cowboy newspaper column astrology but the ancient science that has been studied throughout the world for thousands of years. As soon as the unit management were satisfied that I had a sound interest in the subject, they paid for my enrolment fees in the Mayo School of Astrology based in Cornwall. I was given a correspondence course and I collaborated with the principal of the school, Jackie Hudson.

Between my tropical fish project and the astrology correspondence course I managed to keep my time in the unit as positive and constructive as I possibly could.

There's no doubt about it, the Special Unit at Shotts was something else. As soon as you found your niche and got yourself into a daily routine, it was all plain sailing.

On my first day in the unit, I remember thinking to myself that I would have to keep an eye on Jim McLeod, the one person I knew before arriving at Shotts who might be a problem. After all, he had been there a full six months before me, which meant he had the full run of the place, and this was the first time we were going to meet since our time together in Peterhead. I knew he would have poisoned the heads of anyone he could in the unit, bad-mouthing me to whoever would listen to him, but that was to be expected.

I knew I could handle McLeod, so it didn't bother me facing him for the first time. I just had to make sure I wasn't too carried away with myself on the big reunion. I wanted to get off on the right footing, make a good impression and take advantage of all the good stuff the Special Unit had to offer. It came as no surprise to me that he was the very first unit prisoner I saw. I got the impression he had been waiting for me to arrive, and he would have known that I could appear at any moment.

McLeod was standing behind the only locked grille gate in the place, which led in to the main part of the unit. He was holding a champagne glass with some sort of bubbly, non-alcoholic white wine in it. With a big cheesy smile, he approached the grille gate, stuck his spare hand through the bars to offer me a handshake and said: 'All right, Wullie boy, how you doing, mate? Welcome to the unit.'

Impulsively I shook his hand and replied with similarly good-natured remarks. On the other side of this grille gate lay a seventh heaven that could lead to much better things – but only if I played the game and kept my nose clean. Despite his seemingly warm welcome I had an uncanny feeling that I was going to have big problems with McLeod, and my instincts were to be proved right.

While I was in the SSU, I received a visit from my uncle Billy; it was early 1994 and it was the first time I'd seen him since our last meeting at Peterhead the previous year. Billy would come to visit me from time to time to fill me in on what was happening in Glasgow, but on this particular visit he dropped a bombshell. He told me he'd shot and killed a man by the name of Paul Hamilton. I knew all about this as it had been broadcast on the news that Hamilton had been killed at the wheel of his Daimler in November 1993. At that moment it suddenly dawned on me that after the murder of young Arthur Thompson I might well have been in far more danger than I could ever have thought at the time.

Billy never knew that I had hooked up with Paul Ferris soon after I bolted from Dungavel semi-open nick. Obviously, due to being on the run I didn't want to advertise my whereabouts, even to my own extended family, and I was of course also known at that point to many as Gary, in order not to draw attention to my real identity.

Similarly, I didn't know at that time that Billy and Ferris's sworn enemy, Arthur Thompson, were still very close or that Billy was working with him. In fact throughout the time Billy and Thompson knew each other they stayed fiercely loyal, and even when Billy was serving his 15-year prison sentence for the alleged armed robbery on a bingo hall, Thompson stayed in touch with him, making sure he wanted for nothing and even going to visit him occasionally. I also discovered later that when Billy came out of jail in 1989, half the man he had been, he again teamed up with his old pal Thompson, and actually moved into old Arthur's huge property in Provanmill, the Ponderosa. This is how the old school operated; they looked after each other in times of need.

Life can be extremely puzzling and bizarre at times, and it sends shivers down my spine to think that due to my Ferris connection I might well have suffered the same fate as Paul

Hamilton, at the hands of my own uncle, during the bloody Thompson/Ferris vendetta. At the time of Thompson Junior's murder, Billy and I hadn't seen each other since I was a kid living with my grandparents and we would've walked past each other in the street. It was a profound and unnerving state of affairs. Being close to Ferris I'd put myself in the firing line, and it could have cost me my life.

What I have to say about the Paul Hamilton murder will come as a complete shock to a lot of people, especially to Hamilton's family, who for years have believed he was killed by Paul Ferris. This is not so.

Paul Hamilton was a defence witness for Ferris in 1992 when he stood trial for the killing of Arthur Thompson Junior. On that occasion, Hamilton gave Ferris an alibi, but in doing so he upset old Arthur, who was still grieving the death of his son.

Hamilton was also providing Ferris and Tam McGraw with valuable information about what was going on in the Thompson camp, collecting information from Thompson's outfit and then passing it on to their rivals. But Ferris and McGraw showed him no loyalty – they weren't bothered about Hamilton's welfare or what would happen to him should the other side find out what he was up to. As far as they were concerned they had everything under control, and Hamilton was expendable.

Before his own death in March 1993, old Arthur Thompson decided Paul Hamilton had to go, and my uncle Billy took on the hit. But coincidentally, just an hour before Hamilton lost his life, Ferris had called his house and spoken with his wife. In a *Sunday Mail* article from December 2012 she was quoted as saying: 'When Ferris came on the phone, he was chatty and normal. He told me he had some money he owed my husband, and I knew he was in danger that night. I don't know why I thought that, I just did.'

When Hamilton's wife told the police about the phone call from Ferris, they went and picked him up for questioning. Ferris's account of what happened is that the murder squad did indeed question him (and a nephew of Bobby Glover's) and although Ferris was released six hours later, the police charged Glover's nephew with Hamilton's murder.

Ferris went on to say in *The Ferris Conspiracy* that the Procurator Fiscal subsequently dropped the charge against Glover's nephew because of a lack of evidence. However, in the same *Sunday Mail* piece, Glover's nephew stated, when asked if he had actually been questioned over Hamilton's murder, that he hadn't been, and that Ferris's version of events was inaccurate.

Whatever the truth, it is clear to me that Ferris exploited Hamilton's murder for his own cynical ends – to beef up his own tough man image by refusing to say categorically that he had nothing to do with Hamilton's death and no doubt to bolster sales of his books. And of course he doesn't have to worry about this as the police dropped charges. What's worse, Ferris chose to muddy the waters further by suggesting also that Hamilton lost his life because he had boasted too loudly about his involvement in Bobby Glover's and Joe Hanlon's deaths: a load of rubbish. According to Ferris, Hamilton said he drove about Glasgow's East End with their corpses in the back of his blue van. Ruthless, isn't it? I hope that at least the Hamilton family can find some sort of closure from what I'm making public. I am only mentioning this because my uncle is now dead and because I feel it is the right thing to do.

Despite everything starting off so well at Shotts, it wasn't long before storm clouds appeared on the horizon. Every morning at 6.30 I would nip outside for a jog around the unit grounds. It was a great way to start the day. That was, until some inmates who had formed a unit clique started complaining that I made far too much noise because of the way my training shoes were pounding off the concrete slabs outside the cell windows. This was just one example of the pettiness coming from some of Scotland's so-called most dangerous prisoners, and it got worse.

Every Wednesday at 1 p.m. on the dot, the unit management and staff would sit down for their weekly conference. This meeting was a very important part of the unit's strategy, as it helped to bring everyone up to date with any concerns connected to the running of the place. The unit management got the chance to talk freely without having to worry about prisoners being about. The weekly meetings only lasted for an hour. Staff from both shifts would usually attend these meetings, including the hands-on guards, the governors and sometimes a higher-level authority from the Scottish Prison Service. It gave the unit staff an opportunity to talk openly about any potential problems that the prisoners had security within the unit would always have been near the top of the agenda.

I had often thought about breaching unit security by eavesdropping on the Wednesday meetings, so I came up with an unpretentious but very effective technique of doing just that. On my request, one of my visitors successfully smuggled a Dictaphone in to me during a visit, and once I had this simple piece of equipment I came up with a nifty plan. I knew I would be taking a massive gamble, risking everything and putting my neck on the chopping block, but despite all of that I was determined to go ahead. Minutes, possibly seconds, before the guards started locking the cell doors, I sneaked back into the visiting area where the meeting was due to take place. Then, with a little help from a piece of duck-tape, I managed to stick the Dictaphone underneath one of the tables. I pressed play and record and rushed back to my cell. It was as simple as that.

Now the success of my plan was out of my hands. I didn't know if, for instance, the visiting area would be searched for such devices. The first time I pulled off this plan, I sat in my cell for a nail-biting 60 minutes wondering what would happen if they found my little tape recorder. When the guards came back and opened up the cell doors, I knew immediately that they hadn't twigged, so I made my way back to the visiting area in order to retrieve my Dictaphone.

To my sheer exhilarated delight, I bent down and collected the tiny piece of equipment from beneath the table, stuck it in my pocket and made my way outside for a walk around the unit grounds. I took along some headphones and I began rewinding the small cassette with anticipation, sporadically pressing play and having a listen just to make sure I heard talking all the way through. After I hit the play button, for the next hour I engrossed myself with a heart-pounding array of unprecedented and unique material. I had breached Shotts Special Unit security – and not another soul knew about it apart from me.

Surprisingly enough, my name wasn't mentioned on the miniature cassette tape the first time I tuned in, but then again I wasn't exactly giving the staff much cause for concern. The governor was more concerned about the unit clique, and he spoke freely about the drug problem that had gripped the place, indicating that perhaps it was about time they arranged a dawn swoop with sniffer dogs and a team of riot-squad officers. The drug problem didn't affect me since I was never one for taking them, but it was definitely an issue in the unit, and the governor clearly intended to deal with it.

Now that I had started eavesdropping on the unit's meetings I knew that come the following week I would be itching to do it all over again. The mere thought of being able to listen in to what the staff were saying, as well as being able to build an understanding of how these weekly meetings ticked, proved too much of a temptation. The next week I carried out my nifty plan, and again everything went like clockwork. This went on for a few weeks, and all that time no one knew a thing about it apart from me.

On either the fourth or the fifth week it became clear from the conversations I had been listening to that the management had come to an agreement on conducting a full search of the unit, with special attention going to two specific prisoners who they felt were responsible for bringing drugs into the unit. They appeared to have been somewhat hesitant about the crackdown at first, but now they were turning up the heat on the druggies, and it got to the stage where the sniffer dogs were about to come storming in.

Faced with a dilemma, I had to decide if it was in my interest to alert the prisoners in question. It was a tricky one, but I had to make up my mind fast. In terms of solidarity, I knew there was only one option open to me – that I should mark those prisoners' cards and warn them as to the danger that awaited them. On the other side of the coin, there was no solidarity among the prisoners in the unit, and I knew that sharing the information would most definitely land me in hot water should the unit management find out I had been taping them for weeks. I still believed in the criminal code, the done thing, so I felt a strong compulsion to warm my fellow inmates. But before doing anything, I decided to seek some advice. I approached Chris Howarth, whose cell was next to mine. Chris was the quietest man in the unit and probably one of the most sensible and level-headed. I set the Dictaphone before him and wound through to the bit where the governor was going on about bringing in the sniffer dogs.

'All right, Chris,' I said. 'I want you to do me a favour. Can you put on these headphones and have a listen to that?'

I handed Chris the equipment, stood back and waited for his reaction. Immediately he raised his eyebrows, and his eyes widened at what he obviously thought was exciting stuff.

'Is that what I think it is?' he asked me, looking a bit panic-stricken.

'Yes, Chris, just keep on listening. I want your take on this. I want to know what you think I should do.'

He continued listening to the tapes for a few minutes more, until he got the full gist of what was going on.

'That's heavy stuff, man. What are you going to do?' he asked.

'Well, that's exactly what I was about to ask you ... What would *you* do?'

'I don't know, mate. It's really up to yourself,' came his reply.

I'd put Chris in an awkward situation, and it was obvious he didn't want to commit himself to anything. But I wanted an answer.

'Come on, Chris, what do you think I should do? Should I mark their cards or what?'

'Well, it would be a bit out of order if they got caught with something and you hadn't marked their cards ... but there again, it's your thing and the ball is in your court. It's entirely up to you, mate.'

I'd heard all I wanted to hear and, based on this, I asked Chris's permission to call one of the prisoners named on the recording into his cell so that I could tell him what was happening.

'Yeah, that's cool. Shout him in,' Chris said unashamedly.

Now the cat was out the bag and I felt a weight lift off my shoulders, but then again my inner voice was screaming at me that I was making a big mistake.

I shouted Jimmy 'Fur Coat' McLeod into Chris's cell and

told him exactly what had been happening, that his name had been mentioned in meetings for weeks now, and the only thing I expected in return was that he kept it to himself. This wasn't a lot to ask for, and he should have been grateful for the information. I know I didn't really have much time for McLeod but this wasn't a personal matter. I felt I had done my bit for the prisoners by making them aware of what the authorities were planning. I suppose by doing this I'd hoped to tighten things up in the unit.

There was one other prisoner whose name had also been mentioned in the recordings – the little pest Rab Raiker from Edinburgh – but I reckoned that telling him wasn't my job. I discussed this with McLeod and he assured me he would deal with it and that everything would be all right.

A couple of hours passed, and I was sitting in the concourse reading a newspaper when I saw Raiker run up to the principal officer, who was standing not far from where I was sitting, and scream at him at the top of his voice:

'What's all this about you bringing in the sniffer dogs to search my cell? And don't fucking deny it because I've got it all on tape.'

Astonished, I dropped the newspaper to my knees and turned to watch the barrage of abuse from Raiker. The PO was looking at him as if to say, 'How the hell did you find that out?', his face turning bright red as Raiker raved on.

Now just about everyone in the unit had stopped whatever it was they were doing to tune in to the unfolding drama. This was the mentality of Raiker and, frankly, McLeod was just as bad for not keeping the little pain in the neck on the lead. What was Raiker thinking? That's the thanks I got for marking their cards. This flare-up of Raiker's had, almost immediately, created a divide within the unit.

Now the staff were alert to the fact someone had been recording them. There was no other explanation for what Raiker had blabbed. I slept on it overnight and the following day I approached the same PO and asked him for a word. I thought I should nip it in the bud before it got way out of control.

'It's all my doing,' I told him and I went on to explain that it was me who had taped the weekly meeting, but I said that I had only done it the once. I handed him the Dictaphone – minus the cassette – and apologised, saying it wouldn't happen again and that it had been a foolish thing to do; I didn't know what I was thinking when I did it.

I was hoping that the unit management would treat the situation with leniency since I had handed them the Dictaphone and come clean, so I played it down and made out it was more of a prank than anything else. If I had just ignored the situation as if I didn't know what was going, on then there's no telling what would have happened. At least by taking this stance I still had some control of the situation. I left it with the PO and he assured me my place in the unit would not be under threat, even though I'd embarrassed them severely.

This was the Special Unit and I forgot it was all about helping prisoners stay on the straight and narrow. I felt that I had just got myself out of a sticky situation and I was lucky. As for relations between McLeod, Raiker and me ... if things were bad before, they were about to get worse.

Chapter Twenty-One

The Special Unit and the Silent Cell

Weeks went by, and for me, the unit had lost its appeal. In prison, half the battle is getting on with your neighbours, especially in an environment like the Special Unit. You *must* get on with your peers for the sake of keeping the ship afloat, but these waters had become so stormy now that the ship was about to capsize. I chose to keep a low profile, to get back to my astrology correspondence course, as well as looking after my tropical fish.

The mind games had started. I went into the storeroom one day only to find a tank full of baby cichlids floating upside down on the surface. Someone had put disinfectant into the water. I felt as though I was involved in some sort of psychological warfare. I tried my best to hold it together, but I'm a brooder and I felt that these idiots had gone a bit too far. I'd never liked McLeod and he had never liked me. Now the tension between us was at fever pitch. Things had been gradually going downhill and it got so bad that at one point I started carrying a 12-inch chisel around with me just to be on the safe side. This wasn't what the unit was all about and I could feel myself on the verge of exploding.

I was in the gym one day doing a workout on the punch bag when Pot Duncan, a lifer from Aberdeen, came in and said that McLeod had called a special meeting. Dripping in sweat and still in my shorts, I stopped what I was doing, removed my boxing mitts and slowly made my way round to the concourse.

Everyone was bound to attend these special meetings whenever someone called one. I was the last person to sit down that day and I could sense immediately that McLeod was going to come out with something directed at me. Sure enough, it turned out that McLeod had called the meeting to complain about eggs going missing from the fridge. Here was Scotland's so-called 'toughest' complaining about eggs, but it was all designed to have a go at me.

The way the unit got its breakfast delivered in the morning was different from the way the main part of the jail got its delivery. The cookhouse would send over a metal tray with the unit prisoners' breakfasts in it uncooked and it was then up to the prisoners to cook their own breakfast in their own time. One morning it might be bacon, another morning sausage, and then of course there were the mornings when it would be eggs. The unit clique normally stayed in their beds, which meant they could get their breakfast whenever they got up. However, most of the time no one bothered and these eggs would begin piling up. That's where I came in.

I was training hard in the gym and so any spare eggs I saw in the fridge I would swallow for the extra protein content. I'm talking about eggs that had been sitting uneaten for days. This is what McLeod was really complaining about. It was pathetic and clearly McLeod had called this meeting to embarrass me. I stood up and said to him: 'Hey, Jim ... OK, you've made your point. I'll tell you what: I'll buy a couple of dozen eggs on a special canteen order and I'll hand them to you personally. How's that?' I then walked off, raging, back to my workout in the gym.

I put the boxing mitts on and began battering the punch bag as if my life depended on it. The meeting on the concourse was finished as far as I was concerned I wasn't prepared to sit and listen to much more of that drivel. I worked myself up to such a heightened state that the next thing I knew I had blown my top. I slung off the mitts and stormed out of the gym like a raging bull. I'd had enough.

Everyone had since scattered from the meeting and I knew McLeod would be sitting in the cell belonging to Eddie Burke, a double lifer. I barged in uninvited and there was McLeod, sitting on the edge of the bed along with Raiker, Pot Duncan, Andy Walker (an ex-soldier who had murdered three comrades) and Eddie Burke.

'Here, Jim, me and you around the back of the unit for a square-go. Come on,' I said to McLeod through a load of bodies who had stood up to prevent me going further into the cell.

Instead of taking me on and dealing with it man-to-man, he threw a teacup at me that bounced off the side of my forehead, cutting me slightly just above the left eye. Pot Duncan and Andy Walker stood in front of McLeod as if to keep us apart, but I wasn't impressed at all. There were six of us cramped into that tiny cell, five lifers and myself, and there was a right commotion going on.

'You're a coward, Jim, a dirty coward,' I shouted at him above all the yelling, before leaving the cell and making my way back to my own to arm myself for what might be round two. Now the guards knew what was happening.

I stuck the chisel I had in my cell down the waistband of my shorts and waited, prepared, in the concourse for what the next move would be. You could've heard a pin drop, it was that quiet. The guards' faces and body language showed that they were worried about a potential bloodbath.

There was no movement from Burke's cell, although I knew the five of them were still in there. There's no doubt I'd made McLeod look a right dummy and shown him up for the coward he really was. He'd been as well chucking the cup at me during the special meeting because it had drawn just as much attention. Now we had a situation where everyone was waiting to see what would happen next.

It was a classic Mexican stand-off and probably the worst one I'd been faced with. I felt so extremely aggravated that if McLeod had shown his face then, I'm sure there would've been a murder. Thankfully he stayed out of my sight. Pot Duncan was the first to approach me by gesticulating that he wanted a word in my cell.

'Try and cool down a bit,' he said to me in a troubled voice.

'Cool down! You must be kidding! I went into Eddie Burke's cell to ask that clown for a square-go and you were there, you witnessed what the coward did. It's pointless now because he's brought it all on top. That's like fly grassing and you know it.'

'I know, I know, but you've got to calm down otherwise you'll end up getting kicked out of the unit, and you don't want that, do you?'

He was right about that. I didn't want to get kicked out, but my feelings were running high and who knew what was round the corner. I just had to wait and find out which way the wind would blow. I didn't want to be seen as the aggressor in this case because the unit management wouldn't have taken too kindly to that. I was still trying to recover from the taping incident.

'Tell that mug I'll fight him with blades, with my fists, whichever way he wants. I've nothing to prove to that dope. I know exactly what he's all about. I've already offered him outside and he knows where I am. Tell him that, will you?'

McLeod's cell was right next door to mine so in order to get to his own cell he first had to pass mine. This was the perfect opportunity for him to have another go if he so desired. If he fancied going for round two, then he knew where I was, but come lock-up time he was nowhere in sight. As far as I was concerned, he was the one who'd lost face because all those lifers saw what happened, they were in the cell and heard everything. McLeod knew I would've battered him all over the place and that's why he threw the teacup.

The evening ended without further bloodshed, but that didn't mean to say it was over between me and McLeod. Far from it; it was now a case of whoever got to the other first, and I wasn't prepared to let the coward stick a knife in me when my back was turned.

Then I remembered Rafferty coshing me on the head with the cobbler's last in Perth Prison because I foolishly took my eye off the ball and didn't get him first. There wasn't going to be a repeat of that incident. No way: I had learnt my lesson the hard way. I convinced myself that the only way I could ensure my own safety, and make sure it wasn't me receiving the second prize, was for me to do him first. I'm sure McLeod would've been thinking the exact same thing.

All that night I stayed awake, psyching myself up for when my cell door opened up first thing in the morning, and pacing up and down the floor with the 12-inch chisel in my hand. I thought about my course work, my tropical fish project . . . it had all been going so well for me, yet here I was on the verge of throwing it right down the toilet pan.

It's fair to say I had lost all sense or self-control at this point. All I thought about was heading straight into McLeod's cell as soon as my own cell door opened. I recall stretching my body and limbs, which I hoped would reduce the chances of my bones cracking as I entered, but the likelihood was that he'd be up and ready just like me.

I watched the time carefully, hour after hour passing until 5 a.m., when I heard some movement outside my door. 'That can't be right,' I said to myself. The staff didn't usually start their shift until six. What was happening here? Did I just hear something or was I imagining it? Wearing only a pair of shorts and still holding the chisel I went up to my cell door and put my ear to the space around the door frame. I could hear footsteps, many footsteps. There was something going on outside the cell door. I threw the chisel beneath my desk and stood back from the door. Then the spy-hole flew open and a guard shouted through: 'Right, Lobban! Stand back at the end of the cell where I can see you. We're here to take you to the segregation unit.'

I knew this familiar instruction; I had heard it a thousand times before. It was riot-squad officers, about a dozen of them, dressed from head to toe in full riot gear, helmets, shields, the lot. They'd turned up to remove me from the unit. It was useless arguing with them because they would've simply jumped on me and physically carted me away.

Despite wanting to get at McLeod, I felt a huge weight lift from my shoulders, knowing I could relax a bit from that point on. I'd been so worked up and ready to go into McLeod's cell that I suddenly realised just how close I'd come to the ultimate bloodbath. The unit management had obviously taken the view that it was in the unit's best interests to get rid of me, so I ended up being the fall guy on this occasion.

Looking back, it probably was for the best, because there's no doubt in my mind that there would have been a major incident that morning. The riot-squad officers showed respect by allowing me, still in my shorts, to walk with them to the segregation block over in the main part of the jail.

I wasn't allowed to take any of my belongings with me and I was heavily escorted to the solitary cells. What was going to happen to me now? I had no idea. All I did know was that there was absolutely no chance the governor would allow me back into the unit.

It was about quarter past five in the morning by this time and I felt drained because I hadn't slept all night. My exit from the unit had been swift and precise, and now I had to try and put the whole experience out of my mind. This was a right downer for me, but this was prison politics and all part of the game. Some you win, some you lose.

The segregation cell in which the riot squad placed me was cold and filthy with only a thin mattress on top of a concrete base. There was a stainless-steel toilet and sink, and that was it, nothing else. This was a serious fall from grace after having done so well, and now I had to keep it together until I found out what was going to happen.

Only a couple of weeks before I had been removed from the special unit, the unit governor informed me that I'd qualified under Scottish law to serve only half of my 18-month prison sentence for taking prison officer Terry O'Neil hostage in Perth. As things stood, I was currently serving 14 years but this was actually four consecutive sentences rolled into one. Because I'd received my 18-month sentence after 1 October 1992, I qualified under the new Criminal Justice Act of 1991, which states that anyone sentenced to four years and less will automatically serve only half their sentence. I could've received ten years for taking three prison guards hostage and keeping Terry O'Neil against his will for over 13 hours, but Donald Findlay QC worked his magic on that case.

My earliest date for release was 1998. I still had a few years to serve before I got out and where I would go from the Shotts segregation block was anyone's guess. Where was it all going to stop? It was just one thing after the other. For now, it was back to the drawing board, and back to the big waiting game.

The unit governor made the effort to come and see me later that day. He told me that the decision to move me from the unit had been taken because they'd received information that I was about to kill another unit inmate. No name was mentioned, but it was obvious he was referring to Jim McLeod. It was pointless protesting too much because the governors had their fingers on the pulse and they knew what was going on. They're not stupid.

I was due a family visit the day I was shifted from the unit and my visitors had no idea that I'd been moved. I waited patiently all day, right up until about eight o'clock in the evening, and there was still no sign of my visitors. I knew something wasn't right, and I knew my visitors wouldn't just let me down for no good reason. The spy-hole shot up and there was a guard outside kicking on the door.

'Lobban, I've got a message for you from the prison gate-house. Your visitors have been refused entry into the jail because they didn't have a visit order.'

I sprang to my feet and shouted back angrily: 'And you've waited all day before you tell me this? You might have had the decency to tell me this long before now.'

'Well, you should've thought about that before you got yourself kicked out of the Special Unit,' was the reply.

This was the silly games starting up again, and naturally I felt cheated out of my visit. I wasn't happy at all. The spy-hole went down with a clunk, and I began pacing hastily up and down the cell. Up, down, up, down, my pace was picking up speed with the exasperation of what had just happened, and then I just exploded into a fit of rage. I screamed out at the top of my voice. The whole of Shotts Prison must have heard this almighty yell. In a flash, I lost my rag and any sense of composure I had left. I quickly turned my attention to the stainless-steel toilet pan fixed to the wall.

They said that the segregation cells at Shotts were indestructible, that their design was capable of withstanding any amount of physical violence. Well, with every bit of strength I could muster, I delivered a volley of backward kicks into the tough steel. Blow after blow I struck this steel toilet, and I kept on going until I saw signs of it starting to give way from its holdings. I thought that if I got the steel pan dislodged from the wall, then destroying the rest of the cell would be a doddle.

The noise I made was incredible; I'd flipped and I was going berserk, wreaking total havoc in the cell. I could feel the steel toilet pan was getting precariously weaker by the second. The salvo of backward kicks had obviously loosened the fittings and fixtures and there was water beginning to seep out from the cracks. I grabbed the rim of the pan and with both hands began shoving it wildly from side to side.

Like a man possessed, there I was fighting with this toilet pan, pulling, heaving, and with one last thrust it suddenly fell free from the wall. Now there was water shooting out in all directions. The small copper pipe had snapped as the toilet pan detached itself from the wall. My next focus was on the stainless steel sink, so I began battering lumps out of it. In no time, I had the sink lying on the floor, bashed to an unrecognisable shape. There was water everywhere, spraying out all over the place and on the floor; it must have been at least an inch deep. For at least an hour, I went bonkers in that cell. I had flipped my lid, weeks of frustration and anger all coming out at once. By the time I'd finished I was absolutely exhausted. I fell down on the now soaked mattress, unaware that the riot squad were preparing to come in and restrain me.

They waited for me to tire myself out first; that way it made their job easier. I remember the spy-hole opening and one of them shouting through: 'Right, Lobban, stand at the back of the cell where I can see you.'

As if! I was worn out and the last thing I was going to do was stand at the back of the wall.

'Beat it! I'm too tired to even stand up!' I shouted back.

The door flew open and in stormed the cavalry, flattening me with a fibreglass shield. They then dragged me onto the flooded floor. I will never forget one of them forcefully pressing my face into the water while they had me lying on my stomach. Slowly the riot squad forced both my arms and legs into the approved controlled and restrained position, taking their time to ensure maximum pain. At one point, I thought they were going to drown me.

'He's not a screamer, this one,' I heard one of them say.

The liberty-takers bent my limbs as if they were Plasticine but no matter how hard they tried to hurt me, I still wouldn't give them the pleasure of hearing me yelling out. I remembered Eric Duff, from Perth Prison, once telling me that if a prisoner didn't yell out during a control and restraint relocation then the guards carrying out the assignment weren't doing their job properly. That always stuck in my mind. It took about 15 minutes to carry me 30 feet to my destination – the 'silent cell'.

Every few paces the screws were stopping, putting me down again, and from the beginning it was 'Lock one secure . . . lock two secure' and so on. They would repeat the same procedure all over again and, in the end, my body felt limp because of the pain.

The worst came when they had me pinned down on the floor inside the silent cell. As I tried to get a look at one of their faces to see if I could identify any of them. As I lifted my head to catch a quick glimpse the guard kneeling in front of me said: 'Don't fucking look at me!' before head-butting me flush on the forehead and catching me with one of the metal studs on the visor of his helmet. The force he used almost knocked me out; it burst my head wide open. I still have the scar today.

The prison issue clothes I was wearing were ripped from my body and at this point they made their retreat. For ages I lay motionless in agony on the cold concrete floor, gradually coming to grips with my newfound surroundings. When I finally got to my feet, I could see there was nothing in the cell with me apart from a thick paper piss-pot that sat in the corner. The cell was massive, twice as big as a normal cell, and there were two honeycombed steel-plated cell doors as opposed to the one.

Essentially this was a cell within a cell and if I coughed or said something out aloud, it would eerily echo back at me. There was no mattress in the silent cell. In fact, there wasn't even a concrete slab or foundation on which to put a mattress, only bleak confinement and nothing else. Normally a prisoner spent a few hours maximum in the silent cell, and they called this a 'cooling down' period. At each side of the door there was a four-inch wide fibreglass panel that went from the floor right up to just above the cell door. These fibreglass panels were actually full-length spy-holes that the guards would use to keep their eyes on me. With no running water or toilet, and no natural sunlight, the silent cell was the isolation from hell.

I would spend the next seven months in this cell.

How the prison authorities managed to justify leaving me in a windowless cell for seven months I'll never know. On moral and health grounds, it was wholly unacceptable. The excuse the governor gave me for leaving me in such a cell without ventilation, a window, running water or a toilet for so long was that no prison in Scotland would accept me. This reason might have been half-believable if I'd only spent a couple of weeks under the same conditions, not after I was locked up for more than half of a year.

The day after I smashed up the segregation cell I went in front of Governor Shearer to answer to a charge of destroying prison property. He read out a list of the damage I'd caused and he fined me a total of £800-odd pounds. How I was going to pay that amount, I've no idea, but I'm sure something like 50 pence was being deducted from my prison wages each week. It would take a long time to pay back in full!

I chose to retreat into myself for a while, to enter into my own little world of madness, refusing to communicate even with the guards who came to feed me. I cut myself off from everything, refusing even to have a radio, receiving my food on a plastic plate, which the guards pushed into the cell along the floor. Since there was no toilet or running water, it meant I was the only inmate still slopping out in Shotts. I got my hourly entitlement of exercise every day and it didn't matter if it rained, snowed, or blew a gale, I still made sure I got out there for my fresh air.

The exercise pens were similar to the ones up in Peterhead, with the only difference being that you could see who was in the pen next to you, but they were much smaller. I quickly got into a daily routine of jogging around the tight space; I remember the middle of the three was the better for running in. I used to pace up and down the silent cell all day, seven days a week, and I did this for seven months. I would sing, shout and scream at the top of my voice, and no one would ever hear me – that at least was great!

After a few months of this I started to stare into space for hours on end, only breaking away from this hypnotic state when my cell door opened. One positive thing that happened to me during my time in the silent cell was a visit from Jimmy McIver. The guard opened up my door and said that the man from the Salvation Army wanted to see me. I went into a private room to speak to him where I found him sitting down waving an envelope.

'I've got some good news for you, William,' he said with a big smile on his face. 'We've found your father. Isn't that just great?'

I quickly snatched the letter from his hand and began reading with a mixture of feelings, but predominantly I was very excited. It was my father all right, David Lobban, whom I had managed to locate through the Family Tracing Service, a branch of the Salvation Army. It turned out he was living in West Yorkshire, and he had married for a *third* time – and he seemed to be pleased to have learnt I was searching for him. I took the letter back to my cell and read it over and over. My father included a photo of himself in his younger days, and as this was the first time I'd ever seen what he looked like, it was quite a moment for me.

We began corresponding with each other via the Salvation Army, and this went on for some considerable time until one day he suggested that I might wish to put in for a transfer down south and into the English prison system so that we could share some compassionate visits together. I was over the moon at this suggestion because I could now see light at the end of the tunnel. It meant I had found the perfect solution to the Scottish prison system's headache of where they were going to put me next.

I applied for an immediate transfer to England, but Governor Shearer told me I would first need to go through the proper channels, and this could take up to six weeks.

I thought that, given my circumstances, the process might've been fast-tracked, but there was more chance of me being discharged than that happening. I had to wait the full six weeks before the go-ahead was sanctioned, and every day felt like a month. When word finally came through that I was going south, it felt like I'd won the lottery. The transfer was a temporary one to begin with, although the prison authorities indicated that it would be possible to change that to a permanent transfer provided the visits kept going and everything went well with the relationship with my father. It was time for a fresh start.

The silent cell had been a different experience from anything I'd come across before. It required some serious discipline to get through such a dreadful period. But the human spirit can adapt to just about anything, even when it comes to minimal human contact and maximum sensory deprivation.

I'll never forget the morning I left the silent cell to go down south on transfer. One of the guards on duty that morning was a hard-nosed officer who had shown nothing but contempt for me throughout my whole time there. This man was one of those screws who dislike everything about prisoners and what they stand for, a real hardliner who would've brought capital punishment back if he'd had the opportunity. Just as I was about to leave the segregation block he came up to me, put out his hand and said: 'I've got to shake your hand, Lobban. I don't know how you handled that time in the silent cell because it would've broken me long ago.'

I looked at him and I could tell that he meant every word. Maybe he wasn't so bad after all.

'Thanks for that,' I replied. 'I don't know how I managed it myself.'

I walked out of the segregation block feeling on cloud nine.

It had been a psychologically demanding and challenging seven months at Shotts, but in a sense I believe it strengthened my spirit and made me a much stronger character. I now had a chance to reinstate myself back into the mainstream part of the prison system, albeit the English one.

One falsehood I would like to clear up concerns my move into the English prison system. According to a story that appeared in the press, and in certain other publications in Scotland, the prison authorities had found out I was about to be poisoned, so had sanctioned my transfer. What a load of rubbish – I suppose it sounded plausible to the unsuspecting public since no one had a clue as to the real reason.

The main culprit to weave this blab and put it into the public domain in the first place was none other than King Fibber himself, Paul Ferris. Ferris wouldn't have been counting on me coming out one day to write my own story and to challenge all the lies he's written about me over the years, including that my real father was actually my uncle Billy! I'd imagine he won't be feeling too good with himself when he realises that the public might now see him in a different light as a result of setting the record straight.

Chapter Twenty-Two

The Full Sutton Riot

Moving into the English prison system was a huge relief, not only for me but also for the Scottish prison authorities, who no longer had to worry about which prison governor might be prepared to accept me in his jail. I was undeniably a thorn in their side.

My mother, who had sent me the original copy of her marriage certificate, which I had needed for Jimmy McIver to help trace my father, still didn't have a clue as to why I was suddenly transferring to another prison. It wasn't until I actually arrived in an English jail that she started to become a bit suspicious, asking questions and generally being nosy. She might've been out of her face with booze, but she wasn't daft and could read the game better than anyone I knew. It wouldn't take long before I had to come clean and tell her the truth, but for now I thought it was best to keep it under wraps.

I transferred to Wakefield jail, or Monster Mansion, as it's better known. Currently the largest maximum-security jail of its kind in the whole of western Europe, Wakefield holds approximately 750 long-term inmates, mainly lifers, including 100 Category A and high-risk cons who are some of the vilest and most objectionable child molesters, rapists and murderers you could ever possibly come across. High-profile serial killer Dr Harold Shipman, known as 'Dr Death', committed suicide at Wakefield.

When I moved there in 1995, the Scottish prison authorities hadn't alerted me to the stigma attached to Wakefield nick, not that it would've changed my mind about going there. I'd been through it all already, and there wasn't much I couldn't adapt to.

This was just another road I had to travel – and it was easier in comparison with some I had been down.

The only thing they told me was that Wakefield was the closest prison to where my father lived, in Castleford, West Yorkshire, so I suppose it made sense to transfer me to whichever jail was nearest. David Lobban could drive from his house to Wakefield in less than 25 minutes, so it suited us just fine.

I recall the very first visit I had with my father. It took place in the normal visiting room along with all the other inmates. He brought his wife, Amanda, along with him. The opening visit had been in the pipeline for months and the build-up to it all was unlike anything I'd felt before. This was by far the most enthralling experience I'd ever had. My mother and father had never officially divorced, so the only way he could remarry and avoid the stigma of bigamy was to place advertisements in various newspapers and magazines to the effect that he was seeking the whereabouts of my mother and was trying to re-establish contact with her.

I recall the moment I set eyes on him for the first time. There were the typical butterflies in the stomach. I analysed his every move, looking for a hint or something that would convince me he was in fact my old man. My inner voice kept me sceptical to begin with, but that's because he'd never played a part in my life; he was never there for me as a kid growing up. But it didn't take me long to be sure that it was really him. That first meeting was, as I had hoped, the first of many. This whole new relationship was a breath of fresh air and gave me a real sense of hope for the future.

Before long I applied for my C-Category status, since things had been going so well for me, and I was well within the time limit to qualify. The reports my personal officer was writing were glowing and the visits with my father couldn't have been better, so it wasn't surprising to me when word came that I'd been successful in my application. I was over the moon because here was a great opportunity to get out of Wakefield, move on to an open prison and then progress towards the gate to freedom.

The prison nominated was Wealstun, a C-Category located near the village of Thorp Arch in West Yorkshire, only a 30-minute drive from where my father lived, so it was still convenient for visits. Wealstun was in a different class. Gone were the galleries; instead the halls were of the section type, which housed about 20 cons each. The cells were predominantly single occupancy, although there were a few double cells on each landing.

The only downside for me was that the prison accepted both long- and short-term inmates. In my opinion, it was almost unbearable when the guy next door to you was serving six months and would be back out on the streets in only a few weeks. Even as a long-serving prisoner nearing the end of a 14-year sentence, I found this annoying and I tended to give these fleeting inmates a wide berth most of the time.

Otherwise I found I settled in really well at Wealstun. It was just one of those cushy nicks where there wasn't any hassle and the guards weren't on your back for the slightest thing. I'd say the balance was just right, and that's something you don't come across often. Because of my long-term status, sound penal knowledge and easy approach, I had a lot of new inmates coming up to me for advice on all sorts of stuff. Forget the Citizens Advice Bureau, just pop round and see Billy Lobban, that's what it was like. In Wealstun at its peak I had a hand in just about everything you could possibly think of, including sitting on a prisoner's forum, where I spoke up on behalf of the jail population, as well as studying hard for a business course. It was one of those periods in my life where I felt as if I was floating on air and everything was going my way.

You'd think I would've been content studying for my GNVQ certificate, being part of the prisoners' forum, making great progress in the gym and receiving positive visits from my father, and I was; however, I had something else going on in the background, something that would prove to be my downfall and see me ejected from Wealstun in the end.

As a way of making my own time a bit more comfortable, I would lend other prisoners things such as telephone cards or packets of tobacco, and when they returned them to me, they would pay a little interest on top, a bit like getting a loan from

a bank. For every two items someone took, they would have to pay me three back: it was as simple as that. What started as a few handpicked inmates borrowing a few cards and packets of tobacco here and there soon turned into a thriving business that grew and kept on growing. The guards knew exactly what was going on, but they turned a blind eye. I wasn't throwing my weight around or beating people up. There was no need to; everyone knew the score and would always pay up.

Within a few months, I'd built up a very lucrative business and at its height I was sometimes handing out as much as £200 in cash every week to my visitors. I did this by selling six items for a tenner, and there was never a shortage of takers. Because of the relaxed security it meant there was always plenty of paper money kicking about. Phone cards were a huge currency in jails back then. I had a partner in the business, Peter Snowden, who was connected to the legendary show jumper Harvey Smith, and he decided he wanted to do his bookie bit, so he began accepting bets on the horses at the weekend, and it wasn't long before the amount of items we had stashed was incredible. Each payday I had queues outside my cell door that sometimes took up most of the section. It did get a bit out of hand!

I'll never forget the time a pal of mine came into my cell crying and asking to speak to me. This guy was from Haghill in the East End of Glasgow and he was finishing off a six-year sentence for his part in a drug-smuggling operation in France. He'd had his sentence imposed abroad but after applying for a transfer back to the UK he'd eventually ended up in Wealstun, where we became friendly because of our Glaswegian connection.

'Sit down and tell me what's up with you,' I told him after he walked into my cell looking dazed and upset.

'Will you come upstairs with me to *my* cell so that we can talk?' he asked.

We walked up to the landing above me and entered his cell, which was midway along the corridor. I could tell something wasn't right and I sensed it was something serious, but nothing, and I mean nothing, could've prepared me for what I was about to hear. As I sat down on the end of his bed, I couldn't help but notice a large picture stuck on his cell wall, bang in the middle, in pride of place. The picture was clearly important to him and it jumped out at you the second you walked into the cell. It was a photograph of a beautiful wee lassie with long black hair, and it looked to me like some sort of school photo. While I was taking this in, he delivered the bombshell.

'The governor just asked to see me downstairs in his office and he's given me some terrible news ... It's my 15-year-old daughter. He just told me that she jumped in front of a train and committed suicide.'

It took me a few seconds before these words registered, then my heart started pounding and I hugged him to try to console him. What do you say to a man who has just received news like that? I couldn't believe that such a lovely girl would take her own life in such a way. The news hadn't hit the guy properly, as he'd literally just been told, and I knew I had to keep my eye on him through this sad ordeal.

He never left my sight after that and he got as much support as possible. I spoke to the governor and asked his permission to begin a bereavement fund appeal, where any money raised would go to the rest of the young girl's family in Glasgow. The governor sanctioned this without issue and he even got the appeal fund sheets of paper made up for me, all stamped and addressed to the governor of Wealstun. I went round every prisoner in the jail and raised hundreds of pounds, which the governor forwarded to the girl's mother in due course. Inmates were contributing from their prison wages and personal cash, and some donated as much as a tenner. That's one thing I'll say: convicted prisoners can be very generous when it comes to things like that, and in this case they showed a lot of heart.

Just when I thought everything was going sweetly and couldn't have been any better the heads of the prison management decided they were going to pull the rug from right under my feet.

During the 60-minute lock-up just before the cell doors were due to be opened up for recreation, my cell door came crashing in, startling Peter Snowden and me as we sat chatting away peacefully. At least six unfamiliar guards stood there, saying

they had strict instructions to escort me straight to the reception area. I wasn't given an explanation, just told that I was to hurry up and pack my belongings and that a governor would speak to me over there. I had minutes to gather my things – it would've made no difference if I'd shown signs of dissent. I'd been faced with this same situation before and I knew from experience that it was pointless moaning about it.

The bottom line was that I was being shipped, and there wasn't a thing I could do to stop it, end of story. Although I wasn't told exactly why I was being moved it was obvious it had something to do with my business enterprise; it had to be. Prison is sometimes like a game of snakes and ladders: just when you think you're doing well, you end up right back at the beginning. It later transpired that the last straw as far as the prison authorities were concerned had come when one of the cons who owed money for tobacco slashed himself in order to get himself moved to another prison, thereby getting out of paying back his debt.

I'd just managed to finish my GNVQ and passed with distinction, I'm pleased to say. I also completed my City & Guilds communication skills course and got the certificate at levels 1 and 2. I was going to miss Wealstun, no doubt about that, but now I had to prepare myself for the next stage of my journey.

In mid-1996 three of us awaited our fate in the reception area of HMP Wealstun. We knew we were for the off – we just didn't know where. With me were two of my friends from South Shields in the north-east of England: Gerald 'Gez' Young and David 'Noddy' Rice. We had spent a great deal of time together at Wealstun. We were amongst the more popular cons within the jail population and didn't deserve the treatment being dished out to us, that's for sure – but there was not a thing we could do to prevent this move. The decision had been made, so our time was up at the comfy Cat C. After leaving us to roast for a while, the guards eventually came back and said: 'Lobban and Young, you two are going to HMP Full Sutton. Grab your stuff . . . the van is waiting outside.'

'Where's that?' I asked.

'It's not that far away. Put your arm out to get this handcuff on. And you, Mr Rice, you're going to the best prison in the system . . . Wakefield!'

'Ah, no way! You're kidding me on, aren't you?' Nod replied.

He wasn't too happy, as he knew that Wakefield was mainly for sex offenders. There was no time to tell him about my experience there, as we were moving now.

'Don't worry, lad,' Gez said to his best pal before shaking his hand. 'Just keep your head down; you'll be OK, Nod.'

We both gave Noddy a hug and said our goodbyes before being ushered towards the prison van that waited outside. As the van pulled away to make the short journey through Yorkshire, we looked back at Wealstun one last time. This was yet another fall from grace and a massive backward step. We just sat motionless, contemplating what lay ahead.

When we arrived at Full Sutton, we were taken straight to the reception area, where we were both checked in. Within an hour we were processed, advised of our location, handed an admission kit and told to follow the officer to B-Wing. We couldn't believe our luck that, under the circumstances, we were still together. Normally we would have been split up by now and sent on our separate ways, so it was a right result, and half the battle knowing we would most certainly be spending the foreseeable future together.

Full Sutton Prison is a purpose-built high-security dispersal designed to hold long-term category A and B prisoners. It was also one of the main locations used to house Irish terrorists in England before the signing of the Good Friday Agreement in 1998. It opened in 1987 and lies approximately ten miles east of York in open countryside in the village of Full Sutton, near the town of Pocklington. At full operational capacity Full Sutton can hold more than 600 inmates.

The primary function of Full Sutton is to hold some of the most difficult and dangerous criminals in the country. The prison will not accept convicts who have been sentenced to less than four years, or those who have less than 12 months left to serve. I had roughly two and a half years left of my own sentence at this stage.

B-Wing was a bit like a square. It comprised four sections, each part representing a side of the square, and there were two levels. On the top landing, one of these sections was the guards' offices. The offices that took up the whole section upstairs were out of bounds to prisoners. Each of the other sections housed up to 14 prisoners and had its own television room. Downstairs, on the bottom landing, there were cooking facilities and a huge pantry area where cons prepared their own food. The exercise yard was small and was located on B-Wing; it wasn't much bigger than the modest back garden you would find on an average-sized house.

When I arrived, there were over a hundred hardened criminals housed there. This included 44 Cat-A prisoners, as well as three IRA terrorists: the Harrods bomber Patrick Hayes, John Kinsella of the Warrington bomb attack on a gas works, and Patrick Magee, the maniac who almost killed Margaret Thatcher in 1984. This was B-Wing, and if you weren't on top of your game you wouldn't last long. This sort of environment was very intimidating. I just had to find out exactly who was in the prison, especially if there was anyone I knew, as this could be important in terms of settling in.

Earlier I had arranged with Gez to attend the gym session in the evening, so when the screws opened the cell doors for recreation I quickly made my way there. I could see Gez standing in the queue; he was a big lad and had a presence about him. He was six feet tall and weighed maybe 16 or 17 stone. With cropped bleach-blond natural hair and blue eyes, he wouldn't have had a problem getting the girls, but he was a family man who was married and had two lovely little boys who were his spitting image. He spoke with a Geordie accent and was serving a five-year sentence for the control and supply of drugs on a massive scale.

The gym at Full Sutton was huge. There must have been 30 to 40 prisoners there that night from all different wings, but no familiar faces. It seemed all the regular fitness fanatics had grabbed most of the weights and equipment on offer, leaving not very much to work with for me and my big pal. The gym felt crowded, vibrant, and very busy indeed. It was extremely difficult to find space.

Just opposite to where I was standing there was a con of Asian appearance lying on a bench repping away with the barbell. Suddenly, another inmate picked up a 20-kilo Olympic disk and without warning smashed it down on top of the guy's face. I didn't approve of this type of behaviour in the gym, but that was the type of prison I was in now.

Back in B-Wing there was more violence that evening. Maybe it was just one of those days, or was this the usual routine? A prisoner just a few cells away from me came staggering out into the corridor with his hands pressed against his stomach. There was blood spurting through the gaps in his fingers and he had a look on his face that I had seen many times before. The guy was in trouble and he knew it. Other prisoners just looked on as he made his way down the section towards the office for help. Someone had entered his cell and stabbed him. That rounded off a perfect first day for me!

I have never believed that there's such a thing as coincidence. But what happened next virtually freaked me out. The following day, there, ahead of me in the corridor, I could see a tall figure who stood out from the crowd of prisoners walking towards me. His hair was dirty blond and shoulder length. The manner by which he walked was definitely the same. His tall frame seemed much thinner though, and he wore glasses, but there was no doubt in my mind that the person quickly approaching me was Michael Healy.

For a second it felt like we could just walk right past each other, but then, like old pals who have not seen each other for years, we both flung our arms around one another in an enormous bear-hug.

'How are things?' I asked him as we patted each other on the back.

'What you doing here?' Michael asked me while looking at me with confusion.

I quickly explained that I'd been booted out of Wealstun the day before; that I'd been shipped here, to Full Sutton, and that I was on B-Wing. It was all a bit much for me to take in. Out of all the people I knew, Michael Healy was the last person on earth I expected to bump into. We shook hands quickly and arranged to meet up as soon as he got back from the workshop, where he was going now.

I hurried back to find Gez, so that I could tell him about the bizarre encounter I had just had, but by this time Gez had experienced his own bit of drama.

'What's up with you?' I asked him, as I entered his cell. He replied that he had met one of his adversaries from South Shields.

'I think I'm going to have a bit of trouble,' he went on to say in a shaky voice.

Well, that was just great: we needed that like a hole in the head.

It transpired that Gez had come face-to-face with a young guy called Gary Carruthers who had just been sentenced, along with his brother William. The Carruthers brothers were notorious in the North-east and were the founders of the Boss Gang (Boys of South Shields), which had been terrorising South Shields for years – anyone who stood in their way could expect brutal retribution, including knee-cappings, shootings and beatings. Gez had crossed them numerous times on their home patch and now faced the prospect of a continuation of a bitter feud.

I had my own complications with Michael Healy. Loads of issues required ironing out between us, and for all I knew there could possibly be trouble brewing of my own. Gez and I could only hope for the best and remain positive.

Healy was now serving a sentence of 32 years. Although we had been very close, our friendship had taken a knock in 1991 because of the situation between him, Paul Ferris and me, and I wasn't exactly sure if we had recovered from it properly. The last time we had seen each other was in court at the Old Bailey when Michael had called me as a defence witness at his estimated £6m robbery trial. There's no doubt Michael and I had a whole load of stuff to sort out, but I was quietly confident that I could win him over. I knew his character, and although he had a very nasty side to his nature, I was sure we could work through any obstacles that might stand in our way.

I caught up again with Michael during the recreation period that evening. His cell was in 'the London Section' – the best location on B-Wing. Most of the inmates in this section were

Cockneys, and before you could live there someone would normally have to recommend you.

We sat down for a chat in Michael's cell; it gave us a chance to catch up and fill in the blanks. For the next 90 minutes we exchanged stories and banter. The conversation went well and I never detected any sort of negativity at all.

I was more than content with the situation, but I did raise the issue relating to Gez and the predicament he found himself in with the Carruthers brothers from South Shields. Gez was my friend and without me he would have been entirely on his own, so I made sure he didn't feel isolated in any way; I also made it clear to him that I was with him all the way, regardless of what might happen. I had received assurance via third parties that there would be no funny business with Gez, and this stood for the time being.

Everything ran smoothly on B-Wing and I was beginning to make some pals. As a keen chess player I relished a game whenever possible. Gez was a very good player and we had played a lot back in Wealstun. I would sometimes play a game with the Harrods bomber, Patrick Hayes, who was serving 30 years, in his cell on the London section.

In fact I found I got on best with the Londoners, particularly Dessie Cunningham, who was at the end of a 16-year sentence for armed robbery. Dessie would always come to the gym with me and hold the boxing pads. This involved him putting his hands in the boxing pads, then shouting out instructions that I would follow. A crowd of prisoners would quickly gather just to watch the gruelling session, so it was a bit like performing to a small audience. I think Dessie liked that just as much as I did. By the time we were finished the two of us would be sweating like mad.

Back in B-Wing Dessie would come round to my cell just to show me the bruising to his torso – the result of powerful body shots when he'd been holding the pads close to his side. I remember being on a visit with my father, and just across from me at the next table was Dessie with his visitors. At the end of visiting time one of Dessie's visitors came over to me and said, 'So you're the geezer who has left Dessie black and blue!'

Around this time Gez had arranged to meet up with Gary and William Carruthers outside on the football field in order to sort out their differences. Every weekend offered the chance to go outside to the big playing field, and prisoners from different wings could meet up. While Gez paced up and down with Gary Carruthers, I made a point of keeping my eyes on him just in case things got out of hand.

Whilst I was doing this, Dessie came up to me with a message that his friend wanted to see me. I must say this approach did generate a bit of paranoia. Why did Dessie's friend want to speak to me? It all seemed a bit strange. Dessie pointed over to a con sitting against a wall and said: 'That's him there, his name's Porky. Just go over, he's waiting for you.'

The guy in question was William Edmonds, who had a fearsome reputation amongst his fellow Londoners.

As I walked over I noticed he was wearing a pork-pie type hat. I could tell he wasn't that tall. He had a reddish face with short blond hair. He was sitting against a wall by himself and he waved to me in acknowledgement as I approached.

'You all right, mate?' he asked in his Cockney twang.

'Yes, I'm fine. Your friend Dessie told me you wanted a word,' I replied.

He produced a document from under his sweater and said: 'Your name is William Lobban, isn't it? What you make of that, then?'

'What is it?' I asked as I took the document from him. I was totally baffled. It turned out that the paper was actually a Police Annual Review of some sort, and there within the pages and as clear as day was my name alongside his.

I didn't know what to make of it and I couldn't quite get my head around it. In the document, the police were implying that we were carrying out gangland hits as favours for one another. The police were also suggesting that we were good friends. The thing is, this meeting was the first time that we had ever set eyes on one another.

We chatted for a while and I found Porky to be down-to-earth, smart, and humorous too. We clicked and from this moment on we would become really good pals. Before we all headed back to the wing I discovered that Gez had sorted out his problems with Gary Carruthers and his brother. I would say that, all in all, it had been a good day.

The end of the year was fast approaching. Every weekend I spent socialising with Porky Edmonds outside in the football field. We would walk slowly around the perimeter fence during each session of exercise until the guards shouted it was time to go back inside. I must admit, I did feel somewhat privileged being able to walk around with Porky during those weekend exercise sessions. I mean, this guy was on the ball and he just didn't tolerate fools. He was very selective in whom he spoke to, and even the IRA men wouldn't go near him unless he said it was OK. That's just the sort of man he was. In prison it's often not what you know but who you know that really counts.

At long last I managed to get myself a cell change. Dessie Cunningham had applied for a move to C-Wing so that he could be closer to his good comrade, Porky. His moving had been on the cards for a few weeks, so when his cell became available on the London section I moved straight in. Getting myself onto that section was a positive move; it was quieter and the majority of cons who lived there were top-drawer crooks I could learn from. Patrick Hay and John Kinsella, the IRA men, were just opposite me. Then there was the bold Mick Healy, who was way down at the end of the section close to the screws' office.

Not long after Dessie moved to C-Wing, around 6 p.m. on Monday, 20 January 1996, I sat in the television room to watch the movie *Braveheart*. It was one of the very few nights I wasn't at the gym. I had just settled in my comfy chair with a cup of instant coffee when suddenly someone came in shouting a riot was on the verge of kicking off.

'Bill . . . Porky is at the window over in C-Wing and he sent me to get you. He wants a word.'

I knew immediately that something was wrong. As soon as I left the TV room I noticed an atmosphere which hadn't been there ten minutes before. I nipped into the nearest cell that faced onto C-Wing and when I got to the window I shouted across to Porky, so that he knew I was there.

'Bill . . .the screws have taken Dessie to the segregation block and they're giving him a real beating.'

I could see prisoners running up and down the section corridors from the open cell doors in C-Wing. There was a right commotion going on over there.

'I reckon it's going to explode in B-Wing as well,' I shouted back.

Prisoners in B-Wing were beginning to congregate in the section outside. Whatever had happened over in C-Wing, it looked very serious. I got the feeling it was going to be a long night. B-Wing was on the verge of a full-scale riot and the guards were trying their best to get prisoners to go behind their doors. Within minutes the whole atmosphere had changed. Experience had taught me not to go behind the cell door

A group of prisoners, including myself, had made our way downstairs. The guards did try desperately to lock up as many people as they could, but they were having a hard time doing so. Messages of the heavy disturbance over in C-Wing would have been heard on their walkie-talkies, so they knew that B-Wing could potentially follow and erupt at any second. I couldn't see Michael Healy anywhere. I think he had voluntarily gone into his cell and closed his door behind him. That was his choice and he can't be criticised for that.

My friend Gez, whom I had quickly searched for, was nowhere to be seen either. I was sure he wouldn't have taken part in any sort of trouble. Everyone I looked at had a frantic expression on their face. Prisoners were milling around in small groups. Everyone was staring at each other, waiting for that signal, the spark that would ignite the flame.

Suddenly, two prisoners wearing homemade balaclavas emerged from one of the cells nearby. Holding what appeared to be wooden chair-legs they ran towards the corner office where two guards could still be seen through the Perspex windows. Realising that the office door was locked from the inside, the prisoners in balaclavas turned their attention to hammering away at the thickened Perspex.

All hell had now broken loose and there were perhaps five or six different prisoners, with their faces covered, battering away at the office windows as if their lives depended on it. Blow after blow they continued to strike the windows with mop-buckets, mops, anything they could get their hands on.

The guards, who had been standing inside the office, soon made their escape through an emergency exit-door at the back. There was no sign of any other prison guards anywhere; they had abandoned their posts and now B-Wing was in the hands of the prisoners. It was absolute pandemonium. A group of prisoners had converged and surrounded the corner office by this stage. Still they pounded away, trying to break through, but the planners who'd built the structure had obviously taken this sort of incident into account.

Not wishing to appear the odd man out I grabbed hold of an industrial ironing-board which lay in the section corridor two feet from where I was standing and, with all my strength went running like a javelin-thrower along the corridor towards the office, shouting: 'Move out of my way!'

Crash! The whole thickened Perspex window went flying into the office, leaving a huge hole for everyone to climb through. But there was a problem as I had made a fundamental error in assuming the guards had completely gone from the office.

With everyone preoccupied and focused on attacking the windows, no one seemed to notice the female guard's face through a six-inch square window in the emergency exit door. With the ironing board still in my grasp, I looked across and saw her face pressed up against the small glass square staring back at me. She had witnessed me as clear as you like ramming the ironing board through the window. I immediately let go of the board, dropped my head in embarrassment, turned and walked hurriedly away back along the corridor. From that moment I knew I was in serious trouble.

Prisoners began to barricade the doors leading into B-Wing. Others continued on their rampage by causing as much damage as they possibly could. The television rooms were smashed to pieces. Furniture was piled high against the main door leading into the wing. Toilets and sinks were ripped from the walls and water began to flood the floors in every section. It was absolute mayhem on a grand scale. I had been involved in chaotic disturbances in the past, but none of them had come close to this madness. And this was just the beginning.

I made my way through the heaps of broken furniture that were strewn across the flooded floors, went upstairs and pressed on towards Gez's cell. When I opened up the peep-hole, I could see him standing inside. I told him about my inauspicious encounter with the female prison guard downstairs, and explained that the screws had run off and abandoned the wing, and the cons were smashing up everything in sight. To think that only a quarter of an hour before I was sitting in the TV room, relaxed. It was unbelievable how fast the riot had erupted.

By the time I got back downstairs, a group of about a dozen prisoners had gathered at the main gate leading out to the exercise yard and were trying to wrench the steel gate from its hinges – a proper task, considering the size and weight of the thing. Someone wedged a wooden door between the steel gate and the wall, and prisoners began pulling and heaving until it came loose. There was no shortage of muscle; everyone took it in turns to yank on the door. After a lot of sweat and determination the gate slowly slackened from its holdings. Then, without warning, the whole thing went crashing to the floor. The steel gate was so heavy that ten or twelve prisoners had to carry it – and the damage this gate did afterwards was just incredible.

I think every prisoner that night was very surprised that the riot squad hadn't made any effort to regain control. Perhaps Full Sutton wasn't prepared for a disturbance of this magnitude. As both B-Wing *and* C-Wing had erupted, maybe there wasn't enough trained manpower available to deal with it on the spot. Whatever the case, another 12 hours passed before the riot teams eventually made an appearance.

With a firm hold on the steel gate, the cons managed to carry it awkwardly upstairs and onto the London section. From there I saw it being used as a sort of battering ram to smash a way into the offices that were strictly out of bounds to prisoners and which contained sensitive information about every inmate on B-Wing. But before this could be achieved a bit of manoeuvring was required. Some cons took the steel gate into the shower room and from there battered a hole in the wall which led out onto the foyer of the offices and the entrance to the wing. Then, using the steel gate, they battered another hole through the wall which led into the offices themselves.

People lit small fires downstairs and the smoke started to drift along the sections. No one had any control over who did what, but the small group I was with realised that those starting fires had now put the lives of the prisoners locked in their cells at risk.

A barricade had been erected right outside Mick Healy's cell, so I along with a couple of others began removing all the furniture and debris from outside his door just to be on the safe side. Someone with a grudge could've played havoc with a match. The smoke from the fires was getting worse, and there were people walking around with bits of clothing pressed against their mouths to help prevent inhaling the fumes.

When the rioters broke through to the offices, they wasted no time in finding the prisoners' files. Everyone was so keen to get their hands on their own file that it just became a mad rush. There were inmates all over the place and there was no order whatsoever. It was just a mad free-for-all, total chaos. After a short while one of the Cockneys handed me a file and said:

'Cop for that, Bill. It's got your name on it!' When I gazed around me, most people were busy reading through their security files. The important stuff we kept safe and read later on. Everything else got destroyed. Here we were, rummaging through the private offices of the B-Wing management. It would never have been envisaged that prisoners would be able to get this far, and I had never seen so much devastation in a jail. It was completely trashed. A prisoner began parading comically down the corridor wearing an officer's hat and tunic. Framed photographs of family members of prison staff that once sat proudly on top of desks were lying smashed to pieces. There was broken office equipment all over the place and heaps of paperwork lay scattered on the floor. Some prisoners even made phone calls!

As soon as the novelty wore off and everyone was satisfied that nothing else could be destroyed, people began to leave and make their way back downstairs. Some bright spark then came up with the idea that it was time to turn the lights out.

The electricity supply was switched off and B-Wing was plunged into darkness. As I walked around the shadowy wing, smoke from the fires that were started earlier still hung in the air. Every now and then I passed prisoners wearing homemade balaclavas and carrying wooden table legs. Their identities concealed, there was no way of telling who they were. I have a clear mental picture of these events and I can tell you it was a very eerie and threatening scene. It must have scared the life out of a few folk, especially as B-Wing housed so many dangerous men.

Access to the exercise yard wasn't a problem since the steel gate had been removed earlier. Prisoners began to take broken furniture outside to make a bonfire. You would have thought it was Guy Fawkes Night. Right in the centre of the exercise yard the furniture was piled high, then it was set alight to produce an enormous blaze. As the fire took hold more furniture was applied until the flames were bigger than B-Wing itself. At one stage it was impossible to stand in the yard because of the intense heat.

The fire brigade, which was on standby outside in the prison grounds, began aiming their water cannons over the rooftops in the hope it would extinguish the flames. However, they had to pull back when prisoners threw steel door handles and other missiles in their direction. Later reports said that the flames and smoke could be seen for miles. If that wasn't bad enough, some idiot started a fire up in the offices. This wasn't a wise thing to do because the sections on each side of the offices held prisoners who were still locked in their cells. On one side there was Mick Healy, and on the other side my pal Gez was trapped, as well as a couple of other prisoners I didn't really know. These guys were terrified, as smoke was coming at them from all directions.

Gez had at one point become so freaked out by it all that I had to shout out instructions to him, advising him what to do. Braving the intense heat and flames I told him to roll up a poster into a long tube so that he could use it to breathe through the window. He was panicking but did as I suggested. You could see this white tube-like poster poking out from his window and Gez at the other end inhaling the fresh air like a man possessed. It was bad enough for me being outside with all the fires and smoke. It must have been absolutely terrifying for those locked up in their cells, especially when they knew there was no one who could rescue them. People could quite easily have died that night.

The disturbance carried on throughout the night and right into the early hours of the morning. At no time did the riot squad try to regain control. Every prisoner who took part in the unrest was simply left to his own devices. Food that had been stored in fridge-freezers on the wing, such as chicken, beef and sausages, were brought outside and placed on the fire to cook. There was also homemade booze being passed around. It was just like a massive barbeque at an open-air party.

As the fires died down so did people's energy. Everyone was exhausted. I had stayed with the same group of people throughout and helped defuse the situation where possible. I also did my bit by putting small fires out that I felt were a risk to prisoner safety.

The Prison Service decided it was time to act, so they put into effect the Operation Tornado programme for dealing with serious unrest. Reinforcements were sent to Full Sutton from other prisons in Yorkshire and the North-east. The mufti mob were on their way. The riot squads finally appeared at around 6 a.m. but by that time the crowds had dispersed into cells, in groups of at least two to reduce the chances of being harmed or beaten up. The idea was that if there were witnesses the riot squad would think twice about injuring anyone. In the cell I was in, there were six of us.

When the riot squad started to break down the barricade at the wing entrance, I stood peering at the end of the section to witness them coming through. I could hear cell doors slamming shut and a voice telling me to hurry up, but curiosity got the better of me and I just had to witness these final moments. I was the last prisoner to go behind the door that morning. I still have a clear picture of the riot squad bursting down that barricade and yelling out 'Clear!' As they began inching their way forward, their riot-shields moving ever closer, it was time to sprint back to the cell. It was over.

As the riot squad shuffled slowly along the section, emptying each cell in turn, we all looked at each other and said, 'Well, this is it, lads . . . here they come,' before shaking hands, embracing, and patting each other on the back as an inevitable farewell gesture. None of us had any idea what would happen when the cell door was opened, but one thing was certain – we knew we wouldn't see each other again for a long time, if ever. It had been quite a night, and we were all utterly exhausted.

I recall the intensified level of apprehension the second our cell door swung open. All the Londoners and I were standing facing the door as we were greeted with the familiar sight of blue overalls, helmets and transparent fibreglass shields. The riot squad shouted at us, 'OK, first one out – hurry up, get a move on.' One by one, we left the hot, crammed cell, which by this time was stinking of body odour after the night-long madness.

I was the third-last prisoner to leave the cell that morning, and I didn't have a clue where those who had left before me had gone. When I stepped into the corridor, there to greet me was a sea of riot-squad officers that stretched as far as I could see. I'd seen a concentrated spate of guards in full riot gear back in the Scottish jails, but nothing like what I witnessed in Full Sutton that day. There must've been literally hundreds of them, lining the corridors. It was a massive show of strength. Every so often, one of them would utter some sort of sarcastic remark as I walked along, but this didn't intimidate me in the slightest.

I ended up at the inevitable destination in such circumstances – the reception, which was a trek and a half from the cell I'd set off from. Just outside the reception building I noticed loads of white Group 4 prison vans sitting parked with their engines running, which could only mean one thing. In the reception itself, in a specially converted area like a small hangar, there was a mountain of prisoner's private property, just lying there stacked in a heap so high it almost touched the ceiling. I saw prisoners' personal family photographs strewn across the floor. I saw expensive stereos and hi-fi systems lying smashed to bits. There were personal clothes, toiletries, bedding and other unidentifiable items from cells all thrown together in a massive heap. The scene resembled a rubbish tip: it looked as though a lorry had just tipped its load in the middle of the floor. I've no idea how the prison management could justify such cavalier treatment of prisoners' personal property. I'd never seen anything like it before, and I'd bet a lot of money no one got their property, particularly electrical property, back in one piece.

I was cuffed and bundled into the back of one of the vans, and along with five other prisoners was taken to a privately run jail near Brough in the East Riding of Yorkshire called Wolds. That was the last time I would ever see Full Sutton. The riot was the last dramatic event I'd ever be a part of before my release some two years later.

I found out later what had been going on over in C-Wing, and why it had kicked-off there. It transpired that Dessie Cunningham, who had moved over to C-Wing to be next to Porky, had been badly beaten up and taken to the segregation block because he'd been accused of stabbing someone in the exercise yard. Apparently during a brief lock-up the guards dragged Dessie from his cell shouting and screaming while beating him severely all the way to the segregation block. Just before 6 p.m. on C-Wing, Porky went to Dessie's cell to look inside. When he looked through the spyhole he could see blood splattered on the walls and furniture turned upside down.

Because of the appalling violence meted out to Dessie, Porky gathered a group of prisoners together to confront the guards outside their office. One thing led to another and this is what caused the riot. The prison officers who removed Dessie from his cell that afternoon must surely have felt the wrath of their superiors because the damage caused in that incident alone cost the Prison Service in excess of £2 million. It took six months before prisoners could inhabit both wings again.

Sadly, Dessie Cunningham hanged himself at Whitemoor Prison on 31 December 1998. I was living in Darlington when I received the shocking news from Porky Edmonds on New Year's Eve shortly before the bells.

Nearly ten and a half years after receiving the six-year sentence for the rent office hold-up in Rutherglen in 1988, the English prison authorities released me from Hull prison, where I had ended up after various transfers, on 18 June 1998. I cannot emphasise enough just how euphoric this made me feel after spending more than a decade incarcerated. That said, there was no room for complacency. What bothered me the most is what the Glasgow Serious Crime Squad thought about my exit from jail as there was no doubt in my mind they still had a keen interest in my movements and what I would do with myself once released.

Because I finished off my time in the English prison system I had to abide by English protocol. Scotland and England have different sentencing policies when it comes to consecutive terms being added to your original sentence, so I missed out on three months' remission I would've benefited from had I finished my sentence north of the border. The English authorities classed my consecutive sentences as one single term of 14 years, whereas in Scotland I would have qualified, under the Criminal Justice Act of 1991, for half remission on my 18-month sentence for taking prison officer Terry O'Neil hostage.

I was devastated and fought hard with the Home Office to have this decision reversed, but it was no good. As a result I spent a supplementary three long months banged up in an English system all because the small print contained in the document of my temporary transfer to see my father wasn't explained to me properly.

I still had the Full Sutton riot hanging over me, as well as an ongoing police inquiry into it, so it was hard to believe the prison authorities had ever contemplated letting me out at all. I wasn't proud of my actions on the night of the riot, though I did everything I could to help those locked in their cells, and I think this particular disturbance showed just how easy it was to get caught up amid the pandemonium and determination of countless prisoners hell-bent in causing as much damage as they could. One moment you can be serving your time as a model prisoner, the next all that can change. Although I'd been liberated at the end of my sentence, the Full Sutton riot would remain a burden in my life for some time after my release – right up until the point of a Crown Court trial, which would go on for eight tiresome weeks in early 1999.

For crimes I'd committed purely for financial gain, I'd accepted my punishments, served out 80 per cent of my time the hard way, and I paid back my debt to society. You'd think that having spent so long behind bars, not to mention the way I had behaved during much of my incarceration, that the prison authorities would have made a concerted effort to offer me some sort of viable rehabilitation to prepare me for life back outside in the community. This wasn't the case. I received *no* form of help in reintegrating back into society. Instead, the guard in the reception at Hull jail handed me a giro cheque for £70 as I left to face a whole new world outside prison walls.

Afterword

It's hardly surprising that shortly after my release I did go back to crime, and that that stage of my journey took me to places as far afield as Holland, Spain and Morocco, where I rubbed shoulders with some of the biggest underworld figures and drug dealers in Europe. And three days into my freedom I met a stunning Spanish girl who would later give birth to my beautiful daughter, Tamara. But this all belongs to another chapter of my life, which is no less eventful and about which I am currently writing.

In this book I've taken the reader on a journey from my childhood to the end of my prison days in 1998, and I've tried my best to share some of the experiences I've had in an attempt to show how grim things can be when your life is dominated by crime, and how there are so few opportunities and little encouragement to break the vicious cycle.

In doing so I've managed to make sense of much of my own past and to come to terms with the person I once was. I can channel this fresh, positive energy into things which are a million miles removed from those that defined my life before. Since February 2013 I've been helping a friend and his family deal with a very difficult time as a result of his son suffering from autism. Twenty years ago I would never have dreamed I would be involved in something like this. But my own life experience has given me a different perspective on all sorts of things, and if this can be channelled into something worthwhile, then some good will have come out of all the dreadful years.

Writing has also given me a newfound purpose, a sense of direction, and an enthusiastic aptitude to move forward in a different light whilst simultaneously putting the past firmly behind me. In doing this it has given me a new sense of identity and hope for the future.

Above all, I have been lucky finally to have disentangled my life from the negative influences – the Glasgow curse – that dominated it for so long, though it took a huge amount of determination, not to mention support from others, to resist a way of life that could ultimately only ever drag me downwards. Many others who feature in this book have not resisted that temptation.

We are who we are, there's no getting away from that, and in many ways we are shaped by circumstance. From a very young age my life was never easy; on the contrary, it was always a struggle, a constant battle, and who knows what it would've been like if I'd have grown up in a secure family environment. There's that saying, 'You can choose your friends, but not your family.' This is very true. For me, being related to some of the most violent, hardened criminals in Glasgow meant only one thing – that I would turn out the same as them. With so many of them having had their lives cut terribly short, I can only dream about what it would've been like if they were still alive today, or what they might have been like if they'd been brought up under different circumstances. While the average person might experience the loss of a loved one once or twice leading up to the midway point in their lives, I have known dozens of people who have met violent ends, and that's in addition to close family members who are no longer with me.

Yet it is also true that we have to take responsibility for our own actions. I've never claimed to be a saint, and I only did what I believed in and thought was right in a criminal sense, but I also took my chances and as a result ended up as a scapegoat, expected to take the fall for others.

One of my biggest regrets in life is escaping from Dungavel semi-open prison in 1991. I didn't know it at the time, but the decisions I made then were to shape my life for years to come. I did what I thought was right when it came to helping out Ponny Shannon, someone who had played an important part in my early life and who I had considered a friend. Fate had other ideas, however, and dealt me a dreadful hand, and my life would never be the same again. If I had had a sneak preview of how my life would turn out – my further involvement with the Shannons, with Paul Ferris, my time in prisons all over the country – I can assure you there's no way I would've absconded from Dungavel that day. But what's past is past, and whilst it can't be undone, at least I have learnt how it is possible to mould the future in a better way, and that's a process that never stops.